MONARCHS
OF THE GLEN

MONARCHS OF THE GLEN

A History of Deer-Stalking in the Scottish Highlands

DUFF HART-DAVIS

JONATHAN CAPE
THIRTY BEDFORD SQUARE LONDON

First published 1978
© 1978 by Duff Hart-Davis

Jonathan Cape Ltd 30 Bedford Square, London WCI

British Library Cataloguing in Publication Data
Hart-Davis, Duff
Monarchs of the glen.
1. Red deer hunting – Scotland – Highlands
– History
I. Title
799.2′77′357   SK301
ISBN 0-224-01463-3

Printed in Great Britain by The Anchor Press Ltd
and bound by Wm Brendon & Son Ltd
both of Tiptree, Essex

My delight it was to rise
With the early morning skies
    All aglow,
And to brush the dewy height
Where the deer in airy state
    Wont to go . . .

And sweeter to my ear
Is the concert of the deer
    In their roaring,
Than when Erin from her lyre
Warmest strains of Celtic fire
    May be pouring;

And no organ sends a roll
So delightful to my soul
As the branchy-crested race
When they quicken their proud pace
And bellow in the face
    Of Ben Doran.

From 'The Praise of Ben Doran'
by Duncan Ban MacIntyre, translated
from the Gaelic by Professor J. S. Blackie

Contents

Illustrations

Chapter One

The Highland Deer

The red deer is certainly the largest, and arguably the most beautiful, of all the wild animals that survive in the British Isles. In England, however, there remain scarcely any open spaces big enough to accommodate so wide-ranging a creature: only Exmoor in the West Country, the New Forest, Thetford Chase in Norfolk, and parts of the Lake District carry red deer herds of any size. There are no wild red deer in Wales, and only a few in Southern Ireland. It is in the Highlands of Scotland that *Cervus elaphus* has its last real stronghold: at least 250,000 red deer still inhabit the bare mountains to which, over the centuries, they have gradually been forced to withdraw.

The reason they survive there in such numbers is simple, if para-doxical: it is merely that the stag, with his grace, power and nobility, has always offered an incomparable target for the hunter, ancient or modern. Deer-stalking as practised today began only in the early 1800s; yet for hundreds of years the deer in the Highlands have been pursued – and therefore preserved – with the keenest enthusiasm.

Moreover, just as the hills have given refuge to the deer, so the deer have strongly influenced the pattern of life in the mountains. What would have become of the Highlands *without* the deer it is impossible to say: but it was undoubtedly burgeoning Victorian enthusiasm for the new-found sport of deer-stalking that caused the building of the Highland lodges and the construction of innumerable bridges and miles of hill-paths, and brought about a general opening-up of the glens. Merely by being there, the deer drew millions of pounds into the area, in capital expenditure, in sporting rents and in wages; merely by being so warrantable, they ensured that the Highlands were preserved largely for sport.

The excitement of first setting eyes on the deer in the Highlands was admirably caught by Eric Parker in his book *English Wild Life*:

You are looking at the most splendid view of its kind, hill and glen
and water, that you have ever seen. The curve of the hill below you
is a great green cup, with the far side broken out of it to show you
other slopes and ridges and smaller cups, and many miles away the
water of a loch shining in the sun, and beyond that, peak after peak
of fainter and fainter blue. And for the moment you get a sense of
vast, empty space—though the stalker is looking intently, slowly,
this way and that.

And then—I wish it may come to you the first time, that wonderful knowledge, as it did to me—you suddenly realise that the whole
landscape below you is dotted with deer, light brown, tiny bodies of
deer, some of them moving, some of them still. That is one of the
great herds, there on the green floor far away.

And yet, splendid though the mountains and the deer still are,
neither the setting nor the animal is more than a shadow of its former
self. The barren hills now celebrated for their purple heather were once
clothed in trees to a height of 2,000 feet or more, and the deer were once
double their present size. Their diminution is due almost entirely to
the destruction of the forest: increasingly deprived of shelter, they have
had to devote more and more of their energy to the business of keeping
warm, with the result that their physical stature has progressively
declined.

The disappearance of the primeval forest is a phenomenon at once
tragic and mysterious. In some of the glens a few remnants are to be
seen of the ancient Caledonian forest of birch and pine, and thousands
of acres of the lower ground have been artificially restocked, either
during the great burst of planting which took place between 1750 and
1850, or during the present century. But elsewhere there are thousands
upon thousands of acres which seem totally barren: huge expanses of
moor and bog on which nothing grows except heather, moss and a
few reedy grasses.

A casual visitor may well surmise at first glance that these upland
deserts can never have supported trees; yet if he walks any distance
across a hill, he will soon find evidence of the forest that stood there
long ago. In the sides of the hags (or holes) in the peat, gnarled and
twisted pine roots protrude from their slimy black resting places. Often
they are five feet or more beneath the present level of the ground, and
they are preserved in astonishingly sound condition: so hard is the
wood that one can scarcely believe that its age should be measured in

hundreds of years, or even in thousands. Nor is it only roots that survive in this way: all over Scotland, whole trunks have been exhumed from peat-bogs: oak trunks forty feet long with a diameter of three or four feet are no rarity – and many lie ten feet deep in peat beneath land which could not possibly grow an oak today.

When did those trees live and why did they die? Did they all succumb at once, or did some outlive their fellows? How did the sterile peat build up to such a depth above their remains? Such questions tantalise any stalker today who sets foots upon the hill.

The subject of this book is the Highland red deer, and the way in which man has pursued them over the years. Yet no account of stalking would be complete without a brief explanation of how their environment was so drastically transformed.

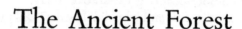

Chapter Two

The Ancient Forest

A convenient starting point for this inquiry is the end of the last Ice Age, which in Scotland is now thought to be about 9000 B.C. For thousands of years before that the Highlands had been intermittently buried beneath gigantic sheets of ice, which in places were 5,000 feet thick. When the glaciers began their final retreat, the pace of their withdrawal was irregular, quickening and slackening according to minor fluctuations in the climate; but experts have calculated that the average rate of retreat in Scotland was one mile in sixteen years, or six miles in a century. In other words, it must have taken the ice front about 1,500 years to withdraw from the site of modern Perth to that of Inverness, and as long again for it to reach the northern extremities of Sutherland and Caithness.

Hard on its heels (speaking in geological time-scales) came the trees spreading northwards as the tundra thawed and the earth became ready to receive falling seeds. Such is the accuracy with which palaeo-botanists now interpret their finds of pollen grains and other organic remains that they can calculate not merely the speed at which the forest advanced, but also the distance which separated the trees from the edge of the ice. For trees with light, winged seeds, like birch, willow, alder and pine, which have the greatest capacity for spreading them-selves, the rate of advance was probably some 220 yards a year. Those with heavier seeds, like oak and hazel, achieved about 175 yards a year; and in places the front line of the forest advanced to within 300 yards of the melting ice ramparts.

Silvicultural experts vigorously dispute the precise nature of the forest which gradually spread over Scotland. They agree that much of the lower ground was covered by dense deciduous forest, in which oak predominated, and that the highest reaches of the woods were no more than thick, short scrub of birch or hazel. The main argument concerns the extent to which Scots pine (*Pinus sylvestris*) dominated the middle and upper slopes.

The Scots pine is the most widely distributed conifer in the world, and some authorities believe that it was the principal constituent of Scotland's primeval forest. 'Even to walk through the larger of them [the remaining natural pinewoods] gives one a better idea of what a primeval forest was like than can be got from any other woodland scene in Britain,' wrote H. M. Steven and A. Carlisle in *The Native Pinewoods of Scotland*. 'The trees range in age up to 300 years ... and thus there are not very many generations between their earliest predecessors about 9,000 years ago and those growing today; to stand in them is to feel the past.'

Others believe that the Scots pine played a relatively minor role. In his monumental, two-volume *A History of Scottish Forestry*, published posthumously in 1967, Professor Mark Louden Anderson reasoned that most of the land newly freed from the ice was so rich in minerals that it must have been occupied by more demanding species:

Scots pine is unable to compete with other tree species on sites which carry soils of more than moderate fertility, and, prior to the general soil degradation which has gone on over the past 7,000 years, the extent of fertile sites in Scotland must have been enormously wider than now. Hence, the opportunity for pine to become dominant must then have been much smaller.

In any case, the experts agree that, whatever its exact composition, a vast forest spread over the length and breadth of Scotland, and that by the arrival of the period known as the climatic optimum, about 5000 B.C., when conditions for tree growth were more favourable than ever before or since, trees of one kind or another covered perhaps sixty per cent of the surface of the country (compared with about five per cent today).

For anyone who knows the Highlands in their present state of desolation, it needs a strong effort of imagination to see the hills as they were 7,000 years ago – a real wilderness, untouched by man, the mountains tree-clad to a height of 2,000 feet in the west and 3,000 in the east. The most open areas must have been in the west and north, in Ross and Sutherland, where the glaciers had left myriad outcrops of rock completely bare, or with too thin a covering of soil ever to grow trees. But nowhere was the forest anything like as solid and regimented as the cultivated woodlands with which modern man is familiar.

Instead of trees in serried ranks, one must imagine a haphazard and open kind of forest with many glades offering good feeding and shelter and – another fundamental difference – trees of every age intermingled. Even the few stands of Caledonian pine that remain (for instance in Abernethy) bear little resemblance to the primeval forest in which their forbears grew; for now the surviving trees are all of great age – between 200 and 300 years – and beneath them not a single sapling grows: the vegetation is mown to a smooth sward by the grazing of sheep and deer. In the ancient woodland, by contrast, trees of every age stood among each other, from saplings to full-grown giants.

In this great forest there flourished a rich variety of wildlife, not least the ancestors of today's red deer. Their remains are abundant in the marl clays – the oldest lake deposits – formed not long after the close of the Ice Age, and still more bones and antlers have been recovered from deep in the peat bogs, showing that the original red deer ranged over every part of Scotland, including Orkney and Shetland. Mesolithic man, who reached Scotland in perhaps 5000 B.C., hunted the deer for their meat and their skins, also using the antlers and bones for tools. How he managed to capture an animal so fleet of foot one can only conjecture: probably by digging pits or by climbing trees to lie in wait above forest trails and hurling down primitive spears, or merely heavy stones, from his ambush. In any event, he had plenty of success; as James Ritchie remarked in his book *The Influence of Man on Animal Life in Scotland*, 'there is scarcely a settlement where he or his successors dwelt that does not contain its [the red deer's] remains.'

These original red deer were of a size to make modern stalkers groan with envy. In 1781 the skull and antlers of a stag were dug up from beneath the roots of an ancient tree which stood on the Meadows, outside Edinburgh, and though the head was irregular, it was of splendid proportions. The right antler was thirty-six inches long, and the left forty-six inches, and together they carried seventeen points. The beam (the maximum circumference of the antler) measured eight-and-a-half inches. (A good modern royal – a head of twelve points – would measure thirty-two or thirty-three inches and have a beam of about five inches.)*

---

* Deer's antlers are often incorrectly referred to as 'horns'. The difference between the two is that whereas horns grow once and remain on an animal's head for its lifetime, antlers are cast and regrown every year. The word 'head', used of a stag, generally refers not to his skull, face and so on, but to his antlers considered as a pair.

The remains of another stag, a nineteen-pointer, came to light during the draining of Loch Linton, in Roxburghshire. An entire skeleton was exhumed from the marl bed beneath ten feet of peat. The bones were broken up by the workmen, but the skull and antlers were preserved, each antler measuring thirty-three inches, and their span forty-four (a span of thirty-five inches is today considered outstanding). Another fine head, of twenty-one points, was found at Ashkirk, and in about 1830 a peat-bog at Smeaton-Hepburn, in East Lothian, yielded a complete skeleton which today is preserved in the Royal Scottish Museum in Edinburgh. Although only a twelve-pointer, this stag stood four foot six at the shoulder, and measured seven feet ten from his nose to the base of his tail. A big Highland stag of today stands only three foot six at the shoulder and measures five foot eight inches from nose to tail: his ancestor from Smeaton-Hepburn, in other words, was more than a third as large again, and must have weighed more than double.

Ritchie, who was a great champion of the magnificence of the original red deer, pointed out that, during man's casual excavations in the peat bogs, 'the chances are all against the discovery of the best heads'. Most likely, he claimed, the animals discovered so far were run-of-the-mill stags — what stalkers would contemptuously dismiss as 'rubbish' today. Perhaps he is right; and if he is, what monsters they must have been, the primeval monarchs of the glen.

Even they, however, were dwarfed by the colossal, mis-shapen creature known as the Gigantic Irish Elk. *Megaceros giganteus* did not survive until the formation of the peat-bogs: its remains are found only in the early marl beds, and it may well have been extinct in Scotland before man appeared to hasten its doom. As the naturalist Frank Fraser Darling aptly remarked in his book *Natural History in the Highlands and Islands*, 'the organism itself was heading for disaster.' Its antlers had evolved far beyond any practical size, and by the end were nine or ten feet wide, weighing eighty or ninety pounds. The effort of growing so much bone tissue every year proved fatally debilitating for the poor Irish elk, and soon it gave up the struggle.

Other species of deer flourished, among them reindeer, which ranged through Scotland, including Orkney, and the European elk, which was common from the borders to the extremities of Sutherland. Roe deer, judging by the paucity of remains, seem to have been scarce. Another monster was the wild ox, which stood six feet at the shoulder and was the ancestor of the few wild white cattle that remain.

B

The wild boar was also abundant, and much larger than its descendants which inhabit the forests of Europe today. The brown bear flourished: the skull and rib of a large bear were found at Shaws, in Dumfriesshire, in a stratum of peat bog associated with the remains of red deer, roe, wild ox and reindeer. Other finds of bones suggest that bear was a regular item in the diet of Neolithic man. In the lochs and burns the beaver was active, felling trees and building dams, as it now does in Canada.

The main predator that controlled the herds of herbivores was the wolf, which must have prowled the primeval forest in strong packs. Another ferocious carnivore was the European lynx, with its elegantly tufted ears: remains were found in a cave near Inchnadamph, in Sutherland, associated with relics of human habitation.

For as long as the forest remained intact there was room – and food – for this great wealth of wildlife. But as soon as the woodland began to decline, there was a battle for survival among the animals, and in due course all but two of the species so far mentioned became extinct: only the red deer, and on a small scale the roe, survived the destruction of the trees.

It is impossible to pinpoint the moment at which the decline began; but it can fairly be said that although man was to blame for much of the devastation, the climate also played a decisive part. Here, too, there is a difference of opinion among experts. Many writers (Ritchie among them) postulate a series of violent climatic swings to account for the sudden death of whole regiments of trees, and for the build-up of the huge deposits of peat which buried them. Guided by the successive layers revealed in excavations (see Figure), Ritchie outlined the forest history as follows.

After the main retreat of the ice, Ritchie thought, the warmer, drier climate ushered in the first forest of birch, hazel and alder, which found footholds in the valley floors and climbed the hill-sides to a height of 2,000 feet (Level 1). But then there followed a much wetter and colder period, during which the glaciers returned to some of the valleys, and many areas of the first forest were swamped by the development of boggy pools and sphagnum moss. The trees were killed; their roots rotted, and the trunks fell into the bog and peat moss (Level 2).

Then drier conditions brought in the great forest whose extent I have already outlined – only for another violent swing of what Ritchie called the 'climatic pendulum' to produce a second cold, wet period, which sent millions of hitherto healthy trees to their graves in new deposits of peat (Level 3).

Other specialists believe that the trees may have died off without any violent climatic fluctuations. Anderson, for instance, pointed out that streams can easily become blocked by small natural dams of fallen branches and leaves, or merely by the activities of beavers.

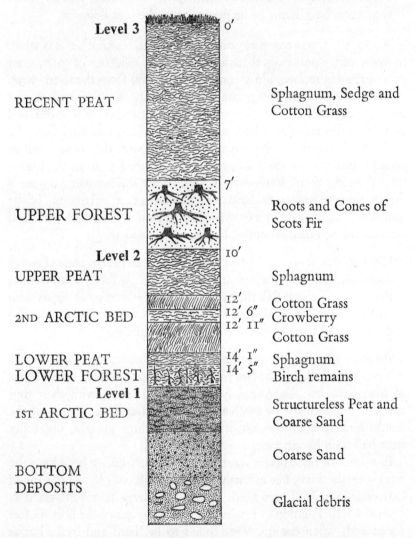

Level 3	0'	
RECENT PEAT		Sphagnum, Sedge and Cotton Grass
UPPER FOREST	7'	Roots and Cones of Scots Fir
Level 2	10'	
UPPER PEAT		Sphagnum
2ND ARCTIC BED	12' / 12' 6" / 12' 11"	Cotton Grass / Crowberry / Cotton Grass
LOWER PEAT	14' 1"	Sphagnum
LOWER FOREST	14' 5"	Birch remains
Level 1		
1ST ARCTIC BED		Structureless Peat and Coarse Sand
BOTTOM DEPOSITS		Coarse Sand
		Glacial debris

Diagrammatic section of upland peat moss in Lowland Scotland (Merrick and Kells District) showing relationship of former plant deposits and of the Lower and Upper forests.

The resultant water-logged areas thus became ideal habitats for marsh plants and for sphagnum mosses. The tree roots found themselves deprived of oxygen and died off, so that the trees themselves must have been killed in masses. The bog plants and mosses continued to develop and to build up accumulations of peaty matter, which ultimately buried the fallen trunks and branches. In this way in many cases the numerous remains of forest trees and of forest vegetation have come to be preserved in the peat deposits.

Water, then, was one main cause of destruction. Another was wind. In many of the peat-bogs there is unmistakable evidence of gales, most of which seem to have blown (as they do today) from the south-west. In a 500-acre bog in the parish of Kilbarchan, in Renfrewshire, for instance, eighteenth-century excavation of peat between seven and nine feet deep revealed a bed of white clay which had once been the forest floor. On it lay the remains of many oaks, the stumps still in position and the trunks — snapped off some three feet from the base — ranged neatly from south-west to north-east. 'Wherever you see a stump, you are sure to find a tree to the north-east,' wrote one of the numerous local eyewitnesses who contributed to the Old Statistical Account of Scotland compiled between 1790 and 1805:

> How an oak tree could break over at that particular place, I never could understand. But we may be allowed to form a conjecture, that before the tree fell, the moss [peat] had advanced along its stem and rotted it there. Wood, immersed in a wet body, is found to decay first at the ring between the wet and the dry.

Another case of hurricane damage was exhumed at Coldstone, in Aberdeenshire, during the late eighteenth century, when a whole forest of pine trees was discovered lying in serried ranks, with their tops towards the east, ten or twelve feet down in the peat. Some of the trunks had been broken off, leaving the stumps upright, but other trees had been blown clean over, roots and all.

In neither of these places was there any way of telling how long the trees had lain there, but in many similar burials oaks have been found extraordinarily well preserved. Parts of one large tree, discovered in 1780 at Castle Huntley in Perthshire, were dug out of the peat six feet down and, when cut up, were found to be 'hard and fresh, but as black as ebony'. Another mighty tree, with a trunk forty-three feet long and three feet in diameter, was found near Cortachy Castle, in

Angus, in 1833. 'The wood was thoroughly dried,' reported the New Statistical Account, 'and portions of it were made into beautiful pieces of furniture.'

Fire – sometimes started by lightning – was yet another agent of destruction. On one occasion during the nineteenth century, when attempts were being made to reclaim land near Tongue, in Sutherland, diggers came upon large tree trunks which had been cored out by fire for most of their length; and in 1925, when experimental trenches were cut through several feet of peat near Fort Augustus, in Inverness-shire, they revealed, on the mineral soil below, stumps of pine and a thin layer of charred wood, which showed that a fire had swept the area hundreds (or perhaps thousands) of years before.

Such fires, of course, may well have been caused by man. But the evidence from the peat-bogs does not allow any accurate estimate of early man's influence on the forest. Several of the reports in the Statistical Accounts mention signs of human interference – axe marks on the trunks, and trunks lying severed from their roots – but there is no means of telling the date at which the primitive woodcutters were active.

And yet, even if it cannot be precisely measured, human influence on the forest must have steadily increased. Mesolithic man, who inhabited Scotland from about 5000 to 2000 B.C., probably did little damage, for his numbers were small and he kept mainly to the coast and to the valleys. It was the Neolithic people, with their oxen, sheep and goats, who brought the first real threat. Until the advent of domestic grazing animals, any part of the forest burnt or felled would have had a good chance of regenerating itself naturally; but then, with the arrival of concentrated and controlled eating power, the clearings must have been gradually extended and much larger grazing grounds established.

As Anderson points out, to Neolithic man the forest was an enemy, not a friend: it harboured wolves and encroached continuously on newly won land:

This enemy he could fight with his cutting tools, with fire and with the help of his flocks. Doubtless he very quickly discovered how the largest of the trees could be killed simply by a complete girdling, or ring-barking, and he must have used this procedure to prepare forest land for shifting cultivation.

The Bronze Age (1900–250 B.C.) stepped up the human attack: bronze axes were far more efficient than flint ones, and enabled their owners to clear wider areas. Settlements also became more permanent. The Iron Age (150 B.C.–A.D. 80) intensified the assault still further and set a trend which has persisted almost to the present day. Not only were Iron Age men furnished with better cutting tools, which could tackle oak as well as softer kinds of timber: they also invented one of the most destructive processes known to forestry – the art of smelting iron with charcoal. Their small furnaces were established all over Scotland, and thousands upon thousands of trees were slowly incinerated. Small wonder that W. Aiton, who in the early 1800s examined buried trees in all the counties of Scotland, declared:

> I have seen many thousands of trees that had evidently been cut with an axe, or some such tool, and the roots or fangs still fast in the earth in which they grew ... The mark of the axe is seen in many trees dug from under moss. Some have been split, and the wedge remaining in the tree; others have been found with holes bored through them, and some partly burnt.

Never from the Iron Age until the middle of the present century was there any let-up in the erosion of the Scottish forests. The process has been chronicled in immense detail by Professor Anderson, and here it must suffice to list the outstanding causes. The smelting of iron was probably the most persistent, for it was carried on throughout Britain continuously for at least 2,000 years, first in hundreds of small, isolated foundries (also known as bloomeries) to satisfy purely local needs, and later, in even more destructive forms, as a commercial enterprise. So inimical was smelting to forestry that in 1556 Elizabeth I banned the process by law in Sussex, and in 1563 another act abolished smelting at Ulverston, in Lancashire.

The effect of these and similar measures passed in England was to drive the smelters northwards into Scotland in search of new fodder for their fires. About 1610 Sir George Hay obtained the use of the woods of Letterewe, in Wester Ross, for smelting, and from then millions of trees in the area of Loch Maree were sacrificed to the production of iron. English miners were brought into the district and built up a considerable industry, casting cannons, among other implements, and using, according to one historian, 120 acres of woodland a year. The inevitable result was that the forests of Letterewe were largely destroyed.

For several centuries the most distant Highland forests were preserved by their own remoteness, and by the supposed wildness of their inhabitants. An act of Parliament of 1609 referred to woods which 'by reason of the savageness of the inhabitants thereabouts were either unknown or at least unprofitable and unused'; but soon Crown surveyors reported the presence of very large pine trees, suitable for ships' masts, on the shores of Loch Arkaig, and so the exploitation began.

It was the Jacobite rebellion of 1715, and the consequent British military occupation of the Highlands, that really showed southerners the way to the forests of the north. One curious fact about the smelting industry was that the iron ore was more compact — and so more portable — than the timber used to reduce it; it was easier to transport the ore to the wood than vice versa, and thus a form of creeping blight progressed through the forests, as one furnace after another was established on virgin ground. The voracity of the process was terrible, as one example will indicate: in 1728 60,000 trees were bought for £7,000 from the forest of Sir James Grant of Strathspey, to be made into masts for the navy. Then, however, they were found to be too small, so the whole lot went instead for charcoal.

By the end of the nineteenth century there were iron workings scattered throughout Scotland, and that great expert, Professor W. Ivison Macadam, recorded nearly one hundred of them during the surveys he made in the 1890s. In the 1880s the Coalecken furnace on Loch Fyne alone produced 700 tons of pig iron a year, and there — a change from the usual system — the charcoal was brought to the smelting works; in the 1830s and 1840s it had been a regular sight to see strings of ponies coming over the hill-track from Loch Awe, ten miles away, their panniers laden with charcoal.

Another cause of widespread forest destruction was deliberate burning, whether by the Danes, by the English, or merely by one clan seeking to flush another out of cover. At Applecross, a magnificent mountain peninsula on the west coast of Ross-shire, there is an ancient tradition that the local forests were fired by invading Danes; and sure enough, far down in the peat-bog on land where now not a single tree is to be seen, one can find the remains of large trunks, many of which were clearly burnt. Physical evidence apart, there are many historical records of deliberate burning or smoking out, to evict both men and wolves. The creation of pasture was a more constructive, but no less damaging, reason for burning down the trees.

Another voracious consumer was the shipbuilding industry, which flourished increasingly from the thirteenth century. Even when the

forests were still relatively extensive, the amount of timber that one
ship needed was a matter for concern and comment. The *Great Michael*,
built in 1511 at Newhaven, near Leith, at the command of King James
IV, was described by a contemporary historian as 'a very monstrous
great ship, which took so much timber that she wasted all the woods
in Fife, except Falkland Wood, besides the timber that came out of
Norway.'

Even with Scandinavian imports taken into account, the general
timber industry became more and more demanding, reaching its peak
in the eighteenth and early nineteenth centuries. At the height of
exploitation the great pine forests of Rothiemurchus in Inverness-shire
were alone producing an income of between £10,000 and £20,000 a
year, and in her book *Memoirs of a Highland Lady* Elizabeth Grant
of Rothiemurchus left a vivid picture of the timber trade in those
days.

Some of the logs were cut up at sawmills in the clearings, but many
were floated down the Spey to the sea. All the men engaged in 'wood-
manufacture', as she called it, drank whisky 'in goblets three times a
day, yet except at merrymaking we never saw them tipsy.'

In due course indiscriminate felling destroyed most of the Rothiemurchus forests – a disaster that could easily have been avoided, as Miss
Grant pointed out. At one stage her brother William established a
proper plan of management, dividing the wood into sections:

> He allotted one portion to be cleared immediately, enclosed by
> stout fencing and then left to nature, not to be touched again for
> fifty or sixty years. The ground is so rich in seed that no other
> course was necessary. By the following spring a carpet of inch-high
> plants would be struggling to rise above the heather, in a season or
> two more a thicket of young firs would be found there, thinning
> themselves as they grew, the larger destroying all the weaker.

There were many enemies of natural regeneration – principally
grazing animals. But another adverse factor was the gradual deteriora-
tion of the soil and the formation of more and more peat, which
favoured the growth of heather rather than of trees. A long succession
of forest laws had little effect in saving the woods that were left. The
original *Leges Forestarum*, ascribed to William the Lion (1165–1214),
prohibited the taking of fire or domestic animals into the forest, as
well as the cutting of oak. Later acts introduced further restrictions and

repeatedly increased the penalties for infringement, but never with much success.

By no means all the destruction, however, was caused by man. Many stretches of forest must have died on their own, merely of old age, and one fascinating glimpse of such a process was recorded by George, Earl of Cromartie, in a letter sent in November 1710 to the Secretary of the Royal Society. In 1651, when he was nineteen, he was in the parish of Loch Broom, in the west of Inverness-shire, and he went past a small plain 'about half a mile round':

This little plain was at that time all covered over with a firm standing wood, which was so very old that not only the trees had no green leaves, but the bark was totally thrown off; which the old country-man who was in my company told me was the universal manner in which fir woods did terminate, and that in twenty or thirty years after the trees would ordinarily cast themselves up from the roots, and that they would lie in heaps till the people would cut them and carry them away ... The outside of these standing white trees, and for the space of one inch inwards, was dead white timber, but what was within that was good solid timber to the very pith, and as full of rozin as it could stand in the wood.

Some fifteen years after, I had occasion to come the same way and called to mind the old woods which I had seen. Then there was not so much as a tree, or appearance of the root of any kind, but in the place thereof, the whole bounds where the wood had stood was all over a plain green mound, covered with a plain green moss. I asked the country people who were with me what had become of the wood, and who carried it away. They told me that nobody was at the pains to carry it away, but that, it being all overturned from the roots by the winds, the trees did lie so thick and swarving over one another that the green moss there (in the British language called fog) had overgrown the whole timber, which they said was occasioned by the moisture that came down from the high hill which was above it, and did stagnate upon that plain, and they said that none could pass over it because the scurf of the fog would not support them. I would needs try it, and accordingly I fell in to the armpits, but was immediately pulled out by them.

Before the year 1699 that piece of ground was turned into a common moss, where the country people were digging turf and peat, and continue to do so. The peats, as yet, are not of the best, and

are soft and spungy, but grow better and better, and, as I am reliably
informed, it does now afford good peats.

There, in a few paragraphs, is the process that reduced many parts of
Scotland, and in particular the Highlands, to the state which they are in
today. One small consolation is that at least some of the remains of the
forest can be recovered and put to good use: it was the digging of peat,
for fires, that revealed the subterranean relics of former ages, and for
years the roots of the ancient pines (generally known as 'bog-fir') were
dug up and dried to provide light in the winter: in many places they
were the only form of artificial lighting that the country people could
afford.

It is no longer possible to tell at exactly what stage the shrinking
forests became too small to support the various species of animal. Bears
are thought to have become extinct by the tenth century, although a
folk memory of them lived on in the Gaelic name *Magh-ghamhainn*, the
'paw calf' – according to Ritchie, 'a rough, dark, grisly monster, the
terror of the winter's tale'. The beaver survived longer; it was known in
Gaelic as *Dobhran losleathan*, the broad-tailed otter. Reindeer also
survived at least until the twelfth or thirteenth century: many remains
confirm the tradition recorded in the Orkney Saga that in the twelfth
century the *jarls* (earls) of Orkney used to cross the Pentland Firth to
hunt reindeer in the wilds of Caithness.

The wild boar, which flourished in the days of the great oak forest,
when acorns were abundant, is remembered in many Highland names,
among them Slochd-Tuirc (Boar's den), Druim an-Tuirc (Boar's
ridge) and Beannan Tuirc (Boar's mountain). The date of the pigs'
demise is unknown; but when in the nineteenth century the Earl of
Fife tried to reintroduce the species on his estate at Mar, it failed for
lack of a natural food supply.

One of the most tenacious survivors was the wolf. A menace to
man and to domestic stock, it was vigorously persecuted throughout
historic times; but the ancient forests afforded it an impenetrable
retreat, and not until the cover had been greatly reduced was the last
wolf exterminated in the middle of the eighteenth century – by which
time the species had already been extinct in England for some 250
years.

In a memorable phrase, Bellenden, translator of the medieval
Scottish historian Hector Boece, described the wolf as 'rycht noysum
to the tame bestiall in all partis of Scotland' – and so it was; known as

'the herdsman's foe', it was also the terror of humans. In the sixteenth century wolves were so numerous that spittals, or refuges, were built in lonely places to give travellers shelter for the night (hence names like Spittal of Glenshee), and in many areas people had to take special precautions to prevent wolves digging up the dead. In Atholl coffins were made of five flagstones, and a well known tradition, reported in several different sources, records that the inhabitants of Edderachillis, in the west of Sutherland, had to transport their dead to the island of Handa and bury them there to render them safe. Much the same was done at Loch Maree, where the island was used as a safe burial place, as was the Green Island in Loch Awe, in Argyllshire.

From the earliest times wolves had prices on their heads: according to Holinshed's Chronicles, Dorvadil, the fourth king of the Scots, decreed that anyone who killed a wolf should have an ox for his pains; and Ferquhard II (an exceptionally futile monarch who died in 668)

followed in chase of a Wolfe, the beast, being enraged by pursuite of the houndes, flew back uppon the King, and snatching at him did wounde and byte him right sore in one of his sides, immediately whereupon ... he fell into a most filthie disease.

Eight hundred years later, in 1491, the bounty for a wolf was only 5s., but by 1621 in Sutherland it had risen to £6 13s. 4d. In many areas the sheriffs and other inhabitants were obliged by law to go wolf hunting three times a year – and indeed hunting the wolf was considered a fine sport as well as a duty. An outstanding early practitioner was Lady Margaret Lyon, wife of the third Lord Lovat, who flourished in the late fifteenth century and is described by the Wardlaw Manuscript as 'a stout woman, a bold huntress, she would have travelled in our hills a-foot, and perhaps outwearied good footmen.' According to the nineteenth-century book Lays of the Deer Forest, 'she lived in Phoppachy, by the sea, in a stanck house' [one with a moat], and from there she conducted such vigorous warfare on the wolves in the Aird district (north of the Beauly Firth, in Inverness-shire) that they were exterminated from their principal stronghold in that range. It was her habit to have the wolves driven to her through a pass on Mount Caplach, where she engaged them with her crossbow, and for generations afterwards the site of her redoubt was pointed out to passers-by.

Such local purges, however, can have done little to reduce the overall wolf population, and in the early seventeenth century large tracts of forest were burnt to flush out the predators. *Lays of the Deer Forest* records that

> on the south side of Beann Nevis a large pine forest, which extended from the western braes of Lochaber to the Black Water and the mosses of Rannoch, was burned to expel the wolves. In the neighbourhood of Loch Sloi a tract of woods nearly twenty miles in extent was consumed for the same purpose.

Many stirring accounts were handed down of individual man–wolf combats, a particularly celebrated one being that of the brothers Chisholm in the time of Charles II. A litter of cubs had been established in a cairn in Gleann Chon-fhiadh – the Wolves' Glen – and the mother had killed some of the local people. The Laird of Chisholm and his brother, two gallant young hunters, set off along Strath Glass, and having tracked the she-wolf to her den, discovered from traces that she was out. The Elder Chisholm crept into the den and began slaughtering the cubs with his dirk, but almost at once the mother returned, and on hearing the yelps rushed at the entrance. Chisholm the Younger, standing guard, hurled his spear but missed, shattering its point. His brother met the desperate animal as it entered the den; fortunately he was wearing the left-handed *Lamhainn chruaidh*, or steel gauntlet, much favoured by the Highlanders, and this iron fist he thrust down the wolf's throat, stabbing her in the chest with his dirk. The Younger Chisholm, meanwhile, clubbed the animal's hindquarters with his broken spear, and in a short time the wolf was dragged out dead.

The honour of having killed the last wolf in Scotland was claimed by many different people in different districts; but, wherever the final death took place, the species is known to have died out during the 1740s, by which time the forests which once had furnished it with such secure retreats were substantially diminished.

Through all these vicissitudes, both animal and vegetable, the red deer gradually performed an astonishing feat of adaptation. Originally denizens of the lowland forests, they transformed themselves, out of necessity, into upland animals, able to live on the open, desolate moors and mountainsides. Over the centuries, as the forests were felled or burned, and more and more land was taken for agriculture, the deer withdrew northwards on to the higher ground, until, by the end of the eighteenth century, there were practically none left except in the Highlands and Western Islands.

The change to a far less comfortable habitat brought about a severe reduction in the deer's size. Inferior feeding was one adverse factor; but an equally important one was lack of shelter. In the primeval forest the deer had always been able to find cover during storms and wintry weather; in the Highlands they often had—and have—none. The result is that much of the energy gained from food is used not in physical development but in keeping warm.

The difference that shelter and good feeding make is striking and easily observed. A modern Highland stag which weighs sixteen stone clean* is considered an excellent beast; an animal weighing twenty stone is a monster—and probably the half-dozen such beasts which are shot in Scotland each year have had access to farm crops or other low-ground feeding. In Thetford Chase, in Norfolk, by contrast, a mature stag of twenty stone is a runt, and a good one weighs thirty or thirty-five, almost double its Highland counterpart. The same is true of the stags in the forests of Central Europe, where, although the winters are colder than in Scotland, the cover and feeding are incomparably better.

There is no genetic difference between the animals in all these places: they are all red deer, and the variety of their physical achievement depends solely on their environment. Living proof of this fact can be seen in the Highland Wildlife Park at Kincraig, in Inverness-shire, where stags brought in from the hill already mature, have, with good feeding and shelter, grown to magnificent proportions. Had these animals remained at large, they would never have been half so fine.

There is no means of telling either the date at which the decline began or the rate at which it progressed. There seems no doubt that the primeval stags weighed thirty stone or more, and would in every way have been a match for the best that now survive in Europe's forests. Later remains show that the deer of the early Christian era, though already diminished, were still much larger than today's. In the sixteenth and seventeenth centuries, unfortunately, no one seems to have been much interested in the weight of the quarry: the head was everything, and there are no records of weights. One reason, no doubt, was that the animal was generally dismembered on the spot where it fell, rather than being taken whole to a place where there was a set of scales. Not until the middle of the nineteenth century, when stalking became fashionable, was weight considered important.

* The weight of a stag is traditionally that of the animal bled and gralloched—that is, with its stomach and intestines removed, but with the heart, lungs and liver still in place. All weights in the book are given in this form unless otherwise stated.

Nor is it possible to reconstruct any information about the size of the red deer population through the ages. It might be thought that, with the elimination of the wolf, numbers would have increased; but for the last few generations of their existence in Scotland the wolves themselves cannot have been numerous enough to have had much effect on the deer. By then man had long established himself as the main predator: it was human pursuit, and the competition of other grazing animals (mainly cattle), that kept the deer herds down.

It is a sad irony that the inhospitable and windswept hills which the deer now perforce inhabit should be described as deer forests. A Scottish deer forest is essentially a tract of open country which contains no trees at all, or at best a few in the glens: the name comes from the medieval term *afforestation,* which meant not large-scale planting of trees, but the setting aside of huge areas for hunting. Often in England, and indeed in Scotland 500 years ago, such areas were heavily wooded: the New Forest is an obvious example. But the term was still applied in the nineteenth century, when most of the Scottish deer forests were created, and by then the trees had gone.

Chapter Three

The Tinchels

Bones, skulls and antlers found among cave deposits and in burial mounds show that man hunted the Scottish red deer from the earliest times, perhaps by digging pits and waylaying the animals on trails through the primeval forest. There is also evidence of a different kind which shows the means to which the hunters resorted when the trees had gone and the deer had taken to open country: on several of the Western Islands, as well as on the mainland, traces were visible until a couple of centuries ago of the long, converging stone walls between which the deer were driven into an enclosure where they could be slaughtered.

In an account of the Island of Jura written in 1549 Dean Monro described how the deer there were driven by men and dogs through the isthmus between Loch Tarbert on the west and Tarbert Bay in the east; and in the Old Statistical Account of Scotland printed in 1796 the Reverend Donald Maclean gave a clear account of a similar operation on the Island of Rhum:

> Before the use of firearms, their method of killing deer was as follows: on each side of a glen formed by two mountains, stone dykes were begun pretty high in the mountains and carried to the lower part of the valley, always drawing nearer, till within three or four feet of each other. From this narrow pass a circular space was enclosed by a stone wall, of a height sufficient to confine the deer; to this place they were pursued and destroyed. The vestige of one of these enclosures is still to be seen in Rhum.

Similar walls and enclosures were reported on Skye, and an eighteenth-century account of deer-hunting on the mainland shows that sometimes the walls of the final trap were made of stakes and brushwood instead of stones. The ring of men who drove the deer was called the Tinchel, or *Tainchell*—a Gaelic word applied also to the whole method of hunting. The enclosure was known as the *Eileirg*, and anglicised versions of the term (elrick, or elrig) are used as place names to this day. In many a forest there is a hill known as 'the Elrig', especially in Perthshire and Argyllshire. The Victorian artist and author J. G. Millais reported that in the 1880s traces of old stone dykes were still visible on Ben Griam, in Sutherland, as well as in the forest of Dunrobin.

In historical times the deer became royal game, to be hunted only by the king or by those to whom he had granted the right of forestry; and occasional scraps of information show that during the Middle Ages royal hunting forays took place in many areas from which the deer have long since disappeared. David I (1124–53) maintained a hunting lodge at Crail, in Fife; and in 1169, when Walter the Stewart founded the abbey of Paisley, he granted the monks a tithe of his hunting, with the skins of the deer killed in his forest of Ferenze in Renfrewshire. In fourteenth-century records there are several references to deer in the forest at Selkirk, and Robert the Bruce (1306–29) was said to have been repeatedly baulked during his hunting expeditions in the Pentland Hills by the appearance of a white hind—the demise of which, superstition held, would inevitably bring bad luck.

These lowland hunts were no doubt conducted in much the same fashion as their equivalents in England. Those taking part rode horses, and hounds pursued the deer, either pulling them down or bringing them to bay. The huntsmen were armed with swords and daggers, and sometimes with bows and arrows; but the main agents of destruction were the dogs. For centuries pursuit by dogs was the essence of the chase: other means of taking deer, such as girnes (snares), nets and crossbows, were considered unsporting, and forbidden by law; and firearms, when they became available, excited particular disapproval.

The use of half-hags (arquebusses) and pistols was prohibited by several sixteenth-century acts; but these measures were clearly ineffective, for in 1551, during the reign of Mary Queen of Scots, a statute was passed complaining that deer, roe and other beasts had been 'clean exiled and banished' by shooting with half-hag, culvering and pistolet, and forbidding 'our sovereign ladies lieges' to shoot any such animals under pain of death and the 'escheat of moveables', that is, the confiscation of goods.

A later act, of 1579, outlined the penalties for infringement of the forest laws in greater detail. The fine for a first offence was £10, for a second £20, and for a third £40. But if the malefactor was 'not responsible in goods', that is, if he could not pay, he was to be given eight days in the stocks, prison or irons, on bread and water for the first offence, fifteen for the second, and for the third was to suffer 'hanging to the death'.

Other means of conserving deer stocks had already been tried, among them the introduction of a law in 1474 which forbade the killing of any deer until it was at least one year old, and set some sort of close season in the winter. But in spite of the laws and vicious penalties, the deer in the Lowlands dwindled away: harried by human predation and by the constant expansion of farming, the survivors withdrew to the mountains farther north.

There, in the wilderness of rock and bog, no conventional method of hunting was possible. No horse and rider could travel at any speed across the rough territory which the red deer made their home: although sturdy ponies could pick their way slowly through the hills, most of the ground was too steep, too rocky, or too wet for any form of chase on horseback.

The answer was the Tinchel; and although in some places walls and enclosures were built so that the deer could be positively corralled (as described above), the more common practice was simply to manœuvre the herds towards a particular glen or pass where the royal or noble party was lying in wait with dogs.

A large number of men would be involved, and the initial ring would be several miles round. Having completed their cordon – a manœuvre that might take several days – the beaters would gradually drive the deer inwards, forcing the herds together and pushing them towards the ambush. In the last moments before the encircled animals made a bolt for freedom, there would be a brief and bloodthirsty massacre, as the men flung themselves on the deer with any weapon they could muster – bows and arrows, swords, dirks, spears, stones and Lochaber axes, which were like modern forestry slashers, with chopping blades fixed on the ends of long handles.

A Tinchel attended by royalty was a tremendous social event, staged with recklessly extravagant display. Perhaps the most magnificent ever recorded was that given in 1528 by the Earl of Atholl in honour of James V. The King was accompanied by his mother and by an ambassador of the Pope, among many others; and as the historian Lindsay of Pitscottie remarked, their host did everything possible to make the visitors feel at home:

C

This noble earl gart make a curious palace to the king, and his mother, and the embasador, where they were as honourably eased and lodged as they had been in England, France, Italy or Spain ... [It] was builded in the midst of a fair meadow, and the walls thereof was of green timber, woven with green birks [birches] that were green baith under and above, which was fashioned in four quarters, and in every quarter and neuk [corner] thereof, a great round, as it had been a block-house, which was lofted and joisted the space of three house height, the floors laid with green scarels, spreats [both forms of wild grass] medwarts and flowers, that no man knew whereon he zeid, but as he had been in a garden.

Farther, there were two greit rounds in ilk side of the gate, and a greit portcullis of tree falling down, with the manner of a barrace, with a draw brig, and a greit stanck [moat] of water of sixteen foot deep and thirty foot of breadth ... Farther, this earl gart make such provision for the king, and his mother, and the embasador, that they had all manner of meates, drinks, and delicates, that were to be gotten at that time in all Scotland, either in burgh or land; that is to say, all kind of drink, as ale, beer, wine, both white and clared, malvesy, muskadel, hippocras, aquivite. Farther, there was of meats wheat bread, maine bread, and ginge bread, with fleshes, beef, mutton, lamb, veal, venison, ghoose, grice, capon, coney, cran, swan, partridge, plover, duck, drake, brissel-cock [turkey], and pawnes [peacocks], black-cock, muir-fowl [grouse], cappercaillies; and also the stancks that were round about the palace were full of all delicate fishes, as salmons, trouts, pearches, pikes, eeles, and all other kinds of delicate fishes that could be gotten in fresh waters, and all ready for the banket.

Syne there were proper stewards, cunning baxters, excellent cooks and potingers, with confections and drugs for their deserts; and the halls and chambers were prepared with costly bedding, vessels and napery, according for a King, so that he wanted none of his orders, more than he had been at home in his own palace.

The King remained in this wilderness at the hunting the space of three days and three nights, and his company, as I have shown. I have heard men say it cost the Earl of Atholl every day in expenses a thousand pounds.

Would that Lindsay had described the hunt itself in as great detail! As it is, there is no record of the bag, or of what sport the King enjoyed.

Yet the occasion was long remembered in the area, and for 200 years at least a narrow pass in the forest of Atholl was known as 'the King's Seat', and was said to have been the place from which he observed (or perhaps took part in) the slaughter.

Another great hunt took place on Atholl ground in 1563. This time the royal guest was Queen Mary, and fortunately one of her courtiers, William Barclay, left a vivid account of the proceedings.

Two thousand Highlanders were employed to drive to the hunting-ground all the deer from the woods and hills of Atholl, Badenoch, Mar, Moray and the countries round about. As these Highlanders use a light dress, and are very swift of foot, they went up and down so nimbly that in less than two months' time they brought together two thousand red deer, besides roes and fallow deer.

The Queen, the great men and a number of others, were in a glen when all these deer were brought before them. Believe me, the whole body of them moved forward like an order of battle. The sight still strikes me, and ever will, for they had a leader whom they followed wherever he moved. This leader was a very fine stag, with a very high head. This sight delighted the Queen very much, but she soon had cause for fear, upon the Earl saying— 'there is danger in that stag, for if either fear or rage force him from the ridge of that hill, let each look to himself, for none of us will be out of harm's way; for the rest will all follow him; and, having thrown us under foot, will open their passage to this hill behind us.'

What happened a moment after confirmed this opinion; for the Queen ordered one of the best dogs to be let loose upon a wolf; this the dog pursues, the leading stag was frightened, he flies by the same way that he came, the rest rush after him, and break through the thickest body of the Highlanders. They had nothing for it but to throw themselves flat on the heath, and to allow the deer to pass over them.

It was told the Queen that several of the Highlanders had been wounded, and that two or three were killed on the spot; and the whole body had got off, had not the Highlanders by their skill in hunting, fallen upon a stratagem to cut off the rear from the main body. It was of those which had been separated that the Queen's dogs and those of the nobility made slaughter. There were killed that day three hundred and sixty deer, five wolves and some roes.

Several elements in this description strike false notes. First, it seems impossible that the driving-in of the deer could have taken two *months*. With no means of communication except messengers on foot, it would have been impossible to coordinate so protracted an operation; besides, in all that time there would have been so many changes of wind and weather that deer shifted by one part of the advancing cordon would have become thoroughly alarmed by the scent of men reaching them from many different directions, and would surely have broken through some part of the Tinchel while the beaters were still widely strung out. Impressed though he was by the Highlanders' fleetness of foot, Barclay nevertheless underestimated their speed over the hill: in two months they could have driven most of Scotland to their Queen, let alone one area – albeit substantial – of the Grampians.

Another anomaly is the description of the impounded herds being led by a particularly fine stag. This sounds like a flight of fancy invented to suit the royal occasion. A red deer stag does not lead a mixed herd in this way: far from being a chivalrous pioneer, he cravenly keeps himself well to the rear, and almost invariably the lead is taken by some crafty old hind.

In spite of these discrepancies, Barclay's account has a general ring of truth, and the site of the great massacre is remembered to this day: it seems to have been on the western marches of what is now the forest of Fealar, and as the deer were driven up into a steep pass that goes out over the shoulder of Ben-y-gloe, the Queen watched from an outcrop of rock above Loch Loch still known as *Tom nam ban righ*, 'the Queen's hillock'.

An even better idea of the style with which the Tinchels were held is given by John Taylor, an agreeably eccentric traveller who visited the Highlands in 1618. Known as the Water Poet, Taylor was described in one edition of his works as:

a sailor, a waterman, a poet, a composer – on the shortest possible notice and on the most reasonable of terms – of nipping satires, epigrams, anagrams, odes, elegies, and sonnets; a custom-house officer, an adventurer by sea and land, a licensed victualler, writer and publisher of short pieces in prose and verse for upwards of forty years, a peripatetic bookseller, a tuft-hunter, a very great schemer, and a firm Royalist with a lame leg.

This ebullient versifier amused himself by making difficult journeys, and often financed himself by taking bets. He went on one such wagering adventure to Germany in 1617, and for his trip to Scotland in the following year undertook to travel from London to Edinburgh and back without using any money of his own, 'neither begging, borrowing or asking meat, drink or lodging'. He went, he wrote:

> for no other ends,
> But to get money, and to try my friends.

Tried his friends certainly were, in more senses than one: Taylor got 1,600 subscribers to put up 2s. each towards the cost of the pamphlet in which he would describe the journey. But when *The Penniless Pilgrimage* was published some 800 people refused to buy the booklet on the grounds that the poet had broken his own rules, spending some of his own money on the journey.

In any case, Taylor went to Edinburgh, Stirling and Perth, and there heard that his friend Sir William Murray had gone to 'the great hunting to the Brae of Mar'. Following in Murray's tracks, he became increasingly alarmed by the wildness of the country, which he later described in typically quipping style:

> The next day I travelled over an exceeding high mountain, called mount *Skene*, where I found the valley very warm before I went up it; but when I came to the top of it, my teeth began to dance in my head like Virginal's jacks; and withal a most familiar mist embraced me round, that I could not see thrice my length any way, withal, it yielded so friendly a dew, that did moisten through all my clothes: where the old Proverb of a Scottish mist was verified, wetting me to the skin ...
>
> Thus with extreme travel, ascending and descending, I came at night to the place where I would be, in the Brae of Mar, which is a large country, all composed of such mountains, that Shooter's Hill, Gad's Hill, Highgate Hill, Hampstead Hill, Birdlip Hill, or Malvern's Hills, are but mole-hills in comparison, or like a liver or a gizard under a capon's wing, in respect of the altitude of their tops or the perpendicularity of their bottoms.

In Braemar Taylor found a fine gathering of nobles, dressed to a man in kilts, stockings and flat blue caps, with their tartan plaids, or cloaks, thrown over their shoulders: the uniformity of dress was such that it seemed 'as if *Lycurgus* had been there, and made laws of equality'. So rigid was the sartorial formality of the occasion that Taylor himself was obliged to change into Highland dress; and thus attired, he found himself warmly welcomed, the recipient of splendid hospitality. The entire hunting party consisted of some 1,500 men, and they moved camp every night, finding a new site each evening beside some burn, always in the wildest country: it was twelve days, Taylor recorded, before he saw 'either house, corn field or habitation for any creature, but deer, wild horses, wolves, and such like creatures'.

He began to doubt whether he would ever see a house again, but in the meantime he was far from uncomfortable:

I thank my good *Lord Erskine*, he commanded that I should always be lodged in his lodging, the kitchen being always on the side of a bank, many kettles and pots boiling, and many spits turning and winding, with great variety of cheer: as venison baked, sodden, roast, and stewed beef, mutton, goats, kid, hares, fresh salmon, pigeons, hens, capons, chickens, partridge, moor-coots, heath-cocks, capercaillies, and termagants [ptarmigan]; good ales, sack, white and claret, tent (or Alicante), with most potent *Aquavitae*.

All these and more than these we had continually, in superfluous abundance, caught by Falconers, Fowlers, Fishers, and brought by my Lord's tenants and purveyors to victual our camp ...

The manner of hunting is this: five or six hundred men do rise early in the morning, and they do disperse themselves divers ways, and seven, eight or ten miles compass, they do bring or chase in the deer in many herds (two, three or four hundred in a herd) to such or such a place as the Nobleman shall appoint them; then when day is come, the Lords and gentlemen of their companies do ride or go to the said places, sometimes wading up to their middles through bournes and rivers: and then, they being come to the place, do lie down on the ground till those foresaid scouts, which are called Tinchels, do bring down the deer; but as the proverb says of the bad cook, so these Tinchel men do lick their own fingers; for besides their bows and arrows which they carry with them, we can hear now and then a harquebuss or musket go off, which they do seldom discharge in vain.

Then, after we had stayed there three hours or thereabouts, we might perceive the deer appear on the hills round about us (their heads making a show like a wood) which being followed close by the Tinchel are chased down into the valley where we lay; then all the valley on each side being waylaid with a hundred couple of strong Irish greyhounds, they are let loose as the occasion served upon the herd of deer, so that with dogs, guns, arrows, dirks and daggers in the space of two hours fourscore fat deer were slain.

When they returned to camp 'there was such baking, boiling, roasting and stewing as if Cook Ruffian had been there to have scalded the devil in his feathers.' So thrilled was Taylor with the sport that he composed two sonnets extolling the delights of Highland hunting, and its superiority to the Lowland chase. In neither can he be said to have done his subject justice, and there is only one memorable line:

Mongst craggy cliffs and thunder-battered hills

in either of the poems.

Often the Tinchels were less innocent than the one which Taylor described. Under the pretext of hunting, the chiefs would collect their men together for an attack on a neighbouring clan. Such was the covert purpose of the gathering described by Sir Walter Scott in *Waverley*, the first of the series of novels known by that name. The book was published in 1814, but its action is set in 1745, the year of the great rising and a time of political ferment. Young Edward Waverley, the hero, is taken to the rendezvous by Fergus, the Chieftain with whom he is staying, attended by 'about three hundred of his clan, well armed, and accoutred in their best fashion'. Scott's account of the Tinchel is clearly based on the earlier writers already mentioned, but his imagination furnished the drive with a vivid climax:

But now the main body of the deer appeared at the head of the glen, compelled into a very narrow compass, and presenting such a formidable phalanx that their antlers appeared, at a distance, over the ridge of the steep pass, like a leafless grove. Their number was very great, and from a desperate stand which they made, with the tallest of the red-deer stags arranged in front, in a sort of battle-array, gazing on the group which barred their passage down the glen, the more experienced sportsmen began to augur danger.

The work of destruction, however, now commenced on all sides. Dogs and hunters were at work, and muskets and fusees resounded from every quarter. The deer, driven to desperation, made at length a fearful charge right upon the spot where the more distinguished sportsmen had taken their stand. The word was given in Gaelic to fling themselves upon their faces; but Waverley, on whose English ears the signal was lost, had almost fallen a sacrifice to his ignorance of the ancient language in which it was communicated.

Fergus, observing his danger, sprang up and pulled him with violence to the ground, just as the whole herd broke upon them. The tide being absolutely irresistible, and the wounds from a stag's horns highly dangerous, the activity of the Chieftain may be considered, on this occasion, as having saved his guest's life. He detained him with a firm grasp until the whole herd of deer had fairly run over them. Waverley then attempted to rise, but found that he had suffered several very severe contusions; and, upon further examination, discovered that he had sprained his ankle violently.

Temporarily disabled by his injuries, the hero has to limp home; but the rest of the clans hold a stirring parade and then march off on some secret expedition. 'Waverley', remarks the author, 'was surprised that Fergus had not mentioned this ulterior destination when they set out upon the hunting party; but his situation did not admit of many interrogatories.'

Even if a Tinchel was quite innocent, held purely for hunting, its setting-up called for careful organisation. Records preserved in the charter room at Blair Castle show clearly how the great concourse of men and dogs was assembled. Every autumn, at the beginning of August, from the glens scattered about the fringes of his forest, the Duke of Atholl would summon his fencible men, that is, those between sixteen and sixty who were fit for military service. In 1710, for example, the orders went out in the first week of August to many parishes round about. 'These are ordering you to advertise our Vassals and a fencible man out of every merk land belonging to us either on property or superiority,' said a typical summons. Some men were told to bring six days' rations, some eight, and all were to present themselves 'in their best arms and apparrell'. A rider added that they were to bring as many dogs 'as possibly they can get'. A week later invitations went out to two of the Duke's neighbours, Farquharson of Inverey and Mackenzie of Dalmore: 'I designe to have a deer-hunting this year, which is to begin on Wednesday, the 23rd. inst. in Beaniglo. If you please to come there, with some pretty men and as many dogs as you can provide, you shall be welcome.'

On the 23rd all the men were duly drawn up on a hill called Druim na h-eachedra, and before the Tinchel was sent out the following orders were read aloud:

1. That none shall offer to fire a gun or pistol in the time of the deer-hunting.
2. That none shall offer to break up a deer or take out a gralloch [the intestines] except in His Grace's presence ...
3. That none be drunk or swear an oath.

Whoever shall transgress any of the said rules shall by fyned and taken into custody, as His Grace shall appoint.

In spite of these prohibitions, the Tinchels were clearly accompanied by a great deal of roistering (in 1704 a mild scandal was caused when it was reported that during the autumn hunting the Duke had drunk out of Dundee's skull). The bag for 1710 is not recorded; but in the following year the first day yielded nothing, the second twenty-five deer, and the third thirty-two. The climax of each drive must have been barbaric in the extreme – a frenzy of slaughter. At one Tinchel, it is recorded, John Robertson of Easter Tyre and John Stewart of Blair Atholl each cut a stag clean in half with a single blow of his broadsword.

Chapter Four

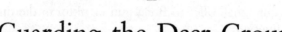

Guarding the Deer Ground

In the accounts of early deer-hunting, it is no accident that the Earls and Dukes of Atholl are mentioned more often than any other landowner, for the huge forest of Atholl is one of the oldest in Scotland and deer have been preserved on it for several hundred years. Just as the ground itself occupies a central position in the Highlands, lying to the east of the main road that now runs from Perth to Inverness, so the Forest of Atholl is central to the history of deer-stalking, not least because a rich hoard of family papers preserved at Blair Castle gives many fascinating insights into the early management of the forest.

Great landowners like the Atholl family were both helped and hindered by the vagueness of the forest laws: by the beginning of the eighteenth century it was commonly agreed that although acts such as that of 1551 had never been formally repealed, their barbaric penalties (including prison, the stocks, amputation of the right hand and even death) were obsolete and should therefore be disregarded. Yet if such laws were still officially in force, so too were the ancient traditions whereby the monarch had conferred on the great barons the privilege of forestry, which included the right to kill deer for their own use and to confiscate all cattle found straying within the forest bounds – two-thirds of them to be given to the monarch, and one-third to be kept for the landowners themselves. In 1714, when a dispute broke out between the Duke of Atholl and his neighbour John Robertson, the laird of Lude, the Duke invoked hazy but impressive historical precedents:

The Duke of Atholl and his predecessors being invest in the Forrest of Freechrombie comprehending Beaniglo and Beanivurich and several other hills, and in possession past all memory of man of

Hunting and Shooting of deer and debarring others from pasturing and shealling [grazing cattle during the summer] within the bounds thereof ...

'Past all memory of man' was accurate enough: nobody could refute the Duke's claims, because nobody could remember, or had any documents to show, exactly what the original depositions had been. It was thus mainly on a base of tradition that the family exercised its rights over such an enormous area.

The early foresters' duties were fourfold: first, to guard the ground assigned them against incursions by unauthorised persons; second, to keep out other people's grazing animals; third, to kill vermin; and fourth, to shoot deer for the chief's larder. In the seventeenth century no laird dreamt of pursuing deer on his own; though he would gladly direct a Tinchel, with all its pomp and excitement, he would never himself descend to the menial task of going after venison, which could be delegated to one of his forest staff.

The provision of venison for the laird's family and friends was perhaps the forester's most congenial job. Two hundred and fifty years ago he was paid a regular salary to work at what others now give small fortunes to enjoy – a long season of deer-stalking throughout every summer and autumn. No records remain to show how this early culling was carried out, but as only a small number of men were involved, it seems most likely that one of them crept up on the deer alone, his primitive rifle reinforced by the presence of a powerful deerhound which could quickly bring to bay any animal wounded but not killed outright. It was thus among the servants rather than their masters that the practice of stalking originated.

There seem to have been no close seasons for male or female deer: stags (then known as harts) and hinds were shot indiscriminately, the only requirement being that the deer should be in good condition for eating. In 1718 the Atholl foresters were ordered to take care that the beasts they killed were:

sufficiently well grown deer for the season they are killed in ... in consideration of all which we doe hereby allow you twenty pounds Scots money yearly ... and if ye doe not kill the number of deer you are bound to yearly by yr. commission, which is twenty yearly each of you, there shall be kept of your wages forty shillings Scots for each deer deficient of the said number.

In June 1719, while the Duke was living at Huntingtower, near Perth, some twenty-five miles from Blair Castle, he ordered his foresters to kill as many deer as possible – 'at least two a week' – and to take a horse with them right into the forest, so that the carcases could be sent straight back to Blair and forwarded to him with the minimum delay. 'Take care that they don't spoill the deer by cairning them [leaving them out on the hill overnight]', he ordered, 'nor by any means cairn them at all.' To his man at Blair he wrote: 'Be sure if the weather be hot, that you do not travell betwixt ten in the morning and four in the afternoon.'

Between them, the foresters must have killed a considerable number of deer. In 1715, for instance, John McIntosh was commissioned to kill twenty beasts a year, and Thomas Stewart, described as a stalker (the first time the word appears in the records), to kill twenty-five.

The early foresters were invested with sweeping powers. A warrant issued to Innerslaney and Thomas Mackenzie on June 28th, 1706 gave them positively Draconian rights for keeping the ground quiet:

> These are ordering and impowering you to dispossess all persons whatsoever of what Shealls they presently possess within our Forrests of Atholl except they produce our warrand in write for the same ... You are likewise hereby ordered to shoot any dogs you shall find within our Forrest in regard they scare the deer, and to exact 20p. Scots from the master of each dog found there. As likewise we order you to kill or bring in alive any eagles old or young you can take or shoot in the Forrest, and for your encouragement we shall give you a warrand for killing a deer for your own use for each eagle old or young brought in.

Three years later, in 1709, the foresters in Glenfernate were instructed that they

> shall not suffer any stranger or Countryman to shoot guns or Harigbuts within any part of the Forrests without apprehending of them and taking their guns from them and revealing the same to the said Duke ... They strictly keep the marches and meiths [boundaries] of the said Forrest against all persons without find or favour ... they frequently frequent and travel through the bounds of the Forrests at all times of the year according to their ability.

The exact disposition of the marches was evidently a matter of some doubt, and depended more on men's memories than on precisely drawn maps. In 1717 one of the Duke's senior foresters was ordered 'to perambulate the bounds and marches of His Grace's Forrest ... and all the neighbours adjacent to the said Forrest, having called some of the most knowing men to the said march, with other men, that they might know the marches in tyme coming.' The document concludes with an immensely detailed description of the march, corrie by corrie, hill by hill, ridge by ridge.

This exercise, however, by no means settled the matter, for in 1803, nearly a century later, a fresh argument broke out between the fifth Duke and General William Robertson of Lude, who proved a disagreeable neighbour. The disputed ground was a 1,900-acre stretch of moor lying high on the ridge to the east of Glen Tilt. Both landowners claimed the right to shoot over the area, and, in the words of the Atholl record,

> Lude, in order to annoy the Duke, encouraged his tenants to poach both deer and grouse on it, undertaking to pay their fines in the event of their being prosecuted and convicted. The General is said at times to have taken a cannon to the march of the commonty, and by discharging the piece endeavoured to scare the deer on the other side of Glen Tilt, and thus spoil His Grace's sport when out in the forest. On other occasions he fired his cannon at the deer when grazing on the commonty. Three of these balls (five pounders), found afterwards on the hill by some of the Glen Fender tenants, are at Blair Castle.

Over the years the powers assigned to the foresters were gradually diminished. Thus in 1706 Innerslaney had been empowered to shoot dogs on sight; by 1750, however, Duncan Robertson was ordered only to 'seize the dogs, guns or netts of all strangers who shall attempt to destroy the deer or game.' Nor was he allowed to confiscate grazing animals, as his predecessors had been: he was merely to 'seize and apprehend all the bestiall that he finds within the said bounds and to poynfold and detain them until they pay conform to the Forrest Laws.'

By 1767, the Duke's men had instructions to be even more polite and correct in their manner when finding strangers abroad in the forest. Orders given to the gamekeepers in that year enjoined them:

carefully to watch His Grace's grounds in their severall districts, and when they observe any person or persons come to hand thereon with dogs, guns or netts, they are to order matters so that a clear proof may be brought by the Testimony of two concurring witnesses ... who can swear to the identity of the person, that they saw him shoot, and saw him sett his dog in the field, no matter whether he miss or kill.

And for a greater certainty the gamekeepers or servants who watch the ground, after hearing or seeing any shott, are in a Discreet way to talk to the person or persons that are shooting or hunting and let him or them know whose ground they are hunting on, that they are by their own master's orders to watch, and ask their names in a civil way, that they may report to their master for their own ex-oneration lest they lose their bread.

The reason for this tentative approach was that the landowners had become less and less sure of the legal ground on which they stood. It was rather as if they found themselves in the middle of a huge peat-bog: though perfectly sure that all the land for miles around belonged to them, they could not take decisive or aggressive steps for fear that they might plunge into a quagmire of legal uncertainty.

One problem was that, in spite of all the historical precedents they might invoke, they were still not certain to whom the deer belonged. In 1711 a proprietor had tried to prosecute a person who had killed deer on his land, but the case had failed because the court held that the forest laws did not make wild animals the property of a landowner: creatures that were free to roam from one property to another and could not be identified individually were *ferae naturae*, and therefore belonged to nobody, so that the killing of deer on unenclosed ground could never be counted a theft.

Another ancient statute – that of 1617 – laid down that landowners who had been invested with the privileges of forestry 'shall have full powers, privileges and jurisdictions to call, convene and pursue before them whatever person or persons that shall be found hereafter to transgress the said Acts and Statutes.' In other words, a laird had the power to form his own court, and to act as judge in it – an invincible combination. But as more and more people defied this, the most oppressive of all the old forest laws, the proprietors found they could only resort to civil actions, the outcome of which was far less predict-able than it would have been in a court of their own convening.

In view of all this uncertainty, it is hardly surprising that intruders were not co-operative when challenged by the foresters. In 1770 the Atholl forester Paul Robertson reported finding four army officers shooting on the Duke's best moors. When he confronted them 'they asked him if he had a warrant from the Duke for preserving his hills. He told them he had. They then desired him to stop the warrant in his backside, and were very abusive to him.'

The foresters were lucky if no more than abuse came their way: many of the poachers were violent and desperate men, quite prepared to shoot rather than be caught. In November 1762 a vivid report was sent in to the Duke of Gordon's factor by Robert Willox, the forester in Glenavon, about an occasion the previous month on which he had seen a wounded stag, and two men following it. He had given chase:

> and when I came within musket shot of them I presented my Gun and swore I would make Sun and Moon shine through some of their Bodies if they did not stand. At last they stood ...

Finding that the leading poacher was Lewis Grant, a soldier, 'full armed with Gun and Dirk,' Willox challenged him 'in a very harsh manner,' but, being the weaker party, was not able to disarm the intruders. Next day, he joined another of the Duke's foresters, John Stewart, and his son, and again caught Grant in the forest:

> He made off as hard as he could. I cryed at him to stand but he would not. John Stewart having my Gun in his hand I desired him to shoot him. On hearing this – he had two Guns himself – he put one of the Guns down by his side and presented the other and swore he would make light shine through us if we did not stand back.
>
> I took my Gun out of John Stewart's hand and presented her at the fellow's breast on which he swore the second time he would make my Guts ly on the ground if I would put the hindmost foot forward and still kept his Gun on bend at his Eye. I holding my Gun still on bend, taking my Thumb off the Doghead I swore I would make his Lights fly out behind his shoulders if he did not surrender his arms. Having my Gun still in the same Pouster I flew in on him and dis-armed him.
>
> After having him a prisoner he offered me five Guineas if I would give him the Long Gun. I told him I would not take twenty-five Guineas.

During the 1760s and 1770s the Duke of Gordon's foresters were persistently harassed by a notorious poacher called John Priest, of Glenkiness. At one stage he kept threatening to burn down the forester's house in Glenfiddich, and his violent nature emerges clearly from a series of incidents that took place in March 1773. He was seen going into the forest of Glenfiddich and, as he later boasted, he killed two deer with one shot. The beasts were found by two of the Duke's men, who carried off the bodies and hid them in their house.

The next night—one of 'bright moonshine'—Priest set out to attack the house in the forest, accompanied by his brother Francis and by three local women, who can have been scarcely less rough than their men. At the foresters' house, George Storach and James McInnes were asleep in the garret when the raiders arrived; and Priest, after uttering 'many dreadful expressions, threatening to kill such persons as he found in the house', tried to gain access to the garret by climbing up a plank laid against the wall.

Storach, 'apprehending himself in danger', picked up a spade, swung it, hit Priest in the face, and 'struck him back to the ground' so sharply that 'he was pretty much wounded in the head' and lost a great deal of blood. In spite of this setback, he and his cronies continued to bombard the house with stones till Storach 'cryed out from the inside of the house that he had a loaded gun which he would fire out upon them if they did not desist ... '

A forester's life in those days was evidently a tough one; but often the keepers never managed to get to grips with the poachers: sheer fitness and speed over the hill won the day, for in those immense open spaces the safest way for a man to avoid being brought to justice was to outdistance his pursuers and so escape positive identification.

During the eighteenth century the methods used for killing deer gradually changed. A note in the *Chronicles of the Atholl and Tullibardine Families* (a privately printed selection from the family papers) records that the Tinchel of 1713 was 'the last of the old Highland deer-huntings held in Atholl.' What this means is not quite clear, for several later references speak of large-scale manœuvres in the autumn: in September 1800, for instance, Lady Elizabeth Murray, a daughter of the fourth Duke, wrote to her brother, James, 'Papa had a famous deer hunt yesterday: there were above 200 tenants there, who formed a line four miles in length. They surrounded about twelve hundred deer, but they broke through their line and got off, so that they only killed six of them.'

These latter-day hunts, though similar in many ways to the originals, must have been conducted in slightly different fashion. It was no doubt the social and political upheaval of the rising of 1715 which disrupted the traditional pattern; and the even greater disturbance of the Forty-Five, which brought the old clan system more or less to an end, put paid to many of the ancient customs. No longer could a chief send out orders to his fencible men to attend his pleasure; and even if— as in Atholl— the laird was still powerful enough to summon 200 tenants to his hunting, the social nuances of the occasion must have been quite different from those of the old days.

Another innovation, made, quite early in the eighteenth century, was that members of the laird's family began to go out after the deer singlehanded— or at least attended by only a handful of retainers. In Atholl, perhaps earlier than anywhere else, the young nobles discovered how amusing and exciting, and what good exercise it was, to go out stalking. In 1732 Lord George Murray, younger brother of the second Duke, set up his summer quarters in Glen Tatinich, whence he sent home a steady supply of grouse and venison, keeping his wife posted with a series of letters whose natural charm is much enhanced by the eccentricity of the author's spelling:

I have got the most ample wrote order from my Brother for killing Dear and Hunting and Fooling [Fowling] in all his forests etc & there are great plenty of Moorfooll [grouse] hereabouts so I really belive there is no day but there five hundred Dear within five miles of me, & many in this very Glen.

I have delightful Divertion in Hunting etc. [he wrote on July 5th] As I sat down at a burnside in the Forest about one o'clok to take chak, we were disturbed by a dog runing a Fan [Fawn], & the Hind not only defending her Fan, but with great fury ataked the dog, & made him not only quitt his Grips of the Fan, but if we had not interposed and hunted the rest of our dogs at the Hind, I really belive she had demolished the greay hound. However, the Hind escaped, which I was very glad off, seeing she had behaived so valiently for her young.

We shott a Hind about nine in the morning, and I shott another at seven at night. They were both kild in our own Glen ... the Hind, which I sent, tho' it be not fatt, will make very good broth & colops, I hope the nixt will be better. Please also receve a leg of the Fan, which I belive will be very good meat ...

D

Murray clearly had some trouble in approaching the deer, for on July 12th he wrote that he hoped he would 'have better luke than yesterday, for we got nothing.' Even so, he was enjoying himself immensely:

> I am just now on the confines of my brother's and the Mar forests, where I have the pleasure of the most noble Divertion in the world ... I am in perfect health, & indeed I never was better, & what at another time would be a fatigue is performed with the greatest ease. I kild two Hearts on Saturday evening of which I sent one and a half to my love ...

By shooting hinds and their young in July, when the calves were scarcely two months old, Murray showed a lamentable lack of concern for the principles of deer conservation. Yet in calling his sport 'the most noble Divertion in the world' he precisely foreshadowed the sentiments of the great influx of deer-stalkers who took to the Highlands a hundred years later: the grandeur of the surroundings, the nobility and elusiveness of the deer, the invigorating exercise – all these were exactly the elements which appealed to the Victorians, and which retain a matchless fascination to this day.

The preservation of so much land for sport later gave rise to many bitter arguments and the great landowners were frequently accused of clearing out the human population for the benefit of the deer. The Atholl family, in particular, was charged with evicting the human population from Glen Tilt in 1784, and this was often said to have been the first of the notorious Highland clearances. No doubt when the vogue for deer-stalking came in fifty years later, humans were in a few cases sacrificed for sport, but mostly the clearances were made for sheep rather than for deer: it was the creation of sheep-walks rather than of deer-forests that caused the depopulation of the glens. The clearances began in the 1780s and reached their climax in the early 1800s when landlords saw sheep as the great moneymakers of the future; but the carving out of deer-forests did not begin on a large scale until the 1830s, by which time most of the glens had been empty for years and the sheep had already taken over.

Nevertheless, the facts were obscured by a smokescreen of emotional writing in books such as McLeod's *Gloomy Memories* published in 1841 and Mackenzie's *Highland Clearances* published in 1883; and so persistent was the disparagement of the Atholl family that in 1911 the Marquis of Tullibardine (who later became the eighth Duke) prepared a detailed refutation of the claims made about Glen Tilt, the long, narrow and spectacularly steep glen that slices north-eastwards through the forest. In a 2,000-word letter to several local newspapers, he demolished one by one the claims that there had been wholesale evictions in the past and that, properly managed, the glen would be able to carry a population of 1,000 people instead of the handful it still supported.

The estate records, he wrote, showed that in 1705 the upper portion of the glen could furnish only thirty-one fencible men (men of all ranks, including servants, between sixteen and sixty). In 1784 – the year in which the wholesale eviction had allegedly taken place – the population can scarcely have been any higher. During the eighteenth century, he pointed out, there had never been more than thirteen smallholdings in the upper stretch of the glen, and over the years these were either amalgamated into larger units or fell in for lack of new tenants willing to take them on, with consequent loss of income to the Atholl family. 'In place of these thirteen dwellings scattered up and down the glen,' wrote Tullibardine in 1911,

there are now, if we include Fealar (a shooting lodge), eight houses inhabited all the year round, two inhabited during the summer months, and two shooting lodges, so that the number of houses today inhabited all the year round is only five less than in 1760. It is therefore, in the first place, the grossest exaggeration to speak of the glen as having been 'cleared' and as 'little better than a desert,' or to suggest, as McLeod does, that there were once 'thirty cottages in one spot' ...

Neither estate records (which, as I have shown, furnish us with the names of holdings, tenants and amounts of rent at different periods during the last two hundred years) nor the voluminous correspondence on family and estate matters preserved in the Atholl Charter Room, contain any reference to any force ever having been used to turn anybody out of any holding in Glen Tilt, or on any part of the estate, for the purposes of sport ... In all the years since McLeod's book first drew attention to Glen Tilt no one has ever given a specific case of an eviction there ... Not only have there been no 'wholesale evictions,' but no evictions or forcible clearances for deer at all on the Atholl Estates.

It seems that the Marquis was scrupulously honest in his exposition of the family records, for he invited anyone who cared to do so to come and peruse them. Thus one must look for some other-than-obvious explanation of the orders issued to the foresters in 1706 'to dispossess all persons whatsoever of what Shealls they presently possess within our Forrests of Atholl except they produce our warrand in write for the same.' Probably the key lies in the words 'except they produce our warrand', and the people to be evicted were squatters who had taken up grazings unofficially.

Another element which the Marquis used in his family's defence was the fact that both land and weather in Glen Tilt were highly intractable: of the various houses that he mentioned, one stood 1,450 feet above sea level, one at 1,250 feet, and several at about 1,000. Although the east side of the glen provided some sheep-grazing, he wrote, the western side 'is quite unsuitable for sheep, being little more than a cairn of stones, with practically no grazing ... I doubt if anywhere in all Scotland men are to be found spending the whole year in a more inhospitable and inclement spot.'

This was one of the deer's greatest strengths—their ability to survive on ground which no other animal could tolerate. There is no evidence to show that during the eighteenth century in Atholl, or anywhere else, men envied the deer the amount of space which they had been granted: everyone could see that most of it was useless for any normal type of farming. What people did resent, however, was that in a poor country, where food was scarce, so much meat on the hoof should be reserved for the nobility, who needed it less than anyone else. Inevitably, venison was highly prized, and poaching was an art assiduously practised by generations of Highlanders.

Chapter Five

The Free Foresters

In a book called *Forest Sketches* published in Edinburgh in 1865, the author (who preferred to remain anonymous, but whose name was in fact William Robertson) gave an admirable account of the Highland attitude to poaching which had prevailed at the beginning of the nineteenth century. In putting the old laws into practice, he wrote, the foresters on the great estates conducted themselves so officiously as to make themselves extremely unpopular. Their right of seizing stray cattle was particularly vexatious, and as the head forester always lived in the forest or near it, he had 'many opportunities of annoying their [the cattle's] owners'. Such were the head forester's powers that the office was highly coveted, 'carrying with it not only direct advantages, but immunities from many evils and hardships, it was one of ambition to small proprietors and cadets of more powerful families.' Once in office, a forester was very difficult to get rid of: the story was told of an Atholl man, who, having been dismissed, returned and murdered his successor, only to be tracked down himself and executed.

Even though it gradually came to be accepted that the deer were *ferae naturae*, and therefore not the property of the laird, prosecutions still took place, according to *Forest Sketches*,

> up to a very recent period; and it might be difficult to determine which was more in the wrong – the man of wealth and power, who knowingly wrested the law and turned it from the course of justice to suit his own ends; or the man who ... poor, ignorant and needy, killed deer because he found it the easiest and most expeditious way of feeding his starving family.

In the Highlands, the anonymous author wrote, the forest laws were particularly oppressive:

People liable to periodical famines, who had occasionally to resort to every possible means for procuring food to preserve their lives, thought it an unbearable hardship to be withheld from using the resources nature had put within their reach. The ownership of the Crown in deer had ceased to be looked upon as a tangible fact ... The deer were looked upon as a gift of nature that might be appropriated without the infringement of any moral obligation.

It was therefore considered in no way derogatory to the character of a man, or of a gentleman, to be known as a deer-stalker, and if he had become the object of the forester's dislike and one that had often baulked well-laid schemes for his capture, he was thought all the more of, and excited all the higher respect and admiration ... It is not to be wondered at that young men of station and family, who had no right to kill deer, were often addicted to the chase, not only from the excitement and fascination of the noble sport itself, but also as a way to fame among their friends and dependents.

Clandestine deer-stalking, the book concluded, was an excellent form of training for any youth who wanted to become a soldier, increasing, as it did, his endurance, his resistance to discomfort, his self-reliance and his cunning.

This constructive attitude to poaching was reinforced by the ancient traditions of the clan system, whereby all the members of a clan were bound by sacred ties to respect each other's privileges. Chiefs would allow their tenants to poach as much as they poached themselves, and a successful *creach*, or foray, was accounted a worthy achievement, to be imitated as often as possible. Like the smugglers who spirited illicit whisky through the glens, poachers were aided and abetted by other members of the community; just as 'a whole country side would unite to baffle the exciseman', watching him and passing news of his movements to interested parties, so the plans and movements of the foresters were passed on as swiftly as possible to the young bloods who disappeared at night to the hills.

After its factual opening, *Forest Sketches* develops into a discursive but vivid narrative about one Robert Graham of Dunurn, a well born though impoverished young man who is struggling to restore his family fortunes by becoming a lawyer. As the story begins he is wrestling with Latin texts in Edinburgh, but his heart is in the hills, and the whole of the rest of the book concerns his enmity with the equally youthful Lord Strathalbane, the laird whose deer-forest lies close by

Dunurn, and with his head forester, James Walker, also known as Sheamus More, or Big James, the swiftest and most powerful man on the hill for miles around.

Whether or not the story is based on fact, it is clearly a parable designed to illustrate the kind of behaviour to which the iniquity of the forest laws gave rise. Robert is the archetype of the heroic, adventurous young stalker; Strathalbane the well meaning but conventional laird, trapped in the web of the old conventions; and Big James, the dogged, unswervingly loyal retainer.

Robert, on all his expeditions, is accompanied by his beloved deerhound Farrum, whose rich cream colour and black muzzle and ears make him no less distinctive a poacher than his owner. Their first nocturnal foray is memorably described.

Leaving home on foot in the evening, ostensibly to visit a relative, Robert turns aside from the road after dark and in an oak wood meets his three retainers, chief among whom is Robbie, armed with a home-made gun so dangerous that his own friends flee whenever he prepares to discharge it (on one occasion, when he fired at some partridges, 'the barrel got away from the stock and went through the air with a most disagreeable noise, and according to his own account killed two of the birds.')

The four men proceed deep into the hills. It is October; already the rut is well advanced and the stags are roaring:

As they went on the roaring became more loud, and ere long it proceeded from all sides, as if they were surrounded by a herd of furious bulls ... Robert Graham felt his hair bristling as one great stag challenged with a mighty voice, and a hundred answered in a hundred different keys, from glen, corrie and mountain-side.

The night's manœuvres yield one hind and two stags, the biggest a monster with a head of sixteen points. As a parting gesture, the friends place the great head on an urn in front of the castle, where it will immediately be seen by the first person who comes out in the morning, and then they borrow Curly, the laird's deer pony, to carry home two of their carcases (the third they split and carry on their shoulders).

Next day Big James and a bailiff descend on Robert's home to try to arrest him, but by then he has resumed the journey to stay with friends which he began the evening before: thus he has not only a long start, but also an impregnable alibi.

In describing another excursion, the author gives a fine idea of the
excitement that the early stalkers got from watching their deerhounds
at work. In this case, a stag has been wounded and Farrum sent after
him:

On came the stag, thundering along the hillside, and Farrum within
forty yards of his haunches, straining every muscle to lessen the
distance. Without looking at the men, the deer held on his course,
his head thrown back and his antlers nearly touching his back: his
nose well up and the nostrils crimson red. It was not a bounding
or a labouring gallop, but a spanking trot, and never a man
looked on more magnificent action. The dog did not gain an inch
upon him, and as they swept past between him and the river, Ronald
flourished his cloak and bounded three times in the air to nearly his
own height, and declared that 'By George, the sight was worth
living and dying to see.'

Eventually the feud between Robert and the young laird culminates
in a great deer-drive and its aftermath. Hearing that Lord Strathalbane's
men 'expect to make a thousand deer pass through Glenbuie before
two o'clock', Robert and Robbie walk all night to be on the ground
before daybreak and to take part — uninvited — in this form of latter-day
Tinchel. They reach their target area, sleep in the heather, and wake to
see the laird and his party coming along the glen below them, all
dressed in green kilts, round grey coats, red and white stockings and
smart little blue bonnets.
    After a long wait, shots begin to go off from points high in the
surrounding corries, and Robert takes advantage of the sporadic
fusillade to down a stag of his own; but at once he sees that Big James
Walker has heard the extra shot, and is hastening towards them to cut
them off. They split, Robbie to decoy and delay Walker by acting the
oaf and pretending to be lost, Robert to head for home. This he does,
but as he passes the place where Lord Strathalbane himself has been
ensconced for the drive, he flushes a magnificent stag, which the laird
knocks over with a rifle shot.

The animal dropped like a stone. The young lord ran to where he
lay, and as he got near it, drew a long dagger from his belt, in order
to bleed the stag. But before he could reach him he got upon his
feet, apparently stupefied, and tried to stagger away. Strathalbane,
dropping the knife, struck the animal a heavy blow with the butt

of his rifle, which made him turn round, and, seeing his assailant, he put his head down and charged him ... The next moment, Strathalbane was thrown down heavily upon the stones, and the stag ... furiously jumped upon him with his feet and tore at him fiercely with his horns.

Robert and Farrum rush to the man's rescue. The dog seizes the stag with its favourite hold behind the ear, and Robert plunges the dagger into the animal's breast. Then he picks up the nobleman, who is 'bruised, helpless and half unconscious', and lays him gently down on the greensward. The young lord turns his eyes, and for a moment they meet those of his 'deliverer'. The next moment he faints.

Walker, meanwhile, has been delayed by Robbie, who, to the intense irritation of the forester, bogs him down with intricate arguments. The delay is enough to give Robert a good start; but then follows an epic chase – one which the author of the book evidently had great relish in describing.

It is seldom that two men such as James Walker and Robert Graham find themselves in the relative positions that they are now in to each other. The one in the prime of manhood, and enjoying the reputation of being unmatched for speed and endurance – the terror of all illicit frequenters of the forest, the pride of his fellow-foresters and the favourite of his master. The other, young and almost untried, but tall and strong and athletic in an uncommon degree, with the promise of indomitable determination and the appearance of pluck and resolution all but inseparable from such patrician blood as flowed in his veins.

On such a contrast as began between the two, much money could scarcely fail to be staked, if undertaken for a bet ...

At first Robert runs well within himself. Fifteen miles of the forest lies ahead before he can reach the safety of the march, and he thinks his lead is enough. Slowly, however, Walker gains on him. Robert 'shakes out another reef', and still Walker gains. He tries going uphill, then downhill, and still Walker gains. Then Robert sees his pursuer's secret: he is being heaved along at superhuman speed by a mighty bloodhound which he has on a chain; it is dragging him forward 'at a pace no unassisted man could rival in speed or endurance'.

But then comes a sudden change. When Walker is no more than a hundred yards behind, he stumbles over a stone, and in doing so lets go his dog's leash. At once the brute dashes forward to attack Robert, only to be met by a counter-charge from Farrum:

> The other dog, seeing him coming, rushed furiously upon him. With marvellous quickness and activity Farrum avoided his savage antagonist, and his own great weight and the force of his onset carried him past. The deerhound sprang at him, and taking him by the flank in his cruel fangs, he with one shake tore him open, and laid him sprawling on the ground, his entrails about his feet.

The incident gives Robert another fifty yards. Walker ignoring his stricken dog, tries a sprint, but to no avail. Then he settles back to wear Robert down by degrees. Robert, still hampered by his faithful gun, Old Thunder, begins to despair.

> On they went, like men terribly in earnest — settling down to their work as if determined to play the game out ... The one did not gain, the other did not lose — was the only result of half an hour's struggle, which took much of the elasticity of the step of each away. They now approached the far boundary of the forest ...
>
> Nothing but his pluck could have carried him so far, and, with that as strong as ever, he could no longer hide from himself that his physical powers were nearly exhausted. He was well aware that Walker was not only a powerful man, but also a sagacious one, and that if he wished to outgeneral him, he must try other than ordinary tactics.
>
> With his mind on this, he came upon a deep hollow that ran right across his course ... He dived into the hollow and was in a moment out of his pursuer's sight. He then turned to the right, and, putting forth his remaining strength, he faced the ascent, and got round a scarcely perceptible projection of the side before the forester could see him. When the latter came to the hollow, and not seeing Graham, he for an instant examined the ground, and seeing a bend in the hollow to his left and below him, he at once concluded that, exhausted as he must be, Robert would naturally go down and not up the hollow; so, without hesitation, he ran down ...

The vital break has been made: Robert has time to sit down, recover his wind, and then to slip quietly away. The sequel to the marathon

unfolds in fairy-tale fashion: Lord Strathalbane, who has to spend ten
days in bed with severe bruising and two broken ribs, sends Walker to
Robert with an invitation to come and shoot, and a letter saying, 'I
believe we have misunderstood each other all our lives.' Later, when
Robert falls dangerously ill with fever, the laird saves his life by arranging visits from the doctor, by sending some of his best sherry, and by
prescribing a special diet. As a reward for bringing Robert round, the
poaching friends give the doctor three legs of salted venison, and in
return they are offered a day's stalk in the forest every year.

Even if its conclusion is trite, *Forest Sketches* does give an admirable
picture of the kind of running battle that was fought between the
owners of the deer-forests and the poachers living round the forest
boundaries – a battle in which physical stamina was the combatants'
greatest asset.

No happy ending awaited Lonavey, a legendary poacher, who had
one hand amputated for his raids in the forest of Atholl and eventually
died in gaol. His real name was Ian Mackeracher, and his nickname
came from his addiction to the chase, *lonach* being the Gaelic for
'greedy' and *fiadh* for deer. His great accomplice was another
Mackeracher – Mackeracher Ruadh, or Mackeracher the Red – and
together they exercised the right of free forestry in Atholl and Braemar,
going to ground, when pressed, in a secret cave with an entrance no
keeper could discover. An account of Lonavey's life is given in *The
Romance of Poaching in the Highlands* by W. McCrombie Smith, first
published in 1904; and although this furnishes no dates for Lonavey,
he seems to have flourished towards the end of the eighteenth
century.

His partnership with Mackeracher the Red ended abruptly when,
one autumn, they were together pursuing a mighty stag whose fame
had spread through Mar and Atholl and set all freelance stalkers on the
go. If a stag of this kind escapes for two or three seasons, the author of
The Romance of Poaching in the Highlands remarks,

> stories begin to circulate that it is impossible to kill him ... that, in
> short, it is a case where only a silver bullet or a silver-tipped arrow
> will be of any avail. In most of these miraculous escapes, however,
> the stag owes his safety more to the excessive anxiety of the hunter
> than to his own charmed life. The hunter becomes so excited ... that
> his thumping heart and shaking hands send all his missiles wide of
> the mark.

Such a beast was the stag which the two Mackerachers were after. For a week they lived in the hills, eating trout and grouse, and stalking separately by day. Then, on the eighth morning, Lonavey heard a shot from the back of a hill called Carn Righ; hastening round the shoulder, he found his accomplice and the great stag locked together in mortal combat. Mackeracher had shot the stag, had gone in prematurely to finish it off with his dirk, and in its death-throes the animal had gored him fatally. Man and beast fell dead together.

Thereafter Lonavey poached alone, a brilliant marksman in spite of the fact that he had only one hand; and *The Romance of Poaching* includes a graphic account of how he adapted the tactics he had perfected for the hill to the more formal circumstances of a shooting contest at Blair Atholl.

Every summer English mowers came north to make hay, and they habitually beat the men of Atholl at shooting with a matchlock. One year, to save local honour, the Earl called in Lonavey, who kept the secret of his method intact by insisting on shooting last. All the other competitors had 'planted their rests at the prescribed distance, had lighted their match, taken a long and deliberate aim, then applied the match to the touch-hole, with the result that more balls had gone direct to mother earth than through the target.'

When Lonavey's turn came, however, he began by stepping back some twenty yards from the firing line. Then, as soon as he had everything ready, he

> seized the rest and the gun and crouching down moved forward silently and quickly till within ten paces of the place he had to fire from. Still preserving his stooping attitude, he next quickly lighted his match ... and sprang forward with amazing swiftness over the remaining ten paces, planted his rest, steadied the barrel on it and on his handless arm, took aim, applied his match ... The report of the gun rang out, and the bullet sped through the target almost in the very centre.
>
> The ten paces he moved forward, crouching, represented the stalk to within range of the deer; the next ten yards and the rapid fixing of the rest, aiming and firing represented the rush in sight of the deer, and the taking advantage of the few seconds that a deer, in such circumstances, takes to view the cause of the disturbance.

By his unique method Lonavey won the championship; he got not only the prize, but 'something additional from the Earl who remarked that if Lonavey must have a shot at the deer now and then, he hoped he would not kill too many.' But a later Earl proved less indulgent to the old poacher, and Lonavey was sent to prison, where he died, having told a fellow inmate that he had left his dirk and gun—the barrel stuffed with marrow oil got from the deer—in his secret cave in the Atholl hills. There the weapons are said to have remained for the best part of a hundred years, until one of Lonavey's free-foresting successors, John Farquharson, accidentally came across their rusting remains.

Lonavey remains a shadowy figure, half fact and half legend; but more is known about Alexander Davidson, who was born in 1792 at Mill of Inver, near Crathie (close to the site of Balmoral Castle). He must have been an extraordinary physical specimen: described by a contemporary as 'a very powerful man', his whole body was 'covered with hair like that of an ox'. One authority gave the measurement of his calf as seventeen inches, another eighteen. Davidson had finely chiselled features, dark hazel eyes, black beard and moustache, and a head of thick curly hair. Altogether he was reckoned one of the handsomest men of his time.

On the hill, his hardiness was almost that of a wild animal: from March to October he slept in the open, disdaining the comfort even of a straw barn, and making his couch from bracken or heather. When he went spear-fishing—at which he was said to be incomparable—he would stand still for hours at a time, up to his neck in the river. He wore the lightest of clothes—in winter a thin tartan coat, waistcoat and trousers, and in the summer a kilt, and when in the open lived mainly on whisky butties—oatmeal saturated in whisky and rolled into balls.

Yet he combined this formidable toughness with a flair for stylish clothes, and when within the bounds of civilisation was generally seen in a rakish white felt hat. He was also an outstanding dancer, and won first prize at a competition organised by the Caledonian hunt in Edinburgh. 'He was incomparably the most graceful of his own time,' according to a contemporary writer quoted in *The Romance of Poaching in the Highlands*, 'and his style was more characteristically Highland than any I have ever seen, while his fine personal appearance, lit by the sparkle of his bright, piercing eye, never shone to better advantage than when he became excited in a Highland reel.'

Davidson began his career as a gamekeeper to the dissolute Lord Kennedy, who had rented the forest of Fealar from the Duke of Atholl, and early in his legitimate career he earned a reputation as a famous shot. But then he took to whisky smuggling and put all the money he had into timber: he bought a large quantity of trees in Glen Derry from the Earl of Fife, and tried to float them down the Dee and thence to market in Aberdeen. When the scheme failed and he lost his money, be became a full-time poacher.

Even so, he did not antagonise the landowning nobility, who were so taken by his natural style and physical prowess that they often treated him as a kind of performing animal. According to one of his contemporaries 'he was a favourite with many of the gentlemen', and was often sent for by them to show his feats of strength and agility:

In 1820 Mr Innes of Durris and Mr Davidson of Balnagask backed Davidson, against Lord Kennedy and Mr Farquharson of Finzean, who had wagered £50, that Davidson would not run naked from Barclay Street, Stonehaven, to the gate of Inchmarlo [some 25 miles away] in a given time. Lord Kennedy and Farquharson thought that Davidson's feet would give way, but to still further ensure their winnings, they ignobly hired a posse of wives armed with stones, their leader, Mrs Duncan, also having a large, knotty stick, to waylay Davidson at the bridge of Banchory and prevent his crossing.

When Davidson came in sight of the bridge and saw the party of Amazons, he rested a minute or two to regain his wind, then charged down on them, and so wild was his appearance, and so terrific the speed with which he bounded into their midst, that their missiles fell harmlessly wide of the mark, and he passed the bridge unscathed, leaving the discomfited wives raging shrilly in the rear. He reached Inchmarlo well within the time ... [*The Romance of Poaching in the Highlands*]

No matter how his social connections might be initiated Davidson exploited them to the full, and in the words of the contemporary record, 'could shoot in a direct line from Braemar to Aberdeen with very little interruption'. Many of the proprietors had given him permission, and others 'winked at him'. He was always extremely polite, and would approach landowners in terms such as these: 'Will you have the goodness to allow me to go through your property when I am on my annual tour? I will not poach it. I will keep the straight line and only kill what may be on my way.'

Thus furnished with a number of permissions – or at any rate non-refusals – he was further helped by the prevailing ignorance about boundaries. Then, as now, the marches of most Highland estates were unmarked on the ground, and by deliberately keeping on or near the frontiers Davidson could always plead inadvertent trespassing should he be so unfortunate as to be challenged.

His early training made him an accomplished stalker, and he was an excellent shot at deer: he seldom missed a stag running even if it was going through trees; yet, curiously enough, he was less certain of hitting beasts lying, on which he had made a stealthy approach. His greatest passion, however, was grouse-shooting, and it was said that 'no millionaire ever rented shootings that would compare with those of Alexander Davidson.' His territory included all the high ground in the shires of Forfar, Aberdeen and Banff, besides a wide sweep in the west of Inverness-shire and the north of Perthshire. 'Nor need any millionaire dream of rivalling Davidson' wrote the author of *The Romance of Poaching in the Highlands*. 'He might possibly include all the ground that Davidson used to include in his three or four months' tour, but, with his effeminate, enervated body, he could no more shoot over it as Davidson did than he could fly to the moon.'

This passionate lover of wild places, who danced so beautifully and also went to church and read the Bible, was found dead on the hills of Glenbuchat on August 25th, 1843: he was lying on his back with his faithful companion, a little brown pointer, seated on his chest keeping guard.

So died the man whom many considered to be the last of the old-time poachers; and certainly, by then, the situation in the Highlands was much different from the one which had prevailed in Davidson's youth. By the 1840s the vogue for deer-stalking was well under way: more and more forests were being let, the ground more intensively keepered and the deer more jealously guarded.

The free forestry that Lonavey and Davidson practised must have been highly enjoyable; for the landowners and their keepers, however, it was a constant irritation, and the other side of the coin is clearly visible in the Atholl estate records, which are full of poaching reports, excursions at night and futile searches for illicit venison. Not only did the poachers kill deer illegally: they also made themselves at home in the bothies, or shooting lodges, far out in the hills, messing the places up and leaving them open to the weather. The bothy at Feith Uaine, built by the fourth Duke of Atholl in 1806, was so much frequented by poachers and furnished them with such a useful base, that in 1826 the estate staff deliberately burnt it; not until the 1870s, when stalking rents had gone sky-high and a Mr Ashley Dodd had become the tenant of Forest Lodge, was the house rebuilt.

Fealar was another lodge to which poachers would sometimes repair; but their use of it was suddenly ended by a sinister accident which was never properly explained. One night two men had gone to the house, and being unable to force the door, had broken in through a window. Needing some water for cooking, one of them began levering himself out of the window backwards, whereupon his leg was seized and savaged by some unseen creature. He roared with fright and pain, and after a violent struggle shook off his attacker. But he and his companion could find no trace near the house of any person or animal, either then or in the morning. The victim carried scars for the rest of his life, and so great was the alarm spread by his experience that poachers kept clear of Fealar ever afterwards.

In the early days some keepers were not above turning poacher, should the occasion seem to justify it. In 1783, wanting a suitable present for George III, the Duke of Atholl summoned his three senior foresters and offered a substantial reward to the man who should bring in the fattest stag within the space of two days. Two of the men set out for the hill on a normal expedition but the third, Peter Robertson, slipped away to the nearby forest of Gaick, where, he knew, there lived a tame stag of exceptional size. This idle beast had been caught as a calf by the Gaick shepherds, and lived luxuriously during the summer with two milk cows that were pastured in the glen; in the winter he withdrew to a barn and feasted on hay, oats, barley and peas, so that by the time he was five he had attained extraordinary dimensions.

Having got the two shepherds blind drunk on whisky, Robertson drove the stag and the two cows slowly down the glen to the point at which he had concealed a rifle, and there he despatched the deer with a deliberate shot. His horse, though a strong one, had difficulty carrying such a mighty burden, and it was evening before he reached home. But his arrival created no small sensation and easily won him the prize.

One persistent trespasser in the forest of Atholl was a blacksmith from Badenoch, who was eventually caught and brought before the Duke, whereupon he was asked whether he would rather go to gaol in Perth for three months or stand a shot from the Duke's rifle at a hundred paces. The man said he would stand the shot, so John Crerar, the head forester, stepped out a hundred paces and handed the Duke his best rifle.

1 A prehistoric Scottish stag (left) compared with a modern one (right):
reconstruction by James Ritchie.

2 Head of the prehistoric Irish elk.

3　Alexander Davidson, the celebrated poacher.　4　Colonel Thornton of Thornton Royal.

5　Gaick Lodge in the 1880s. The gentle slope to the right of the house shows where the old lodge lies buried under the landslide of 1800.

6 Looking for a wounded
deer: one of William
Scrope's own illustrations.

7 Naturalist
extraordinary:
Charles St John.

8 Balmoral Forest, 1860: the Prince Consort with a stag, and Queen Victoria coming up on her pony. From a painting by Edwin Landseer.

9 The recently completed Balmoral Castle. From a painting by James Giles.

The hill men stood by in breathless suspense, looking from the Duke to his human target — and then the rifle went *snap*, only the priming cap having exploded. Calling for a second rifle, the Duke aimed and fired again, but again there was only a snap. 'Well,' he is supposed to have told the blacksmith, 'you are a lucky fellow, for I see your time is not yet come ... but if ever you come after my deer again, my rifle will not miss fire.' Neither gun, of course, had been properly loaded; but the point had been made, and the blacksmith vowed never to trespass in Atholl again.

Even at that early date some poachers were organised in gangs, and although without mechanised transport were strong enough to carry off at speed any deer they killed. Their numbers made the keepers hesitate to tackle them, and often it was found most expedient to take them by surprise in a night attack on the bothy which they were illegally inhabiting.

Sometimes the foresters were helped by the receipt of useful information. In January 1827, for instance, a sly fellow called William Mackintosh wrote to the Duke's factor:

Sir — This is to let you know there is a number of potchers in this place which I will tell you their names as follows [a list of names ensues] likewise Duncan Kennedy in the forest of Clune, a great potcher and entices others to come and hunt with him, especially one Fleming from Ghlasclum. I expect ye will not make me known ... I wish to converse with you concerning the forest and I will let ye know some secret which will be beneficial to His Grace.

Your humble servant,

William Mackintosh

A typical incident occurred during February, 1854, when Atholl woodmen were attracted by a swarm of crows and found — according to their own report — 'the entrails of two Red Deers who had been killed during the preceding night, within ten or twelve yards of each other.' On examining the snow, the foresters found the footmarks of two men and faint spots of blood leading in a westerly direction. They then discovered the place where the deer had been laid out, and later another 'large hart with a strong head of horns was found lying dead about four hundred yards north of where the others were killed. The ball had gone through his body behind the ribs ... the poachers had not found him, as there was no appearance of footmarks about where he was lying.'

E

On the following day the search was resumed, and the foresters raided likely houses under the pretext of looking for an ash tree that had been illegally felled. Nothing was found, however, and the factor wryly pointed out that since the venison was generally buried for a few days as a matter of course, the hunt was all but useless.

Even if a poacher was positively identified, he could usually escape punishment—especially if he was as well connected as Roualeyn Gordon-Cumming, a notorious young rake who later became famous as a big-game hunter. In March 1843 he spent a day at Blair Castle, and then proceeded to abuse the Duke's hospitality by poaching a stag on his way home. The case gives a good idea of the difficulties the lairds had in pinning a poacher down.

Gordon-Cumming was at Blair on March 29th, and the following day he and three other men, together with four deerhounds, were seen, overtaken and challenged by a gamekeeper based at neighbouring Fealar. The men refused to give their names, but the dogs looked newly fed, and when the keeper returned towards Tarf Lodge (one of the bothies) he found the carcase of a freshly killed stag with its head cut off. The door of the lodge had been forced and the beds had been slept in; the intruders had left behind a bottle that had contained whisky and two old newspapers that had been used for wrapping food.

A note in the records, written by the Duke himself, added that, when the keepers had given chase, all the intruders had stopped except for one, 'very fleet of foot and peculiarly dressed in a short brown jacket, who was visibly the leader of the party'. Alexander Campbell, the swiftest of the hill men 'eventually ran him down and took notes on his appearance, as he would not give his name.' Later Campbell was sent to a public house to which the poachers had repaired, and through a partition he both heard and saw Gordon-Cumming boasting about his exploits, so that he obtained a complete identification.

Gordon-Cumming was obviously uneasy about the possible outcome of the incident, for when he returned to England he wrote the Duke a note of explanation:

I went to your forest in search of eagles' eggs for a collection and killed one stag in Glen Tarf to give a young greyhound blood. I did not suppose that *that* would be of any great consequence, as you have far too many deer on your ground, at least double, and I knew that you were not at that season hunting that part of the forest.

I did not break into nor occupy your lodge. I occupied a dilapidated building beside the Tarf without door or window and full of snow. I made *no* promise to any man that I would not return to your forest, but I never returned to Atholl or came within many miles of it after the day I killed the stag in Glen Tarf. Your forester on parting with us, and *after* drinking all our whisky, said to the man who was with me 'I hope you will not return again,' and the man said 'No, we are going straight out of [the] country, and we may never be in Atholl again.'

To assess his chances of a successful prosecution, the Duke took legal advice; a lawyer in Edinburgh summed up the various acts which were theoretically still in force, but concluded that: 'Of these statutes, it appears that the Acts of 1551 and 1587 are in desuetude and not capable of being enforced.' Only a fine, he thought, would be possible; 'but as deer are animals *ferae naturae* and therefore not *property* in the eye of the law, the rights to found upon these statutes would seem to be confined to the public prosecutor.'

The Duke seems to have been discouraged by this advice, for there is no record of any prosecution. That same year, 1834, Gordon-Cumming went to South Africa, where he shot a great many elephants and lions; but later he returned to the Highlands and for years, according to Evan G. Mackenzie, he 'roamed the whole country round, fishing and shooting where he chose, almost as freely as if in the African wilds.'

Gordon-Cumming presented a striking figure, and was said to have the gift of second sight. This, according to Mackenzie, could 'easily be understood by those who ever saw Roualeyn roaming over the hills in the kilt which he constantly wore, a magnificent figure of a man with long hair and long beard, which he must have accustomed himself to in the elephant country and never discarded.'

Second sight or not, Gordon-Cumming came to a sad end. He opened a museum in Fort Augustus, at the western end of Loch Ness, where he exhibited his African trophies, and some Scottish ones too, to visitors travelling to and from the Highlands by boat. At the end of his life he was miserably poor, and lived on the small income that he made from tourists.

Chapter Six

The Southerners Arrive

In the old days of the Highlands, before the deer were driven from the hill, and the people from the glens; when 'the sound of the chase was loud on Ardven,' and 'the song passed away the night in joy,' the harp and cruit were the constant companions of the bow and gun, and poetry and music were as intimately associated with sport as the trumpet with war ...

As the hunter sat upon the hill watching the deer, or waiting for them at the pass—when he lay in his plaid upon the heath or reclined by the hearth in his solitary bothy, his thoughts, like those of Ossian, were 'with his father,' or 'the deer,' and the intervals of physical activity were filled by the activity of the mind. Thus were composed and preserved those beautiful productions of the Gaelic language ... it was thus, surrounded by poetical imagery, that every hunter became a poet.

Seated upon his mountain throne, the blue heaven above, the expanse of free wilderness around him, his mind was elevated and expanded with their space and grandeur, and filled with traditions of the past, affections of the present ...

Thus, wallowing unashamedly in romantic nostalgia, the authors of *Lays of the Deer Forest* looked back in 1848 to what they saw as the golden era of Scottish deer-hunting. If they exaggerated the delights of the old days, they did so with a purpose, for they wished to draw a contrast between the wholesome traditions of the past and the degenerate habits of the modern deer-stalker from the south. 'While he nods in the heather, or dissipates the vigils of his lodge in smoke and cards and whisky,' they wrote, 'the olden hunters beguiled the time with songs and traditions.'

To illustrate the beneficial effect of 'this ancient forest spirit' the authors quoted in full two Gaelic lays, 'The Aged Bard's Wish' and 'The Lament for the Deer', both of which (in translation at least) are of thundering banality.

It is a sad fact that, of all the Gaelic poems published in *Lays of the Deer Forest*, scarcely a line is moving or memorable in English. Clearly a good deal must be lost in translation, for the old hunter-bards were revered and renowned for generations and their poems, chanted to a simple musical accompaniment, brought vividly to the listeners' minds the magic of the hill. No one caught the romance and excitement of deer-hunting more perfectly than the eighteenth-century poet, Duncan Ban MacIntyre, an illiterate forester born in Glenorchy, who recited his poems to a clergyman. Many of his images retain their beauty in translation—the wind-slanted rye grass, the dark eyebrow of cress around the spring—and his celebrated poem 'Oran Beinn Dobhrain' ('The Praise of Ben Doran') lives again in the sprightly version by Professor J. S. Blackie:

> My delight it was to rise
> With the early morning skies
>   All aglow,
> And to brush the dewy height
> Where the deer in airy state
>   Wont to go.
>
> At least a hundred brace
> Of the lofty antlered race,
> When they left their sleeping-place
>   Light and gay;
> When they stood in trim array,
> With their low, deep-breasted cry,
> Flung their breath into the sky
>   From the brae:
>
> When the hind, the pretty fool,
> Would be rolling in the pool,
>   At her will;
> Or the stag in gallant pride
> Would be strutting at the side
> Of his haughty-headed bride
>   On the hill.

> And sweeter to my ear
> Is the concert of the deer
>   In their roaring,
> Than when Erin from her lyre
> Warmest strains of Celtic fire
>   May be pouring;
>
> And no organ sends a roll
> So delightful to my soul,
>   As the branchy-crested race,
> When they quicken their proud pace
> And bellow in the face
>   Of Ben Doran.

The poet also had a memorable knack of describing the movements of the stalker:

> The hind that dwelleth in the glen
>   Is light of foot and airy;
> Who tracks her way upon the Ben
>   Must be full wise and wary.
>
> Softly, softly on her traces
> He must steal with noiseless paces,
>   Nigh and still more nigh,
> Lest she turn with sudden starting
> And, like feathered arrow darting,
>   Cheat the eager eye.
>
> He must know to dodge behind
> Rock and block in face of wind;
> In the ditch and in the pit
> Dripping lie and soaking sit,
>   Stoop, and creep, and crawl,
> Ever with quick eye to note
> Face of earth and clouds that float,
>   In the azure hall.

Another well known poet was Donald MacFinlay, who lived at Fersit, at the north end of Loch Treig, and spent his life in the lovely hills round about, killing deer and wolves with his bow and arrows (for he scorned any more modern weapon). When he died, at an advanced age, he was buried on the brow of a hill overlooking the loch (whose name means Desolation): he had chosen the spot himself, for there, as he had said, 'the deer could couch on his head, and the little calves rest by his side.'

Yet, whatever the quality of their verse, the essential point about the old-fashioned deer-hunters was that they were *Scottish*: their sport was a local one, practised only by natives, and unknown to the English. The reason was not snobbishness or xenophobia on the part of the lairds but rather the physical seclusion of the Highlands: the country in which the red deer lived was so remote, so wild, and so difficult of access that before the nineteenth century very few southerners visited it.

One of the earliest individual stalkers was Cluny Macpherson, Chief of the Clan Chattan, who in 1745 went out on a celebrated expedition with Mr Macdonald of Tulloch. He was about to leave the country for France, where he was to join Bonny Prince Charlie in exile; but before he went he was overtaken by a great wish to kill one more stag. He and Macdonald therefore proceeded to Ben Alder, where they found a solitary stag and stalked it. When they were almost in shot, the beast suddenly went off at a fast pace and ran about two miles before stopping; then, however, it seemed to decide that its alarm had been excessive, for it walked the whole way back to the spot from which it had started, enabling Macpherson to shoot it dead.

Such early expeditions must have been highly picturesque: the stalkers in tartan kilts and caps, and the gillies (or servants) going barefoot, leading the ponies or heaving in the dogs on a leash. The party would leave home in the dark, to be on the best ground by daybreak, and perhaps not come back until night was falling; if a chief had been stalking, his return would be greeted by one or two of his own pipers, whose skirling march — the *caber feidh*, or deer horn — would accompany the dead stags on their last journey from the hill.

Elevated though the thoughts of these pioneers might be, and full of poetry, the stalkers themselves were by no means above seeking physical as well as mental stimulation, and a dram of whisky was from the earliest days an essential companion on the hill, whether carried by the hunter or buried at convenient places in the ground — a practice which was thought to help mellow and improve the fiery spirit. The authors of *Lays of the Deer Forest* left a charming description of the habit of burying whisky by the Clach-an-t-Sealgair, or Hunter's Stone — a square block covered with moss which lay beside the burn:

To save the trouble of conveyance and improve the speed of the gillies, we had divers of these earth-sealed fountains; near customary trysts, or good passes, where the *Deoch-fala,* or blood drink, might be wanted. More than once, however, we were disappointed of our dram by the mice, who, mining over our bottles, found the corks; and probably mistaking them for the spungy stocks of roots, and curious to taste some new kind of pig-nut at their feet, had neatly scooped them out of the glass; when, doubtless surprised with the potent whiff of the spirit within, they burned their noses, with no less dissatisfaction to themselves than displeasure to us.

Still more important than whisky were the dogs. 'Of old,' says *Lays of the Deer Forest,* 'no man went to the hill without greyhounds; they were indispensable attendants upon deer-sport of every class ... for it was justly thought not only a gross waste of venison, but a dishonour to the chase, to allow a wounded deer to get away to die in the corries and be eaten by the ravens.'

The original strains had been carefully preserved by selective breeding to produce hounds of great size and strength: rough-coated, long-legged greyhounds, they stood some thirty inches at the shoulder and weighed up to a hundred pounds. Different forests specialised in different characteristics: the Black Mount dogs, for instance, bred by the Earls of Breadalbane, were second to none in sheer strength, while those of Atholl, though lighter, were famous for their speed. The colour varied too. In the eighteenth century most breeds seem to have been dark grey, but by the 1830s many of the finest strains were yellow or dark red. All, however, had the common distinction of possessing black ear tips, eyes and muzzles. Their names varied very little: there must have been hundreds of dogs called Bran and dozens called Oscar, Buskar, Pheogh and Derig.

When stalking began, the dogs were most frequently used as a back-up for the erratic early rifles and were loosed at a stag which was wounded but still mobile. Sometimes, however, they were set upon a cold, or unwounded, stag, in a form of Highland coursing. The handler would stalk as close as he could to the chosen quarry so as to slip the dog from the shortest possible distance. Much then depended upon the courage and experience of the hounds: young, rash dogs, when they overtook the tiring deer, would go up at once and attack his head – and often they were killed, for the stag would strike immensely powerful blows to either side with his antlers. *Lays of the*

Deer Forest vividly describes the demise of two over-enthusiastic novices:

> Two fine young dogs belonging to the late Glengarry were thus killed in their first run by a gallant stag, which they were driving down the dry channel of a mountain stream—and as they sprang at his throat from either side, with a rapid flourish of his head he struck them right and left and laid them dead among the stones. The experienced greyhounds rarely run at the deer's neck, but come up close by his flank, and shoot up at his throat too close for the blow of his horns, and to effect this they will sometimes for several yards run by his haunch, until they feel the favourable moment for making their launch at his neck.

A vigorous account has survived—in Thomas Speedy's *Sport in the Highlands and Lowlands of Scotland*—of a course organised and witnessed by a party of young bloods on the Isle of Colonsay. Having slept out the night, and spent some time stalking a particular stag, the men found themselves only sixty yards from the quarry:

> The dogs were slipped; a general halloo burst from the whole party, and the stag, wheeling round, set off at full speed with Buskar and Bran straining after him. The brown figure of the deer, with his noble antlers laid back, contrasted with the light colour of the dogs stretching along the dark heath, presented one of the most exciting scenes that it is possible to imagine ...
>
> From the high position in which we were placed, the chase was visible for nearly half a mile. When some rising ground intercepted our view, we made with all speed for a higher point, and, on reaching it we could perceive that the dogs, having got upon smooth ground, had gained on the deer, who was still going at speed, and were close up with him.
>
> Bran was then leading, and in a few seconds was at his heels, and immediately seized his hock with such violence of grasp as seemed in a great measure to paralyse the limb, for the deer's speed was immediately checked. Buskar was not far behind, for soon afterwards, passing Bran, he seized the deer by the neck.
>
> Notwithstanding the weight of the two dogs which were hanging to him, having the assistance of the slope of the ground, he continued dragging them along at a most extraordinary rate (in defiance

of their utmost exertions to detain him), and succeeded more than once in kicking Bran off; but he became at length exhausted; the dogs succeeded in pulling him down, and, though he made several attempts to rise, he never completely regained his legs. On coming up, we found him perfectly dead, with the joints of both his forelegs dislocated at the knee, his throat perforated, and his chest and flanks much lacerated ... Buskar was perfectly exhausted, and had lain down, shaking from head to foot much like a broken-down horse; but on our approaching the deer he rose, walked round him with a determined growl, and would scarcely permit us to come near him. He had not, however, received any cut or injury; while Bran showed several bruises, nearly a square inch having been taken off the front of his foreleg, so that the bone was visible, and a piece of burnt heather had passed quite through his foot. Nothing could exceed the determined courage displayed by both dogs.

A stag not taken on the run would eventually go to bay – that is, it would take up a defensive position, often in a burn, with its back to a cliff or to water, so that it could not be attacked from behind. While the dogs kept it there, yelping and snarling and making rushes, the hunters would catch up with the pursuit and one of them would finish the beast, either with a rifle shot or by going in and sticking it in the throat with a dirk. Sometimes, having regained his wind and strength while the dogs continued to expend theirs, the stag would break the bay and run again, so that all stages of the chase would be repeated.

Such were the expense and difficulty of reaching the Highlands that before the nineteenth century hardly any English sportsmen discovered what the northern hills had to offer. But one notable exception was Colonel Thomas Thornton, who between 1782 and 1789 made a number of visits to Scotland. His book *A Sporting Tour Through the Northern Parts of England and Great Part of the Highlands of Scotland*, first published in 1804, purported to describe one expedition only; but it seems in fact to be a conglomerate account of several trips – and a thoroughly amusing one.

An eccentric Yorkshire squire of impish appearance and exhibitionist tendencies, Thornton was both intensely competitive and endowed with exceptional physical agility. 'His bodily activity was remarkable,' wrote J. E. Harting in a memoir:

In a walking match he went four miles in thirty-two minutes. In leaping he cleared his own height (five feet nine inches) for a considerable bet. In another match he leapt over six five-bar gates in six minutes and then performed the same feat on horseback. At Newmarket, on horseback, he ran down a hare, which he picked up, in the presence of a large concourse of people assembled to witness the feat.

Thornton kept his own pack of foxhounds, and was an outstanding falconer, besides being a keen shot. His preparations for his sporting tours were therefore extensive and on a liberal scale: he and his friends travelled overland to Strathspey, but to transport his heavy equipment – which included his pack of hounds, four good hawks, two bad ones, four setters, six pointers, one deerhound, sundry firearms, eighty pounds of gunpowder, two small boats, a portable kitchen and a housekeeper – he hired a sloop, the *Falcon*, in London and had it sail via Hull to the Moray Firth. After nearly capsizing in bad weather (and almost killing the housekeeper with sea-sickness) the *Falcon* eventually reached Forres, whence its contents were carried, by forty-nine carts, to the Colonel's headquarters at Raitts, near Kingussie, in the broad valley of the Spey.

From this base Thornton made daily expeditions into the surrounding hills, shooting and hawking grouse and ptarmigan, and fishing every loch whose appearance he fancied. Sometimes he set up a temporary camp in a remote glen so that he could be on the hill early in the morning. In general he seems to have shot and hawked wherever he liked: he did, it is true, have permission from one or two landowners, such as Grant of Rothiemurchus, but for most of the time he evidently had no idea whose land he was on, and his erratic progress shows up the low regard in which sporting rights were then held in the Highlands. In the course of all Thornton's forays no one challenged him or tried to turn him off; no one else appears to have been out on the hills; it had certainly not occurred to any of the lairds to charge Thornton rent for the privilege of shooting on their ground, and if they joined his expeditions, it was at his invitation rather than vice versa.

The one sport at which he had no success was deer-stalking. He had come equipped with several rifles, besides the deerhound, and he made a few half-hearted attempts to shoot a roebuck, but on the rare occasions in which he did see red deer, he was invariably armed with the wrong weapons. That he found so few deer is hardly surprising, for during the period of his tours (the 1780s) the deer population of Scotland sank to its lowest-ever ebb, and the amount of land set aside for sport was drastically reduced by the agricultural revolution which changed the entire pattern of rural life in the Highlands.

Under the old system, practised until near the end of the eighteenth century, country people grew small arable crops on communal farms in the glens, and in summer pastured their black cattle, together with a few sheep, on the shielings, or high mountain grazings, which the domestic animals shared during the summer months with the wild deer. The arable farms were organised on the inefficient runrig system, whereby the land was divided into narrow strips and constantly redistributed among those entitled to it, in many cases every year. The mountain grazings, by contrast, were free for all and every spring there took place a complete *transhumance* as the women, children and old people moved with their cattle to the hills, where they lived in small, round, stone-walled huts, leaving their men at home to work the land, repair the houses, and cut peats for winter fuel. The miserable existence which these ancient practices afforded was vividly described by the historian I. F. Grant, who wrote:

> The greater part of the population of the Highlands were living under conditions that would now be considered incompatible with civilised existence ... often on the verge of starvation ... a half-naked hungry people living in mud-floored hovels, peat-smoke blackening their faces, before it drifted through a hole in the dripping roof, the sole room shared all the winter through with starving cattle.

One factor which contributed to the poverty was the sharp increase in population which occurred during the second half of the eighteenth century, for reasons which are now not clear. In Morvern, a parish on the west coast, for instance, the population rose from 1,200 in 1755 to 1,800 in 1795 and 2,000 in 1801. As Philip Gaskell pointed out in his thoughtful book *Morvern Transformed*:

> There can be no doubt that the increase of population alone would have altered the agriculture and society of Morvern in the end. But before its full effect could be felt, it was discovered that certain breeds of sheep would thrive on Highland pastures, and this quickly led to the imposition of an entirely new agricultural balance on the parish.

Not only on Morvern: a mighty flood of Cheviot and black-faced sheep began pouring into the Highlands as a whole, for the proprietors found that by letting their land to southern farmers they could get a far higher rent than they had ever before enjoyed. So began the notorious Clearances, which emptied many a glen of its wretched inhabitants and turned the Highlands into a gigantic sheep ranch.

At first these great changes were to the detriment of the deer: with the creation of the sheep-walks between 1780 and 1830, their numbers sank to their lowest level. One authority, George Cupples, reckoned that in 1811 there were only six forests left in which the deer were actively preserved: Atholl, Black Mount, Glenartney, Glenfiddich, Invercauld and Mar. All these he described as 'remains of much larger formations in much earlier period'. Elsewhere, especially in Sutherland, further large tracts were still inhabited scantily by deer, though not preserved as formally as the forests just listed.

Soon after this nadir had been reached, however, a new idea was born: that of letting one's sporting rights to outsiders. That a land-owner might charge someone else money to come and shoot on his ground was a revolutionary concept: until about 1810 it would have been thought both unbecoming and immoral – and probably when the practice first gained ground, it was looked on as thoroughly regrettable by the more conservative members of the aristocracy.

Nevertheless, the idea gradually became accepted. By an odd historical coincidence, the letting of sporting rights came in at the very moment when the sheep farms were expanding at their fastest. It was not as if the lairds desperately looked round for a new way of making money: they already had a new way of making money. Nor was there any question of the sheep farmers already failing: the market for both meat and wool grew ever stronger for another forty years, and by 1865, when prices eventually began to fall, deer-stalking was already being let on an enormous scale.

The first lets were modest, and huge areas of land could be secured for minuscule rents, partly because the sport was so uncertain and partly because the forests had no facilities whatever: often there was no lodge in which the tenant might stay, and in many cases there was not even a road up which he might drive a horse and cart into his new domain.

Moreover, most southerners were totally ignorant of the conditions which prevailed in the Highlands. In January 1812, when the Duke of Gordon advertised in *The Times* and northern newspapers that the shooting in the forest of Glenfeshie was to let, most of the applicants assumed that the place was some sort of neglected farm that could speedily be brought back into good order (it is in fact a very high tract of mountain country in the Cairngorms, much of it lying above 2,500 feet).

'Having devoted my time and attention for many years to the Science of Agriculture,' wrote William Ozten of Enstone, in Oxfordshire,

I would be glad to convert this large Estate into more valuable and profitable purposes ... I have a method of reclaiming land peculiarly my own which is by no means expensive, and such at the same time as to render it for ever afterwards greatly superior.

To this misguided inquiry the Duke's factor replied:

His Grace the Duke of Gordon desires me ... to mention to you ... that the tract of land which he has advertised to be let cannot be improved for the purposes of Agriculture by any Effort of Science or Industry. Though termed a Forrest, it consists of a range of extremely high Hills covered with masses of Rock on the Tops; and with Gravel and Moss; and is only valuable for the pasture grass it contains skirting the bottoms of these Hills.

To another inquirer he wrote:

I am desired to mentioned in answer that you have misunderstood the terms of the advertisement. The Forrest of Glenfeshie cannot be cultivated by the Plough; nor does His Grace intend to attempt any Improvement on it ... It is to be left in its natural State, either as a Summer Grazing for Cattle, or as a Shooting Quarter to a Sportsman.

'From what you state of yourself,' the factor told yet another prospective tenant, 'I must be candid in mentioning that I do not think the place will be suitable for you; as it has no House; is remote and mountainous; and very inaccessible for want of roads.' Nor did a gentleman who wrote from Scarborough strike the factor as any more suitable: 'The only sportsmen from your part of the Kingdom whom it might probably suit are such as could afford to preserve the land entirely for Deer and Moorgame; and who, being in the prime of life, could encamp for a few weeks among the hills during the shooting season.'

The crucial question – as to how much game the forest carried and what sport it might produce – could be answered only in vague terms. 'My reason for thinking that it will soon be peopled with deer if preserved,' wrote the factor in another letter, 'is because the Forrests of Mar and Atholl, in which they [deer] abound, connect with it, and they are freebooters that take possession where they find the most convenient feeding ground.'

In the end the forest was taken, at a rent of £70 a year, by G. Macpherson Grant of Ballindalloch. Soon afterwards he bought it, and it remained in the hands of the family for more than a hundred years.

Thus began a system of letting which flourishes to this day. Yet it was still possible for sportsmen to roam the Scottish hills with enviable freedom, and one spirited account has survived of an expedition which took place in 1816. On September 2nd four sportsmen set out from Auchry, in Banffshire, and for 'six days, half of them rainy' marched over the hills, apparently into the forest of Mar, for their destination, given as 'Reenacula', appears to be a corruption of Corrie Na Cula, in Glen Dee.

One of them was James Christie, a gamekeeper-poet who afterwards described the tour in rollicking verse: his scansion was uncertain, but in some lines he achieved an almost Chaucerian bounce. The leader was Troup, the local laird, his two other companions Dockar, a crack shot and fiddler, and Dr Cumine of Auchry. They walked hard and slept rough, and kept themselves going with traditional remedies. One evening when two of them staggered into camp soaked to the skin,

> We flew to our whisky, which proved a cure ever,
> And gave them a jugful that warmed their liver ...
> Our gentry never were proud nor yet saucy,
> For breakfast took water brose,★ made in a bassy,
> Into each man's pockets caused put bread and cheese
> And a flask of whisky to drink when we please ...

Although they shot mostly grouse, it was the occasional sighting of deer that provided the main excitement:

★ Brose was a form of porridge—a mixture of oatmeal and water—and not to be confused with Atholl brose, a mixture of whisky and honey. This sovereign concoction has revived countless travellers in the Highlands, among them the playwright Sheridan, who in the 1760s had a stormy passage up Glen Tilt, in Atholl.

A herd of Deer skipped o'er the mountain,
Dockar ran off to spy their marking
For he was dexterous at stalking.
Ere he was one hour o'er the hill
Dockar's servant roared like hell,
Swinging his bonnet round his head
With signs to come to him with speed ...
We both did run blasting like bellows
To know the cause of such great hallows ...
Good news at last rang in our ear,
T'was Dockar, he had killed twa Deer.
We hastened till we saw the harts
Far bigger than twa-year-auld stirks.
He took out a knife and cut their throats
And after that took out their guts.
In our game bag put heart and liver
To make a hash with something ither ...

Altogether the party killed six deer during their six-day trek, and
they came away well satisfied. But as stalking became more organised,
the opportunities for such free-ranging expeditions steadily diminished,
and it was clearly to put a stop to this kind of guerrilla operation that
the lairds began to advertise in the local press on the following lines:

> The Earl of Airlie requests that no Gentlemen will Shoot or Hunt on
> his Estate of Auchterhouse during the present season. Strict orders
> have been given for the detention and prosecution of poachers and
> other trespassers.

As other shootings began to be advertised, word of the possibilities
offered by the far north started filtering down to the country gentlemen
who normally shot nothing more formidable than partridges and
pheasants in the flat fields of East Anglia. According to 'Thormanby',
the pseudonymous author of *Kings of the Rod, Rifle and Gun*, the 'first
man that went in earnest deerstalking in the Highlands' was William
Coke of Norfolk. 'He had a pair of corduroy breeches which Squire
Osbaldeston declared he never took off for a fortnight. Crawling on
hands and knees, he was for a time being a separate Nebuchadnezzar.'
    Other young bloods hastened to try this eccentric new sport, not
least Horatio Ross, a godson of Nelson (hence his Christian name), and

10 The Balmoral stalkers on September 3rd, 1858: John Grant, the head
stalker, is pointing; John Brown has his arms folded, and John Macdonald,
Prince Albert's 'Private Jäger', is on the right.

11 John Macdonald with a stag shot by Albert in Corrie Buie on October
5th, 1854.

14 'The Monarch of the Glen' by Edwin Landseer.

Facing page:
12 The Duchess of Bedford's encampment in Glenfeshie. From a sketch by
Edwin Landseer. 13 'The Return from Stalking': engraving of the
painting by Edwin Landseer.

15 'Mr Briggs is suddenly face to face with the Monarch of the Glen! He is so astonished that he omits to fire his rifle.'

16 'After aiming for quarter of an hour, Mr B. fires both his barrels – and – misses!!!! Tableau – the forester's anguish.' From a series of cartoons by John Leech, published in *Punch* during the 1860s.

a celebrated athlete and shot. In 1828, when he was twenty-seven, he arranged a grand shooting match against Colonel Anson, in which the two men were to walk up partridges at Mildenhall, in Suffolk, from sunrise to sunset, without dogs. This epic event—on which a great deal of money was staked by cronies of the antagonists—was to take place on November 1st, and to train for it Ross rented the deer-stalking in the forest of Fealar from the Duke of Atholl.

I shot eighty-seven deer that season to my own rifle [he recorded in his memoirs]. I worked hard. I was always up at three a.m. and seldom back to the lodge before seven or eight p.m., walking, running or crawling all the time. This was the grandest training in the world. I believe I came to the post at Mildenhall on November 1 as fit to go as the winner of the Derby ever did at Epsom.

Ross's rigorous preparations paid off. On the appointed day, after the rivals had breakfasted by candlelight, Colonel Anson went off at a furious pace; but since there were between 500 and 600 spectators, the noise and commotion made the birds exceedingly wild, and the shooting was difficult. All day the contest remained evenly poised; then, a quarter of an hour before sunset, one of the umpires rode up and told Ross that the Colonel was unable to walk any more, but that he was one bird ahead. Ross—though claiming to feel as fresh as when he had started—settled for a draw; and luckily for him he got no takers when he challenged anyone present there and then 'to go to London on foot against him for £500, or to shoot the same match next day against anyone for £500.'

Stalking in Scotland became one of Ross's principal sports, and in the course of his long life he shot an enormous number of deer: in 1837, for instance, he killed seventy-five in Sutherland, and in 1851, on Mar, 118, including thirteen with fourteen shots in a single murderous day. He was still stalking at the age of eighty, and attributed his exceptional health to the fact that he walked between eight and twelve miles every day, took a 'sponging bath of cold water' every morning, and for many years had 'drunk nothing but light claret, one bottle per diem'.

With sportsmen such as Ross eager to rent shooting, the creation (or re-creation) of forests in the Highlands began apace. Black Mount, for instance, after carrying deer for centuries, had been converted into a number of sheep-walks at the start of the nineteenth century; but in

F

1820 it was restored to its former status by its owner, the Earl of Breadalbane. Gaick, in Inverness-shire, which had been kept exclusively for deer between 1745 and 1788, but had then been let as a sheep-walk, was similarly re-afforested in 1826. During the 1830s the well known stalker Campbell of Monzie created another major preserve alongside the Black Mount ground by clearing the sheep off the ancient forest of Dalness and uniting it with the property that he already owned, Loch Etive. Another famous forest – Ben Alder – was created in 1838. George Cupples in *Scotch Deer-Hounds and their Masters* estimated that between 1811 and 1825 the number of preserved forests was trebled, from six to eighteen, and that by 1842 the total had reached forty.

According to the second Earl of Malmesbury, who himself became an immensely keen stalker, 1833

> was the first year that the Highlands became the rage, and that deer forests were made and rented, but for prices not exceeding £300 a year. Sir Harry Goodricke, who was a leader among the young hunting men, hired Mar Forest, and Lord Kinnaird Fealar, in Atholl ... I went later to the Isle of Skye and to Harris ... and the grouse, deer forest and fishing, all of which were first-rate, were offered to me for £25 a year ... At that time a stranger could fish and shoot over almost any part of the Highlands without inter-ruption, the letting value of the *ferae naturae* being unknown to their possessors.

The hills in which the southerners began to disport themselves still rang with many an echo of the bloody past. In most deer forests there was a loch or a burn or a pass that had been the scene of a clash between the clans, and in many there were caves which had sheltered some noble fugitive, often Bonny Prince Charlie himself. The evocative associations of the forests were beautifully conjured up by Andrew Lang in his brief poem 'Lone Places of the Deer':

> Lone places of the deer,
>   Corrie, and Loch, and Ben,
> Fount that wells in the cave,
> Voice of the burn and the wave,
> Softly you sing and clear
>   Of Charlie and his men!

Here he has lurked, and here
  The heather has been his bed,
The wastes of the islands knew
And the Highland hearts were true
To the bonny, the brave, the dear,
  The royal, the hunted head.

For the Highlanders themselves the hills were peopled also by the spirits of great hunters from the past, not least the old chief Tomas. As Gilfrid W. Hartley wrote in his book *Wild Sport with Gun, Rifle and Salmon Rod*:

Who shall say that when some curious twist carries the fairly-blowing wind to the deer, or when a grey shroud of mist settles down on the hills, blotting them out and making useless the keenest glass, that it is not Tomas and his clan stretching out the arms of protection to their old friends on the hills? And when a bullet goes aside, when it just misses the stag, and sings mournfully into the black glen two thousand feet below, who shall say that it is always the holder of the rifle who is to blame?

Some forests seemed positively haunted — and none more so than Gaick, whose lodge stands in one of the loneliest places imaginable, on the floor of a long glen flanked by immensely steep hills. The old lodge was destroyed in 1800 by an avalanche, which crushed the building beneath a mass of rock and earth, and killed the four stalkers who were staying there. The new lodge (which still stands) was built further out in the middle of the flat plain, with a sloping mound protruding from the face of the hill to mark the grave of its predecessor.

Yet Gaick was full of mysterious creatures long before this accident. One was the Dorman, a giant fish said to inhabit Loch an-t-Seillich, along the side of which one approaches the lodge. The Dorman's mission in life was to prevent the salmon in the river Tromie gaining access to the loch — and in this, it must be said, the fish was none too successful, for salmon were sometimes caught in the loch before its lower end was blocked by a dam. Though no reliable description of the Dorman was ever given, belief in this pleasantly Carrollian creature persisted for generations.

Still stranger — because they have been seen so often — are Gaick's fairies. A typical manifestation occurred some time at the beginning of the nineteenth century, when Murdoch, a celebrated stalker, was out after hinds one morning, and was amazed to see a number of tiny women dressed in green milking the deer. One of the creatures had a hank of green worsted thrown over her shoulder, and as she was milking, the hind made a grab at the cloth and swallowed it. The fairy, in a rage, cried out: 'May a dart from Murdoch's quiver pierce your side before night!' Murdoch, not liking to eavesdrop on so intimate a domestic occasion, departed elsewhere; but when, later that day, he did shoot a hind, he found the green hank in its stomach. On another occasion Murdoch was stalking hinds on the Doune Hill, some distance behind the lodge, and he got within range of a group of beasts. But when he put up his rifle to fire at a hind, the deer immediately turned into a woman. When he lowered his gun, the creature became a deer once more. This happened many times; but eventually he fired, and the animal fell dead in the shape of a deer.

All at once Murdoch was overpowered by sleepiness. He lay down in the heather, and a moment later a voice thundered in his ear: 'Murdoch, Murdoch, you have this day slain the only maid of the Doune.' The stalker leapt to his feet and shouted, 'If I have killed her, you may eat her!' and bolted as fast as he could.

One would dismiss these stories as old stalkers' fantasies – on a par with North Country beliefs that witches inhabit the bodies of hares – were they not corroborated in an extraordinary way by the experience of a modern stalker, Colonel Jimmy Dennis. One autumn in the 1950s he too was stalking at Gaick, and he shot a stag somewhere behind the lodge. Because the afternoon was so fine, he asked the ponyman to take the beast down while he stayed on the hill to admire the views.

As he sat there he became aware of a movement at the head of the burn which ran below him in the glen. At first he took it to be a roedeer – for the object was rusty red – moving quietly about the green moss and flat stones that surrounded the spring. Several times he put his glass on the spot, but the telescope revealed no living being in that place. Every time he put the glass down, the movement was again visible to the naked eye, and at last, by shading his brow, Colonel Dennis made out that the creature was of human form, like a child in a siren suit and pixie hood.

When, however, he tried to approach the place more closely, the attempt proved futile. Never taking his eyes from the spot, he rose slowly to his feet; but at the first pace forward, the object vanished, never to reappear.

Returning to the lodge somewhat mystified, Colonel Dennis told no one except his wife what he had seen. But some years later, when he was out in the neighbouring forest of Glen Bruar, he mentioned his strange experience to the stalker, and the man immediately replied, 'Then ye've seen the sprite of Gaick.'

The first English sportsmen who came north in the early 1800s thus entered an area rich in associations both historical and supernatural. Yet what probably seemed to them much more important was the fact that at first everything was gloriously cheap. Not only were rents low; stalkers and gillies could be hired for next to nothing. John Crerar, head forester at Atholl and a man of some importance and standing, was paid £24 a year – although admittedly he also got a useful amount of extras, including

Six and a half bolls of meat [each worth £1], cows' keeping, potatoes for cows, one suit of short green, one suit of long green, two suits of short grays, four flannel jackets, three pairs of hose, one bonnet, two pairs of hill shoes, one pair of mittens, one pair of grey garters, four pairs of breeches, one greatcoat.

He also got his house rent, valued at £3 per annum, and altogether was reckoned to cost the Duke £68 a year. But an under-keeper's wages were only six guineas a year, and at Achnacarry Lord Malmesbury found 'excellent ponies and very intelligent gillies ready to be engaged at five shillings a week and food.'

The influx of southern money soon began to benefit country people – not only the lairds, who pocketed the rents, and the tradesmen who began to supply the newcomers, but also the former shepherds who became gillies or stalkers. Gradually there grew up a demand for an entirely new skill – that of the professional stalker, who could show a stranger the ground which he had rented (and of which he was quite ignorant), point out to him which stag was worth shooting and which was not (again, a matter about which most beginners knew nothing), and finally lead him up to a firing position within range of the chosen animal. In the old days the stalking lairds had naturally done all this for themselves, although usually in close consultation with their own hill men; but now there appeared an entirely new breed of riflemen –

clueless, clumsy, and unfit – who had to be professionally chaperoned.*

The onset of the stalking craze thus produced fresh employment in the hills; yet many Highlanders bitterly resented the change. The modern stalker, thundered the authors of *Lays of the Deer Forest,*

> is frequently so ignorant, unpractised and dependent on the guidance of the forester, that to be '*taken up to the deer*' has become the modern forest phrase for the approach of the sportsman. This contemptible term and its contemptible practice has only been introduced with the last quarter century [that is, since about 1815], since the prevalence of the stalking gentleman utterly unacquainted with the ground and pursuit of deer.
>
> Of old, the *Sealgair uasal nam beann* was initiated to the hill when yet but a *biorach* of a stalker, and when he became a matured hill man, he should no more have suffered himself to be *taken up* to his deer by an attendant than a Melton fox-hunter to be trailed after the hounds by a whipper-in with a leading rein.

According to George Cupples in *Scotch Deer-Hounds and their Masters*, dislike of the 'cold-mannered southerners' was so strong that many of the old Highland families 'held themselves apart' and refused to sell the newcomers deerhounds:

> If there was one possession that still remained to the Gael unmortgaged, peculiar to themselves, beyond the power of interlopers, it was the pure old Ossianic or Fingalian dog. That they withheld it to no small extent, and that this told prejudicially against the breed, is undoubted.
>
> It was as if the lurking memories of bypast misfortunes to the clan, with the sense of present trouble, could at all events be wreaked after this minor fashion in close connection with what the southern interloper prized so much – his new opportunities of ground, and sport among the north-country hills. It is not too much to say that during the interval from the outset of modern deer-stalking in 1815 until about 1825, all the pure strains were reduced to the lowest point compatible with survival, where they had not become extinct.

And yet, resentful though they might feel, the Highlanders were

---

* Ever since the term 'stalker' has had a double meaning, referring both to the amateur sportsman who owns or rents the forest, and to the professional who lives in or near the forest all the year round, acting as gamekeeper and general factotum.

powerless in the face of the sporting invasion. They desperately needed the money which the cold southerners brought with them: having no other employment, and no other source of income, they could not afford to turn the stalkers away. (Soon, however, good friendships began to be formed between the hill men and their clients; and to this day many rifles find their professional stalkers – with whom they spend whole days alone – the most courteous and delightful of companions.)

One factor which to some extent kept a brake on the rate of expansion was the difficulty of reaching the Highlands. Before the railways were built, a journey from the south of England to the north of Scotland was a major expedition, and if made by coach could scarcely be accomplished in less than a fortnight; besides, it was extremely expensive, and might cost a single traveller as much as £20.

An alternative method, favoured by many, was to go by sea. First sailing vessels and then steamers plied regularly from London to Leith, near Edinburgh, and from there one could travel onwards either by a smaller vessel or by coach. It was also possible to sail up the west coast, and the attractions of this route were much enhanced by the completion in 1801 of the Crinan Canal, which linked Crinan Loch with Loch Fyne, and so cut out a lengthy detour.

A still greater improvement was effected by the Caledonian Canal, which made use of a series of lochs – from the west, Linnhe, Eil, Lochy, Oich and Ness – to open up a navigable channel from sea to sea across the entire breadth of Scotland. Designed and begun by the engineer, Thomas Telford, in 1804, the Caledonian Canal proved a commercial failure, but at least its construction gave employment to 3,000 men for twenty years, and meant that a sportsman heading for the Highlands could sail the whole way to Inverness.

A passage through the canals was – by modern standards – exceedingly slow and awkward; yet for anyone aiming at the Highlands it was clearly preferable to any other means of travel. The Earl of Malmesbury, who for fifteen years rented the forest of Achnacarry, by Loch Arkaig north of Fort William, would go by coach to Edinburgh, cross over to Glasgow, and at Greenock, on the Clyde, embark on the steamer for the north. In his autobiographical *Memoirs of an Ex-Minister* he left some vivid sketches of his journeys. Once after travelling north he reported:

My servants, too, had a very dangerous journey by sea, their steamer having run aground between Aberdeen and Inverness; they saved their lives but lost all their luggage and some of ours.

The drawbacks of a journey to the Highlands were thus not inconsiderable; nor were the northern hostelries all that a well-to-do southerner might expect. Idleness and scruffiness were the characteristics most often found in landlords, recalled Joseph Mitchell, the Scottish engineer, in *Reminiscences of My Life in the Highlands*. He called Donald More, landlord of the inn at Kinlochoilart, 'the worst of innkeepers', and yet 'the most obliging and good-natured fellow alive'.

He was of Herculean dimensions, six foot six inches, stout and well made in proportion, but with indolent tastes and habits truly Highland. Fishing salmon, a shot at a stag or sleeping out on the hillside were occupations especially congenial. Keeping a clean house or providing comfortable fare for his customers never seemed to enter his head, nor did he consider it a necessary part of his profession.

Moreover, some of the natives were still prone to bestial behaviour – as Mitchell witnessed during a Highland gathering at Invergarry during the 1820s:

One feat which I never saw since was twisting the four legs from a cow, for which a fat sheep was offered as a prize. The cow was brought up and felled before the multitude, and the barbarous competition began, several men making the attempt. At last one man succeeded. After struggling for about an hour, he managed to twist off the four legs, and as a reward received his sheep, with an eulogistic speech from the chief in Gaelic.

In spite of these minor hazards – and the much greater difficulty that in many areas the natives still spoke no English – the trickle of sportsmen to the Highlands grew steadily until it became a seasonal migration. In the early years the 'moorgame' – grouse and ptarmigan – were the main attraction in many forests, for the deer were still scarce. At Glenfeshie during the 1830s, for example, when the forest was rented by the Ellice family, the bags of grouse were enormous (3,632 were shot in 1839), but hardly any deer were killed – only three or four in most seasons, and never more than ten. Entries in the Ellices' game-book show what an event it was when deer were sighted:

> *20 August 1839* Immense excitement occasioned by our being informed, after about two hours' shooting, that some of Sir Joseph's deer were on the ground [having come in from the neighbouring forest of Gaick]. Gillies, shepherds and dogs ... started up the Feshie and found about fifty hinds and eight harts just crossing the burn to go home again. A well-drilled *volley* at three hundred yards brought down the best beast of the lot.

The inexperience of the sportsmen, and the novelty of their surroundings, led to some bizarre accidents. On September 9th, 1836 the Glenfeshie party were out after grouse when some of them heard two shots, 'followed by loud cries', proceeding from the top of the hill. They went up as fast as they could, and, in the words of the gamekeeper, found

> Mr Golding lying on the ground with his gun in a hole, in which it appears he had discharged its contents, being in a state of great excitement. We learned from him that he had shot an eagle. Having descended into the hole, I succeeded in extricating the carcase, which to the surprise of all turned out to be a *horned sheep*. I have been fifteen years in the habit of attending Gentlemen shooting, but never saw the like before.

On newly created forests, then, the grouse-shooting was at first the sportsmen's main pursuit. Yet deer seem to have spread, increased and colonised new areas with extraordinary speed. One reason was the removal of the sheep, and therefore of grazing competition. Another was the destruction of vermin, which was begun on an immense scale; between 1837 and 1840 the English tenant of the Glengarry shootings caused the extermination of the following:

11 foxes	301 stoats and weasels
198 wild cats	67 badgers
246 marten cats	48 otters
106 pole cats	78 housecats (gone wild)
27 white-tailed sea eagles	3 honey buzzards
15 golden eagles	462 kestrels

18 ospreys	78 merlin hawks
98 blue hawks	83 hen carriers
7 orange-legged falcons	6 gyr falcons
11 hobby hawks	1,431 hooded crows
275 kites	475 ravens
5 marsh harriers	35 horned owls
63 goshawks	71 fern owls
285 common buzzards	3 golden owls
371 rough-legged buzzards	8 magpies

So immense was this slaughter that it was reported in the *Inverness Courier*, and though the removal of so many predators must have benefited the grouse most, the deer may also have gained a little from the death of the foxes and eagles. Yet it was undoubtedly the removal of the human predators which did most to allow the deer population to build up. The Clearances, by emptying the glens of their human inhabitants, greatly reduced the amount of poaching; and the number of deer which the sporting tenants were able to kill during their relatively brief autumn visits was far smaller than the regular toll which had been exacted throughout the year by indigenous Highlanders on the verge of starvation.

Once again, the paradoxical truth began to be demonstrated, that it is the preservation of deer for sporting purposes that most effectively increases stocks.

Chapter Seven

William Scrope

No one did more to publicise the excitements of the hill than William Scrope, a landed gentleman and amateur artist of repute whose book *The Art of Deer-Stalking*, first published in 1838, at once became a classic and is still keenly sought after today.

It is not clear how Scrope first heard about deer-stalking. He owned property at Castle Combe in Wiltshire and Cockerington in Lincolnshire, but he also had a holiday house in the Borders – The Pavilion at Melrose – and perhaps it was there that he learnt about Scottish deer from his friend and neighbour, the novelist Sir Walter Scott. In any case, on April 18th, 1822 he wrote from Melrose to the Duke of Atholl's factor at Blair Castle:

> Sir – If His Grace the Duke of Atholl has any sporting ground that is good and of great extent, and that will be vacant this approaching season, I shall be glad to treat for it.

The next day, fearing that he had addressed his letter wrongly, he sent another repeating his request, and to further his chances he got Sir Walter Scott to write the Duke a note on his behalf. Scott described him as 'an English gentleman of family and fortune ... I am enabled to say that Mr Scrope is not only a perfect gentleman, and incapable of indulging his love of sport otherwise than as becomes one, but that he is a man of highly cultivated taste and understanding as well as much accomplishments.'

This glowing reference secured for Scrope an association which lasted for the rest of his life. That same summer he rented Bruar Lodge from the Duke of Atholl, and year after year he returned to it until he became almost a feature of the autumn landscape. According to Thormanby,

The Duke had constituted Scrope a sort of amateur head game-keeper, and the fortunate painter-sportsman, luxuriously housed in Bruar Lodge, found himself practically uncontrolled master of a vast tract of moor and mountain forty miles long by eighteen broad, comprising 135,458 acres, of which 30,000 were devoted partly to grouse and partly to deer, whilst 52,000 were reserved solely for deer.

From Bruar Scrope would keep Blair Castle supplied with grouse and venison, and occasionally he would send haunches to his friends elsewhere, among them Sir Walter Scott. One such gift evoked from the great novelist a charming reply:

> Thanks, dear sir, for your venison, for finer or fatter
> Ne'er roamed in a forest, or smoked in a platter.

Your superb haunch arrived in excellent time to feast a new-married couple ... and was pronounced by far the finest that could by possi-bility have been seen in Teviotdale since Chevy Chase. I did not venture on the carving, being warned both by your hints and the example of old Robert Sinclair, who used to say that he had thirty friends during a fortnight's residence at Harrowgate, and lost them all in the carving of one haunch of venison; so I put Lockhart on the duty, and, as the haunch was too large to require strict economy, he hacked and hewed it well enough.

In the wilds of Bruar Scrope soon learnt the ways of the hill and devised his own stratagems for coming to close quarters with the deer. His favourite method was to set out at daybreak or before, attended by three or four retainers, and to stalk, as he put it, 'in quick time'. One man carried his rifles, one held the deerhounds on a leash, and the others were ready to carry out flanking movements, making immense detours and appearing on distant ridges so as to move the deer towards the spot at which Scrope himself would by then be hidden. Often, after they had shifted the herd, the men had desperate chases to cut them off, and the book is full of forced marches, sudden sprints, and breakneck descents of precipitous faces.

It sounds as if Scrope was an excellent shot, and his rifles were the best that money could buy (seven of them now hang in the Great Hall at Blair Castle—all beautiful weapons, in perfect condition still, but bearing on their highly polished stocks the scars and abrasions which they received on the high tops of Atholl 150 years ago). Scrope generally took three rifles to the hill, for muzzle-loaders firing black powder took some time to recharge, and the only way of getting more than one shot at a group of stags was to have several weapons ready at the same time.

Early stalkers had had to make do with sporting versions of the flintlock musket known as Brown Bess, which had been the British army's regulation weapon for more than 150 years. This was notoriously inaccurate and clumsy, weighing over eleven pounds; the bore was ·753 inches, but the bullet was a good deal smaller, being wrapped in a loose patch (small piece of cloth) before being rammed down the barrel during loading. (At a trial held in 1842, twenty men each fired ten shots with muskets at a target six feet high and twenty broad, and at 300 yards only thirty-two hits were made.)

The earliest stalking rifles were similarly ineffective at long ranges, though fairly accurate up to eighty yards or so. In Scrope's day the most popular rifle for deer was the 16-bore (·662 calibre), which fired a ball weighing one ounce, propelled by a relatively small load of slow-burning powder, in a trajectory aptly described by one writer as like a rainbow. Gunmakers found it impracticable to flatten the trajectory by increasing the bullet's velocity, for a bigger charge merely caused the patched ball to strip across the rifling, so that it emerged from the barrel without having acquired the necessary spin needed for it to fly true.

Many hazards beset the sporting rifleman of the 1820s and 1830s. One was wet weather, in which his powder was prone to become damp, so that he had a misfire. Another was the dense cloud of smoke that followed a discharge, blocking the view; unless a brisk cross-wind was blowing, the stalker had to leap up and sprint sideways to gain clear visibility for a second shot. He had also to be expert at judging distance, for the range governed the amount that the round would drop in the course of its flight: at one hundred yards, it might fall only about twenty-four inches, but at 200 the drop would be at least double (a modern, high-velocity rifle bullet drops about one-twentieth of these amounts.) Moreover the amount of drop was substantially increased by firing steeply uphill, and vice versa.

It was as well that Scrope's rifles were strongly built, for by his own account he handled them roughly: 'the gunstocks got much battered,' he wrote, as he 'generally flung down each rifle as soon as he had discharged it – rock or moss, it took its chance.'

The punch delivered by one of Scrope's spherical bullets was far smaller than that available today, and in consequence many a stag went off wounded. Thus it was that the dogs were frequently in action, and a stirring chase by Bran and Derig often ended in a bay. The presence of hounds was the greatest single difference between Scrope's *modus operandi* and methods of stalking today: not only are weapons now infinitely more accurate and efficient, so that the services of dogs are rarely needed, but the great disturbance that a dog-chase causes can no longer be afforded, for forests are much smaller than they were in Scrope's day, and the effect of loosing a couple of deerhounds now might well be to clear one's entire property of deer.

In all other respects Scrope's stalking was extraordinarily similar to that practised a century and a half later: then, as now, the aim was to work up wind or across it, to spy the herd from a distance with telescopes, to select a stag, and if possible to approach within a hundred yards of it before taking a shot. If Scrope did not exactly invent modern methods of stalking (for other people were simultaneously discovering for themselves what worked and what did not), he was certainly the first to describe the process in detail.

The annual pattern of stalking which Scrope enjoyed has scarcely changed. The rifleman first takes to the hill in the heat of August, when the stags are in prime condition and starting to shed their velvet, that is, the soft, furry skin that protects their new antlers while they are growing. At this stage they live far out on the high tops, above the irritation of flies and midges, ignoring the hinds, who are left on their own with their calves. To come to terms with his quarry the stalker must walk far and climb high—and even then he is often frustrated by the sheer size of the stag armies: if there are two hundred beasts in one herd it is a safe bet that all the ones nearest to him will be rubbish, and that the big fellows whom he is after will be impregnably protected.

Then, as September brings in the early frosts, and the first of the hinds come on heat, the stags begin to break out: the odd beast starts to roar, to blacken himself by rolling in peat-hags, and to leave his mates as he goes in search of a harem. Now the rifleman's task becomes easier, for the stags are on the move individually, with their normal vigilance reduced by excitement; and when the rut reaches its peak, in the first week of October, he can pick stags off almost at will, for by then they are so absorbed in the frenzy of procreation that they lose almost all their usual defensive caution, roaring, fighting, defending such hinds as they have managed to round up, and, if defeated by a heavier or fresher beast, rushing off abstractedly in search of newer conquests.

This frantic activity takes a heavy physical toll. From a peak of condition in August, the stags go quickly down until by the middle of October they are scarcely worth shooting, so lean have they grown and so rank has their flesh become. The stalking season thus lasts a mere ten weeks. The culling of the hinds, which goes on between November and February 1st, is almost always left to the professional stalkers, partly because it is considered less exciting, and partly because it takes place in hostile weather.

It is part of the fascination of Highland stalking that none of this has changed since Scrope first took to the Atholl hills. But his own stalking career was short, for the bug had bitten him late in life. In 1822, when he first took Bruar, he was already fifty, and he stalked for only ten years before reluctantly falling back on less violent sports such as fishing. *The Art of Deer-Stalking* came out in 1838, and the book's dedication, to the Duchess of Atholl, showed how keenly the author missed the 'exciting amusement' of the forest. Years had passed, Scrope wrote, 'but the glories of the Highland landscape, though faded from my view, are dear to my remembrance, and I look back, as from out of a cheerless glen, upon those distant and sunny scenes of my life.'

Taken as he was into the heart of the Atholl country, Scrope felt none of the hostility with which other outsiders were sometimes greeted. On the contrary, he soon formed a close and affectionate relationship with the hill men, and in his book the companionship he found among John Crerar, Peter Fraser and their fellows is glowingly commemorated.

In calling him 'highly cultivated', Sir Walter Scott was no doubt correct. A classical scholar at Eton and Oxford, Scrope had made himself a well regarded landscape artist, considered by Scott to be 'one of the very best amateur painters' he ever saw. For the pictures in his own books, Scrope drew or painted the landscape backgrounds, and got friends like Charles and Edwin Landseer to fill in the deer and the dogs.

Scrope's paintings are certainly attractive, and they evoke the Highlands strongly. When he came to write, however, he all too often descended into a vein of facetious silliness which is a severe trial for modern readers. This unfortunate tendency is exhibited in a letter which he wrote (at the age of fifty-four) from Bruar Lodge in 1826, answering a request from the Duke for venison:

I received with gratitude your Grace's indulgent commands this morning, and I have no doubt but I shall be able to stock the larder handsomely if the wind is favourable.

In China a painter advertised as painting 'handsome faces'. Mr. Thomson's son went to him and asked him to paint his handsome face. The Chinese replied, 'Handsome facey paint how can if handsome facey have got no?' So I say in defence, 'Great fat deery kill how can, if great fat deery can find no?'

I have the Honor to be, My Lord Duke, yr. Gr.'s most obliged and obt. servant.

W. M. Scrope

Had Scrope been able to resist this kind of foolishness, his book would have been far better; as it is, the reader has to put up with a barrage of witticisms, an intermittent spattering of quotations in Latin, French and Italian, and long passages of reconstructed dialogue, laced by snatches of all-but incomprehensible dialect which the author claimed represented the actual speech of the Atholl hill men ('Hout-tout! Clish-ma-clavers. I'm ower auld-farren to be fleyed for bogles' is a fair example). Scrope coyly refers to himself throughout as 'Tortoise', in the third person, and switches constantly from narrative in the historic present of his own excursions, to descriptions of natural history, advice about stalking, general history, and any literary allusions that come into his head. The resulting hotch-potch is often fascinating, but also often infuriating.

The book begins with a description of the red deer and their habits. Scrope's observation was excellent, as was his general knowledge: only in one subject was he profoundly ignorant, and that was the age to which deer live. Listening to the old stalkers' tales, he concluded that a stag might live for the best part of 200 years (in fact twenty or twenty-two is the absolute maximum). He based his belief partly on the story of a stag shot by Glengarry in 1826; the animal had a peculiar mark on its left ear and five different foresters, when consulted independently, said it was the mark of Ewan-mac-Ian-Og, a stalker who used to mark calves and had died 150 years before. This meant, according to Scrope, that the beast must have been at least 150 years old, and perhaps 180.

The story of another animal which strengthened Scrope's delusion was that of the celebrated white hind of Loch Treig. Tradition had it that Captain Macdonald of Tulloch, who died in 1776 at the age of eighty-six, had known the white hind for the last fifty years of his life;

his father had known her for the same length of time, and his grand-father had known her for sixty years before that, thus furnishing her in sum with an alleged life-span of close on 200 years. All this – as someone of Scrope's experience should have recognised – was nonsense: no animal could possibly have lived so long, and what the Loch Treig stalkers had been seeing was undoubtedly a succession of white ladies.

In other respects, however, his deer-knowledge was first-class; and what shines out from the book, redeeming its faults, is his great enthusiasm for the chase. Using the ignorance of his companion, Lightfoot, as a foil, he packs a great deal of general information into his accounts of days on the hill.

Thus, when Lightfoot is labouring up a steep slope and hopefully remarks that the top is not far off, he can be told the awful truth which stalkers have to face to this day – that almost always the highest ridge in sight is not the top of the hill, or anything like it, but only a false crest, and that the real summit is hundreds of feet above. Again, when the experienced hill men are spying a far-off stag through their telescopes, and Lightfoot is quite unable to see it, let alone to make out its head, the point is easily made that the distances involved are immense, and that the business of getting within range of a deer is not so simple as a novice might suppose.

In a passage typically embellished with facetious exaggerations, Scrope gives an excellent idea of the physical challenge that the stalker must expect:

Your consummate deer-stalker should not only be able to run like an antelope, and breathe like the trade-winds, but should also be enriched with various other undeniable qualifications. As, for instance he should be able to run in a stooping position, at a greyhound pace, with his back parallel to the ground, and his face within an inch of it, for miles together. He should take a singular pleasure in thread-ing the seams of a bog, or of gliding down a burn *ventre à terre*, like that insinuating animal, the eel; accomplished he should be in skil-fully squeezing his clothes after this operation, to make all com-fortable.

Strong and pliant in the ankle, he should most indubitably be; since in running swiftly down precipices, picturesquely adorned with sharp-edged, angular, vindictive stones, his feet will un-advisedly get into awkward cavities and curious positions; thus if his

G

legs are devoid of the faculty of breaking, so much the better—he has an evident advantage over the fragile man.

He should rejoice in wading through torrents, and be able to stand firmly on water-worn stones, unconscious of the action of the current; or if by fickle fortune the waves should be too powerful for him when he loses his balance, and goes floating away upon his back (for if he has any tact, or sense of the picturesque, it is presumed that he will fall backwards), he should raise his rifle aloft in the air, Marmion fashion, lest his powder should get wet and his day's sport come to an end. A few weeks' practice in the Tilt will make him quite *au fait* with this ... as for sleep, he should be almost a stranger to it, activity being the great requisite; and if a man gets into the slothful habit of lying-a-bed for five or six hours at a time, I should be glad to know what he is fit for in any other situation?

Mercifully, Scrope sometimes stops trying to be amusing, and gives lyrical descriptions of the mountains which he came to love so dearly. There is a fine account of his arrival at Bruar, which he describes as follows:

About eight reputed miles north of Blair Atholl ... you descend into a glen which is of a wild and desolate character. The heather, being old, is rather of a brown than purple colour; but there is some relief of greensward near the lodge, and more in various patches near the winding course of the Bruar.

Huge, lofty, and in the district of Atholl second only in magnitude to Ben-y-gloe, Ben Dairg, or the red mountain, stands dominant. At the right entrance of the pass, the little white and lonely dwelling called Bruar Lodge, lies a mere speck beneath it. It consists of two small tenements, facing each other, encompassed by a wall, so as to form a small court between them; one of these buildings serves for the master, and the other for his servants. There is, besides, a lodging for the hill-men, rather frail in structure, and a dog kennel of the same picturesque character. Close by stands a black stack of peats...

With all its [the house's] apertures, he [Tortoise] loved it dearly; and it may be doubted whether any monarch ever entered a palace or any lady a ballroom with more absolute delight than he was wont to enter this lonely abode. What though the winds would revel freely in it, and heave up the little carpet with an unceasing undulation, still the table-cloth was reasonably tranquil, for the weight of the meal made it retain its station! What though the parlour bell in the passage would ring incessantly during the night, even when the doors were closed, stimulated by the gentle violence of the wind; it was an Aeolian harp to him!

But if he loved the lodge, the High Tops moved him to still greater eloquence: 'And now what do you think of this wild region?' he asks his companion as they sit on one of the summits.

Do you not feel almost as if you were wandering in a new world? Here, everything bears the original impress of nature untouched by the hand of man since its creation. That vast moor spread out below you; and those peaks in the distance, faint almost as the sky itself, give the appearance of an extent boundless and sublime as the ocean ...

Traverse all this desolate tract, and you shall find no dwelling, nor sheep, nor cow, nor horse, nor anything that can remind you of domestic life; you shall hear no sound but the rushing of the torrent, or the notes of the wild animals, the natural inhabitants; you shall see only the moor-fowl, and the plover flying before you from hillock to hillock, or the eagle soaring aloft with his eye to the sun, or his wings wet with mist. Nothing more shall you see except the dun tenants of the waste which we are in search of.

Scrope had many exciting moments on the hill – and not all of them directly to do with deer. On one occasion, as he and his little party sat huddled and drenched in a thunderstorm waiting for the rain to clear, his men were struck by lightning:

The thunder clouds were now vertical; no interval between the fire and the crash, but both instantaneous, like the volleying of heavy ordnance: – another vivid flash, and a loud piercing and protracted shriek was heard from Fraser. The men were driven abroad, as if an engine of war had burst amongst them: each of them had received a violent shock – all of them in the legs; but providentially, no one had sustained a serious injury ... It was evident, from their yelling, that the dogs had received a violent shock also.

Besides recounting his own adventures, Scrope recalled many other stirring exploits in the forest, both old and new. One of the most striking had happened only a year before he wrote, in 1837. A stalker called Donald was going through the forest of Strathmashie, near Loch

Laggan, when he saw the antlers of a stag which was lying asleep in the heather and proceeded to creep up on it:

> He had no rifle, but opened his deer-knife, which he placed between his teeth that his hands might be free, and then threw himself suddenly upon the stag; up started the astonished beast, and sprang forward with Donald on his back, who grasped him with might and main by the horns, to keep his seat in a sportsmanlike manner. No easy matter, I trow, for the animal made right down the rugged side of a hill with headlong speed to a stream in the glen below, and dashed through it, still bearing his anxious rider with the knife in his mouth, which he had neither time nor ability to use.
>
> When, however, this gallant pair reached the opposite side of the glen, and the deer began to breast the hill and relax his speed, Donald was enabled so far to collect his bewildered senses as to get hold of his knife; and he absolutely contrived to plunge it into his throat. The deer fell forward in the death struggle, and Donald made a summerset of course. In consequence of this extraordinary feat, the man has been dubbed by the people with a new and appropriate name in Gaelic, which my authority (Mr Skene) told me he could not pretend either to write or to pronounce.

Altogether, Scrope's book must have seemed a treasure-trove to those who had had only a taste of stalking, or had so far heard about it only by word of mouth. No wonder it was reprinted within a year of publication – and no wonder it sent a lot more novices northwards in pursuit of the 'dun tenants of the waste'.

Scrope's time at Bruar came to an end in the autumn of 1831, and his departure left the Atholl forests vacant, so that young Lord George Murray (later the sixth Duke) had plenty of room in which to work off his formidable energy. So lively was he that the hyperactive Colonel Thornton would surely have made a match against him, could a tryst have been arranged.

Murray's enthusiasm for stalking seems to have increased rapidly. In his private little game-record he entered only six harts and one hind shot in 1831; but in 1832 he killed forty harts and fourteen hinds, and in the following year forty-nine harts and nineteen hinds. In the autumn of 1832 there was a prodigious number of deer on the ground. 'Brought down in the evening to the peat-stacks nearly *4,000* deer,' he wrote in his journal for August 17th, 'but was unlucky in not killing any.'

Even by Murray's own standards, August 20th was an energetic day: a drive was held on Ben-y-gloe, and in his game-book he recorded:

Saw a fine hart come down the hill alone. Set three dogs after it, but they could not see him. I therefore took my horse and galloped after him, he crossed the Tilt near the burn of Auld Brony and went up the hill and I followed full speed till within about fifteen yards. He then began to squint down the hill towards the water. At that moment a dog came up (Canach) and took him as straight down into the river as possible, where I followed and soon shot him.

On September 5th Murray noted that, 'being afraid of being late for dinner, Butter and I ran home (a distance of five miles) in thirty-four minutes.' On September 11th he 'ran home with Mr Scott of Harding from Forest Lodge to Blair [eight miles] in fifty-six minutes after eating a very large breakfast and two luncheons.' The deer must have had a lively time that autumn.

Chapter Eight

Charles St John

After Scrope—chronologically, though not in terms of interest—
another gentleman of independent means stands out in the annals of
deer-stalking: Charles St John. Unlike Scrope, he did nothing to
accelerate the development of the sport; yet he was a fascinating specimen of that odd breed the shooting naturalist, with ideas far ahead of
his time; and by his account of one epic stalk, he immortalised both
himself and the stag which he pursued with such tenacity—the Muckle
Hart of Benmore.

St John was born in England in 1809, a grandson of the second
Viscount Bolingbroke, and from his earliest years was passionately
interested in wild creatures. A school friend recalled how he and
St John were taught to fish at the age of eleven by an elderly pensioner,
and how

> even at that time St John had the zoological bump largely developed.
> His box ... was generally a sort of menagerie—doormice in the one
> till, stag-beetles of gigantic size and wonderful caterpillars in paper
> boxes in the other, while sometimes a rabbit, sometimes a guinea-
> pig or perhaps a squirrel, was lodged below in a cell cunningly
> constructed of the Delphin classics and Ainsworth's dictionary. He
> was scarcely without livestock of some sort.

In due course the country boy went reluctantly to work as a clerk in
the Treasury; but, as a contemporary remarked, he chafed like a caged
eagle at the desk of a government office, and after only four or five
years he left, never to work seriously again. A slight stammer, which
became worse when he had to talk to strangers, increased his natural
dislike for London society, and he was most at home in the wilds of
Scotland, to which he repaired for shooting holidays with friends.

In 1832 or 1833 he was lent a house called Rosehall, on the river Oykell in Sutherland, and there he settled down, living a secluded life, fishing and shooting and observing the wild creatures all round him. This must have been one of his happiest hunting grounds, for it was on expeditions from Rosehall that he both shot the Muckle Hart and secured a wife, Anne Gibson, who was not only well endowed but also willing to adapt herself to his eccentric ways. In the words of his friend, Cosmo Innes, 'as the lady, with a true wife's devotion, accommodated herself to her husband's tastes and manner of life, he was enabled henceforth to live the life of a sportsman and naturalist in the Highlands, which was only modified when the necessity of educating a young family induced them to draw near schools.'

After leaving Rosehall, the St Johns lived for a while on the shore of Loch Ness, and then moved to the south shore of the Moray Firth; there, in a series of rented houses, Charles spent the rest of his active life, constantly fishing and shooting in the immediate vicinity, and making frequent longer expeditions into the hinterland. It was his neighbour at Nairn, Cosmo Innes, who persuaded him to write about his experiences and helped him to get into print: an article by Innes about some of St John's forays was accepted by the *Quarterly* magazine, and then St John himself, stimulated by the receipt of honestly earned money, produced several full-length books, notably, in 1846, *Natural History and Sport in Moray*, also published as *The Wild Sports and Natural History of the Scottish Highlands*.

The picture of the author's home life which emerges from his writing is a delightful one: his house and grounds, wherever they might be, were permanently occupied by a menagerie of birds and small animals, most of which he had himself caught or had brought to him. Owls, hawks, woodcock, blackcock, badgers, mice, jackdaws, rabbits, foxes, squirrels – all seemed to live in remarkable amity, although every now and then an entry in their master's journal takes on a rather pained tone in describing some sudden outrage:

My tame peregrine, after some years of friendship and alliance with our pet owl, ended in killing and eating her! A piece of ungenerous barbarism which I should not have suspected so fine a bird would have committed.

St John's sons were brought up surrounded by animals, and they took to their father's ways at an early age. They were aided and abetted by an aged retainer described in the books as 'Donald', who was in fact an old poacher called Rennie, well known in the neighbourhood of Elgin. One day St John caught him trespassing on land to which he had no right of access, and, rather than prosecute him, took him into his service. Thereafter Donald acted as a faithful servant on the expeditions into the hills, and at home as an extra tutor to the two boys. As Cosmo Innes recorded, 'he was well acquainted with the habits of wildfowl, and could take you up to ... wild geese when the ground seemed impossible. The otters were his own children.'

Tutored by him, and by his own father, young Harry St John shot his first right-and-left at wild geese at the age of ten — a feat which most wildfowlers do not equal until two or three times that age, if ever. The boys were 'the constant companions' of their father's sport, wrote Innes. 'In the evening the drawing-room table was a pretty sight. Some rare bird, or, if no rarity offered, a good, handsome old blackcock, was displayed *en pose* for the artists, and father and children made studies in watercolours of a head, a claw, or a tail of the fine bird.'

St John's own attitude towards wildlife differed markedly from that of his contemporaries, whose blood-lust was unbridled by considerations of humanity or ecology. He had a strong hunting instinct — as he frequently confessed — but, in the words of a friend, 'there was something in him beyond the common slaughtering sportsman', and his desire to kill was tempered by admiration for the creatures he pursued. Not only did he shoot them: he studied them closely, and loved them too. A cynic might suppose that when he killed a golden eagle and then lamented its demise, he was more hypocritical than truly distressed; yet a study of his writing shows that his struggle with his conscience was genuine and unending.

It must be borne in mind that the naturalist of the 1830s and 1840s had no camera with which to record and confirm his sightings. The only way he could be certain of identifying a rare bird was to shoot it or catch it, and have it stuffed and mounted. Taxidermy was then much in vogue; the stuffers (as they were called) did a brisk trade, and collectors were persistent in their demands for specimens. All this helps in some measure to excuse passages like the following, which would sound outrageous in a modern context:

28 May. I heard a most extraordinary singing in some alders today; at one time it was like a person whistling, at another like a very sweet and full-toned blackbird, but always ending in a song like a sedge-warbler. After watching it some time, we shot the bird, which turned out to be a whinchat.

22 April. Drove down to the sea-coast today and after certain trouble, manoeuvring and stalking, I shot a pair of peregrines, male and female ... I had determined to succeed, but I should not have shot the birds for any other reason than to oblige Mr Hancock, and see them live again as stuffed by him.

Peregrines were by no means the only rare hawks that St John shot. Many an osprey succumbed to his gun, as did a number of golden eagles – although the death of an eagle always moved him to spasms of self-reproach:

I must own, notwithstanding the reputed destructiveness of the eagle, that I looked with great regret at the body of the noble bird, and wished that I had not killed him.

In general, St John's attitude to so-called vermin was exceptionally enlightened. Though he killed otters and wild cats readily enough, he did at least reflect about the natural role of predators. 'The owls of this country,' he wrote, 'are far more serviceable to us than we imagine, destroying countless mice and rats.' And again:

It is difficult to determine how far we are right in endeavouring utterly to destroy one kind of animal or bird in order to increase another species. Nature, if left to herself, keeps up a fair equilibrium ... I cannot say, however, that I am at all anxious to see our island entirely clear of what game-preservers call 'vermin'. There is more beauty and more to interest one in the flight and habits of a pair of falcons than in a whole pack of grouse, and I regret to see how rare these birds, and eagles and many others, are becoming under the influence of traps, poison and guns.

In retrospect, it is surprising that any rare birds survived at all, for quite apart from the persecutions of the gamekeepers, St John records that there was already a strong demand for the eggs of golden eagles and ospreys, which fetched £1 or 25s. apiece, as well as for those of other elusive species. Even in the remotest wilds of Sutherland, he found, the keepers had ascertained the value of the eggs of the red-throated diver, 'and were as eager to search for them, and as loth to part with them (excepting at a very high price), as love of gain could make them. Nor had they the least scruple in endeavouring to impose eggs under fictitious names on any person wishing to purchase such things.'

As a naturalist St John is still well worth reading, for his experience of the Scottish hills was immense and his observation close and sympathetic. Whether he is taming a blackcock (which, in captivity, 'soon becomes familiar and attached to his master'), admiring the sagacity of ptarmigan, describing the behaviour of the 'fine bold bird', the long-eared owl, watching the 'gay, lively crossbill', or reflecting on the humours of toads ('like many other individuals of quiet exterior toads are liable to great fits of passion and anger'), he is always entertaining and informative.

Yet it is on his prowess as a deer-stalker that his fame rests, and in particular on his pursuit of the great stag which he immortalised as the Muckle Hart of Benmore. In shooting deer he felt the same compunction as assailed him when he killed birds. 'No man with any feeling can kill a roe without a pang of regret,' he wrote, 'though his natural instinct, as an animal of prey, leads him on to hunt and kill another roe an hour afterwards.'

The stalking of red deer – much larger and less graceful than roe – was less traumatic for him, and he frequently made long expeditions into the hills in their pursuit, sleeping out for the night in the heather or in some distant shepherd's hut. Sometimes he went alone, but more often than not he was attended by his faithful Donald – a professional pessimist who, to keep up his spirits, had constant recourse to gargantuan pinches of snuff. Also present on many of the forays were St John's deerhound, Bran, his Skye terrier, Fred, and a bulldog which he had trained to perfection:

He learned to crouch and creep up to the deer with me, never showing himself, and seemingly to understand perfectly what I wished him to do. When necessary I could leave him for hours together, lying alone on the hill, when he would never stir till called by me. If a deer was wounded, he would follow the track with untiring perseverance, distinguishing the scents of the wounded animal and singling it out from the rest.

Even though forests were by then being made and let on an ever-increasing scale, St John stalked with remarkable freedom. The hill shepherds generally gave him notice of any particularly fine stag they saw on their rounds, whereupon he would set off in pursuit.

Thus it was, one Sunday evening in October 1833, that Malcolm, the shepherd of the shieling at the foot of Benmore, in Sutherland, came to St John's house on his way back from church to report that he had 'crossed in the hill a track of a hart of extraordinary size', and that he guessed it must be that of 'the muckle stag of Benmore'. 'This,' St John reported,

was an animal seldom seen, but [one] which had long been the talk and marvel of the shepherds for its wonderful size and cunning. They love the marvellous and in their report the muckle stag bore a charmed life; he was unapproachable and invulnerable. I had heard of him, too, and, having got the necessary information, resolved to try and break the charm, though it should cost me a day or two.

At sunrise next morning he set out, armed with his rifle, and accompanied by Donald, carrying his double-barrelled shot-gun, and by the deerhound, Bran. On the way up the glen St John shot a wild cat stealing home to its cairn, but otherwise the day produced nothing – not even a track of the mighty hart.

Having slept the night in the shepherd's shieling, the party was again off by daybreak, and spent the whole morning searching the corries fruitlessly. Then, in the afternoon, as they were crossing a bare and boggy piece of ground,

Donald suddenly stopped, with a Gaelic exclamation, and pointed – and there, to be sure, was a full-fresh foot-print, the largest mark of a deer either of us had ever seen. There was no more grumbling. Both of us were instantly as much on the alert as when we started on our adventure ...

We traced the track as long as the ground would allow. Where we lost it, it seemed to point down the little burn, which soon lost itself to our view in a gorge of bare rocks. We proceeded now very cautiously, and taking up our station on a concealed ledge of one of the rocks, began to search the valley below us with our telescopes ... At the farther end were two black lochs, connected by a sluggish stream; beside the larger loch a bit of coarse grass and rushes, where we could distinguish a brood of wild ducks swimming in and out. It was difficult ground to see a deer in, if lying; and I had almost

given up seeking, when Donald's glass became motionless and he
gave a sort of grunt as he changed his posture, but without taking the
glass from his eye. 'Ugh! I'm thinking yon's him, sir. I'm seeing his
horns.'

I was at first incredulous. What he showed me ... looked for all
the world like some withered sticks; but the doubt was short. While
we gazed the stag rose and commenced feeding; and at last I saw the
great hart of Benmore! He was a long way off, perhaps a mile and a
half, but in excellent ground for getting at him. Our plan was soon
arranged. I was to stalk him with the rifle, while Donald, with my
gun and Bran, was to get round out of sight, to the pass by which
the deer was likely to leave the valley.

My task was apparently very easy. After getting down behind the
rock, I had scarcely to stoop my head, but to walk up within shot, so
favourable was the ground and the wind. I walked cautiously,
however, and slowly, to give Donald time to reach the pass. I was
now within three hundred yards of him, when, as I leant against a
slab of stone, all hid below my eyes, I saw him give a sudden start,
stop feeding, and look round suspiciously.

What a noble beast! What a stretch of antler! With a mane like a
lion! He stood for a minute or two, snuffing every breath. I could not
guess the cause of his alarm; it was not myself; the light wind blew
fair down from him upon me; and I knew Donald would give him
no inkling of his whereabouts.

He presently began to move, and came at a slow trot directly
towards me. My pulse beat high. Another hundred yards forward,
and he is mine! But it was not so to be. He took the top of a steep
bank which commanded my position, saw me in an instant, and was
off at the speed of twenty miles an hour to a pass wide from that
where Donald was hid. While clattering up the hill, scattering loose
stones behind him, two other stags joined him, who had evidently
been put up by Donald and had given the alarm to my quarry. It
was then that his great size was conspicuous. I could see with my
glass that they were full-grown stags, and with good heads, but
they looked like fallow-deer as they followed him up the crag ...

Wednesday began briskly with the massacre of two golden eagles
that had sealed their own fate by carrying off one of Malcolm's lambs.
Having found the half-eaten carcase the day before, the shepherd had
dug a hole in the peat close by it, and to this hide St John stole in the

darkness before dawn. He left a vivid account of his vigil in 'the nipping cold before the break of day': the first visitors to the feast were ravens, but soon one eagle swept down – to its death – and not long after its mate followed. As usual, remorse smote the gunner: 'Eager as I had been to do the deed, I could not look on the royal birds without a pang. But such regrets were now too late ...' After an 'incredible breakfast', he and Donald resumed their search for the Muckle Hart, but the day brought no sign of it, and nightfall found them so far even from Malcolm's shieling that they bivouacked on the hill: 'We were content to find a sort of niche in the rock, tolerably screened from all winds; and having almost filled it with long heather, flower upwards, we wrapped our plaids round us and slept pretty comfortably'.

Thursday proved almost equally frustrating; they searched all day, and though they found a few tracks, they caught no glimpse of the animal itself. By the afternoon Donald was thoroughly disgusted with the whole business, but St John's determination was unshaken. 'For myself,' he wrote, 'I looked upon it as my fate that I must have that hart.'

In the evening heavy rain began to fall, and the two men were glad to stumble on a whisky bothy – a den of illicit distillers. They might never have found the place had not St John suddenly heard, above the noise of the rain and the rushing of the burn, what sounded like 'the shrill treble of a fiddle'. He wrote, 'I could scarcely believe my ears. But when I communicated the intelligence to Donald, whose ears are less acute, he jumped for joy. "It's all right enough, sir; just follow the sound; it's that drunken deevil Sandy Ross; ye'll nae haud a fiddle frae him, nor him frae a whisky-still."'

Welcomed in by the revellers, the weary hunters were handsomely entertained; but long after St John had withdrawn to a pile of dry heather in the corner, he had disturbed visions of 'strange orgies in the bothy, and of my sober Donald exhibiting curious antics on top of a tub.' The result was that, the next morning, Donald was out for the count, and St John continued his quest alone, leaving Bran, the deerhound, tied up in the bothy until such time as his handler should recover.

On his own for the first time, St John struck off to fresh ground; but while he was lying high above a loch, scanning a wide range of country with his glass, the weather suddenly changed and the mist came down – a development which, as all Scottish stalkers know, is both disconcerting and potentially dangerous. Not only is it impossible to see the deer from any distance, so that if one continues to advance one runs the constant risk of bumping into them and sending them off at speed; it is also easy to lose oneself, as all bearings are blotted out. If the mist descends, the most sensible course is to keep still and wait for it to lift again.

This St John knew; but he was so cold at this exposed height that he slowly followed a burn downhill until dark began to fall. He realised that he would have to camp out again, and as he had no more food with him, he prepared to shoot a grouse with his rifle. Soon he heard one alight close to him, and he contrived to get the bird's head silhouetted against the sky as it strutted about a hillock. He fired at it, and going up, found that he had killed two birds with one shot. It was, as he later wrote 'a commencement of good luck', for as he took the skinned birds to the burn to wash them, there, fresh in the sand, was a mighty track — the track he had been following for so long.

> Like Robinson Crusoe in the same circumstances, I started back, but was speedily at work taking my information. There were prints enough to show that the hart had crossed at a walk, leisurely. It must have been lately, for it was since the burn had returned to its natural size, after last night's flood. But nothing could be done till morning, so I set about my cooking; and having after some time succeeded in lighting a fire, while my grouse were slowly broiling, I pulled a quantity of heather, which I spread in a corner a little protected by an overhanging rock. I spread my plaid upon it, and over the plaid built another layer of heather.
>
> My supper ended, which was not epicurean, I crawled into my nest under my plaid, and was soon sound asleep. I cannot say that my slumbers were unbroken. I dreamt of the great stag thundering up the hills with preternatural speed, and of noises like cannon (which I have since learnt to attribute to their true cause — the splitting of fragments of rock under a sudden change from wet to sharp frost), and above all, the constant recurrence of visions of weary struggles through fields of snow and ice kept me restless; and at length awoke me to the consciousness of a brilliant skylight and keen frost — a change that rejoiced me in spite of the cold.

So began the sixth and final day of the marathon pursuit; again St John was on his own, for Donald had had no means of telling which way he had gone, and therefore no means of catching up with him (as it later transpired, he had gone back to Malcolm's shieling). St John's own account of his eventual triumph is admirably vivid:

Saturday. Need I say my first object was to go down and examine the track anew. There was no mistake. It was impossible to doubt that 'the muckle hart of Benmore' had actually walked through that burn a few hours before me, and in the same direction. I followed the track, and breasted the opposite hill. Looking around from its summit, it appeared to me a familiar scene, and on considering a moment, I found I overlooked from a different quarter the very same rocky plain and the two black lochs where I had seen my chace three days before.

I had not gazed many minutes when I saw a deer lying on a black hillock which was quite open. I lay down immediately, and with my glass made out at once the object of all my wanderings. My joy was somewhat abated by his position, which was not easily approachable. My first object, however, was to withdraw myself out of his sight, which I did by crawling backwards down a little bank till only the tops of his horns were visible, and they served to show me that he continued still. As he lay looking towards me, he commanded with his eye three-fourths of the circle, and the other quarter, where one might have got in upon him under cover of the little hillock, was unsafe from the wind blowing in that direction.

A burn ran between him and me, one turn of which seemed to come within two hundreds yards of him.

It was my only chance; so, retreating about half a mile, I got into the burn in hidden ground, and then crept up its channel with such caution that I never allowed myself a sight of more than the tips of his horns, till I had reached the nearest bend to him. There, looking through a tuft of rushes, I had a perfect view of the noble animal, lying on the open hillock, lazily stretched out at length, and only moving now and then to scratch his flank with his horn. I watched him for fully an hour, the water up to my knees all the time. At length, he stirred, gathered his legs together, and rose; and arching his back, he stretched himself just as a bullock does when rising from his night's lair. My heart throbbed, as turning all round he seemed to try the wind for his security, and then walked straight to the burn, at a point about one hundred and fifty yards from me.

I was much tempted, but had resolution to reserve my fire, reflecting that I had but one barrel. He went into the burn at a deep pool, and standing in it up to his knees, took a long drink. I stooped to put on a new copper cap and prick the nipple of my rifle; and — on looking up again, he was gone! I was in despair; and was on the point of moving rashly, when I saw his horns again appear a little farther off, but not more than fifty yards from the burn. By-and-by they lowered, and I judged he was lying down. 'You are mine at last,' I said; and I crept cautiously up the bed of the burn till I was opposite where he had lain down. I carefully and inch by inch placed my rifle over the bank, and then ventured to look along it. I could see only his horns, but within an easy shot. I was afraid to move higher up the bed of the burn, where I could have seen his body; the direction of the wind made that dangerous. I took breath for a moment, and screwed up my nerves; and then with my cocked rifle on my shoulder, and my finger on the trigger, I kicked a stone which splashed into the water.

He started up instantly; but exposed only his front towards me. Still he was very near, scarcely fifty yards, and I fired at his throat just where it joins the head. He dropped on his knees to my shot; but was up again in a moment, and went staggering up the hill. Oh, for one hour of Bran! Although he kept on at a mad pace, I saw he was becoming too weak for the hill. He swerved and turned back to the burn; and came headlong down within ten yards of me, tumbling into it apparently dead.

Feeling confident, from the place where my ball had taken effect, that he was dead, I threw down my rifle, and went up to him with my hunting-knife. I found him stretched out, and as I thought dying; and I laid hold of his horns to raise his head to bleed him. I had scarcely touched him when he sprang up, flinging me backwards on the stones. It was an awkward position. I was stunned by the violent fall; behind me was a steep bank of seven or eight feet high; before me the bleeding stag with his horns levelled at me, and cutting me off from my rifle. In desperation I moved; when he instantly charged, but fortunately tumbled ere he quite reached me. He drew back again like a ram about to butt, and then stood still with his head lowered, and his eyes bloody and swelled, glaring upon me.

His mane and all his coat were dripping with water and blood; and as he now and then tossed his head with an angry snort, he looked like some savage beast of prey. We stood mutually at bay for some time, till recovering myself, I jumped out of the burn so suddenly that he had not time to run at me, and from the bank above, I dashed my plaid over his head and eyes, and threw myself upon him. I cannot account for my folly, and it had nearly cost me dear. The poor beast struggled desperately, and his remaining strength foiled me in every attempt to stab in front; and he at length made off, tumbling me down, but carrying with him a stab in the leg which lamed him. I ran and picked up my rifle and then kept him in view as he rushed down the burn on three legs towards the loch. He took the water, and stood at bay up to his chest in it.

As soon as he halted, I commenced loading my rifle when to my dismay I found that all the balls I had remaining were for my double-barrel, and were a size too large for my rifle. I sat down and commenced scraping one to the right size, an operation that seemed interminable. At last I succeeded; and, having loaded, the poor stag remaining perfect still, I went up within twenty yards of him, and shot him through the head. He turned over and floated, perfectly dead. I waded in and towed him ashore, and then had leisure to look at my wounds and bruises, which were not serious, except my shin-bone, which was scraped from ankle to knee by his horn.

I soon had cleaned my quarry and stowed him away as safely as I could and then turned down the glen at a gay pace. I found Donald with Bran reposing at Malcolm's shieling; and for all reproaches on his misconduct, I was satisfied with sending him to bring home the 'muckle Hart of Benmore', a duty which he performed before night-fall.

Oddly enough, St John never described in print the great beast for which he finally accounted, and which so nearly accounted for him. In fact its head was by no means an outstanding trophy: only a nine-pointer, distinguished by no special strength or beauty. The body, however, was exceptional, and weighed thirty stone – a unique amount for a stag that had been bred and reared in the bare hills. Besides, the animal was shot in October, by which time the rut must have been well advanced: one may safely presume that rutting activity had taken several stone off the Muckle Hart before he was killed.

One curious fact about the author's account is that the rut is never once mentioned: there is no roaring of stags, no fighting, no chasing of hinds – and indeed very few other deer feature at all. It seems extra-ordinary that anyone could stalk through the mountains of Sutherland for a week during October without being constantly aware of the rut, and the suspicion steals over the reader that the whole episode may have taken place when the rut was *over* – that is, towards the end of the month, by which time all true sportsmen had laid off for the season. Certainly the few glimpses afforded of the Muckle Hart's behaviour

H

suggest that he had already been at the rut and was through with it, either sated or driven off by fresher stags: always he seems to be on his own, keeping away from other deer.

In 1833, when he shot the stag, St John was only twenty-four and relatively inexperienced: it may be that his youthful enthusiasm drove him on at a time of the year which in later life he would have recognised as inappropriate. In any case, his stalk has passed into history, and the Muckle Hart is easily the most famous stag ever shot in Scotland.

Not until he was thirty-five did St John break into print; then, encouraged by his friend at Nairn, he mined his journals for all the treasure he had laid up over the years. The result was the minor classic, *The Wild Sports and Natural History of the Scottish Highlands*, which combined accounts of his own forays with detailed observations of animals and birds, all pleasantly recorded in an easy, natural style.

For most of his time he seems to have shot and fished around his home on the Moray Firth; but in the spring of 1848 he made a long-range expedition into Sutherland with the object of exploring the north coast and collecting eggs and specimens for some unnamed gentleman. With his favourite retriever, Leo, a friend called Dunbar and an interpreter for conversing with the Gaelic-speaking natives, St John set out in a singular conveyance:

> The vehicle which we travelled in was a small and lightly-built flat-bottomed boat, made of larch and mounted on wheels. It was constructed to ship and unship in half a minute. By simply unscrewing two bolts, it could be taken off its wheels and launched into the water. Being on springs, it made a very easy carriage, and was large enough to hold four persons.

This cart-cum-boat greatly facilitated anti-osprey manoeuvres, which were one of the trip's chief objects. Whenever the site of a nest was reported to them by shepherds or other locals, the party would drive the vehicle as near to the loch as possible, drag the boat to the water, launch it, and row out to the island on which the hawks were established, taking the eggs and if possible shooting the birds.

Although it was not the stalking season, St John's thoughts were often on deer, and in his little book *A Tour in Sutherlandshire*, published in 1849, he described how he called on an old Highland keeper who had been an attendant of his when he had lived at Rosehall. He found him:

winking in the morning sun in a manner peculiar to owls and the inhabitants of cottages full of peat smoke ... Many an old story connected with stag and corrie, shieling and whisky bottle, the old fellow called to my recollection; and I really saw with regret the last of his weatherbeaten face as he bowed and gesticulated to me as long as we continued in sight.

For the Sutherland Highlander, St John reported, deer-stalking seemed an 'invincible passion'.

His constant thoughts and dreams are about the mountain corrie and the stag: get him into conversation on any subject, and by some means it invariably comes round to deer and deer-stalking. He has stories without end, handed down from father to son, of wonderful shots, and dogs that never failed to pull down their stag.

Poaching, he found, was rife, and in spite of the great vigilance of the Duke of Sutherland's foresters, the shepherds managed to kill many deer at all seasons of the year:

Nor is it possible for any number of keepers to prevent this entirely: though they may be as watchful as possible, the shepherd, from being constantly on the hill amongst the deer, and knowing by experience all their haunts at every time of day and at every season, has advantages over the keeper that no vigilance of the latter can counterbalance.

St John described graphically how a shepherd, having spied a stag day after day and having got to know its habits, would lie in wait for it, all day if necessary, and gun it down with a blast of slugs. He would then dismember it, carry home each quarter individually, and privily sell the venison. By then a good pair of antlers was another source of profit, for the gun-smiths or bird-stuffers had begun selling them to visitors in Inverness, or even 'to sportsmen who, taking the stag's head to England with them, pass it off as a trophy of their own skill and prowess'.

Behaviour like that of the shepherd who murdered a stag in cold blood had St John puzzled, and once again he tried to express the conflict between the killer and the naturalist that persisted unresolved inside him:

Without pretending to disown my love of deer-stalking, I find an enjoyment in watching unseen, and patiently, the animal in a manner

which one *could not* do, supposing oneself to be rifle in hand; for
then, such is the passion of mankind for the chase, that I fancy few
people exist who would not be more intent on killing the stag than
in quietly looking at him.

Perhaps if St John had grown into a mellow old age he would have
sublimated his hunting instinct altogether. As it was, he never had the
chance; for in 1854, when he was only forty-three, as he was going out
to shoot he was struck down by paralysis of the whole left side. His
friend, Cosmo Innes, recorded, 'He was carried home quite powerless,
assisted by a Major W. Pitcairn Campbell, 23rd Fusiliers, but retaining
his senses entire.' He recovered sufficiently to go south for a change of
air and for medical treatment, but he never regained the use of his
limbs. He died in 1856 at Woolston, near Southampton, and he was
buried there with the skull of his beloved dog, Leo, set at his feet inside
his coffin.

Chapter Nine

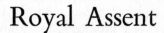

Royal Assent

At five o'clock in the morning of Monday August 29th, 1842, Queen Victoria and Prince Albert, both of whom were then twenty-three, left Windsor by rail for London. Their party crossed the capital in carriages, and at Woolwich, where a large crowd had assembled to see them off, they embarked on the *Royal George*, a man-of-war converted into a yacht. So began the Queen's first visit to Scotland; so began also a love affair with the Highlands that lasted the whole of her life.

The voyage itself proved tedious. 'It was thought derogatory to the dignity of Her Majesty to come in a steamer, and consequently she came in a man-of-war towed by a steamer,' wrote a friend of Captain Washington, the pilot in charge. This ludicrous device naturally made progress very slow, and on the second day of the voyage the Queen recorded in her journal:

> We heard, to our great distress, that we had only gone fifty-eight miles since eight o'clock last night. How annoying and provoking this is! We remained on deck all day, lying on sofas; the sea was very rough towards evening, and I was very ill.

On the morning of the third day the Queen learnt, to her 'great vexation', that they had been making only three knots during the night. But at last, at 1 a.m. on September 1st, they anchored at Leith, near Edinburgh, and from that moment the royal couple were enchanted by everything they saw – she by the novelty of the surroundings, he by their apparent similarity to some of his former haunts in Europe. 'We drove through *Dalkeith*, which was full of people, all running and cheering,' the Queen reported. 'Albert says many of the people look like Germans.' In Perth, 'Albert was charmed, and said it put him in mind of the situation of *Basle*.' In Birnam Wood 'Albert said, as we came along between the mountains, that to the right, where they were wooded, it was very like *Thüringen*, and on the left more like *Switzerland*.'

Greeted everywhere by the firing of guns, by sword dances and reels, by pipers playing, by processions, and by bonfires blazing from the hill tops, the royal pair proceeded to Drummond Castle, where they were the guests of the Breadalbane family. There, on September 12th, Albert had his first experience of deer-stalking. He had already done a good deal of ordinary covert-shooting: he was used to pheasants, partridges, and hares, and even to driven roe and wild boars; but skirmishes against the deer on the Scottish mountains were something entirely new to him.

He got up at 5 a.m., and because he thought he should not be seen at the castle in anything but formal dress, he changed into clothes suitable for the hill at an isolated farmhouse. All morning the Queen waited anxiously to see how her beloved would perform:

At length, a little before three, to my joy, Albert returned, dreadfully sunburnt and a good deal tired. He said that the difficulty and the exertion were very great ... Campbell of Monzie (pronounced 'Monie'), a young gentleman who has a place near here, went with him, and was, Albert said, extremely active.

Into those last two words a good deal can be read. Albert, though young, had come straight from the lush pastures of London, Windsor and Osborne, and was evidently none too fit; Campbell of Monzie, by contrast, must have been wiry as a pointer from constantly scrambling about the hills, and no doubt took the opportunity of giving the royal visitor a violent work-out. But at least Albert was rewarded for his exertions: he shot two stags, and afterwards reported enthusiastically in a letter to Victoria's half-brother Prince Leiningen:

Without doubt deer-stalking is one of the most fatiguing, but is also one of the most interesting, of pursuits. There is not a tree or a bush behind which you can hide yourself ... One has therefore to be constantly on the alert in order to circumvent them [the deer]; and to keep under the hill out of their wind, crawling on hands and knees and dressed entirely in grey.

That first taste of the Highlands whetted the appetites of both Victoria and Albert for further visits, and two years later, in September 1844, they again sailed for the north, this time to stay with Lord and Lady Glenlyon at Blair Castle. At the start of the journey the Queen was in delicate health, for she had given birth to Prince Alfred only five weeks before; but her spirits soared as soon as they reached the mountains. 'Oh! What can equal the beauties of nature!' she wrote soon after their arrival at Blair, 'What enjoyment there is in them! Albert enjoys it so much; he is in ecstasies here.'

For his benefit, the entire forest had been kept quiet throughout the season: no shot had been fired at either bird or deer. As a result the hills were teeming with game, but there was none for the royal party to eat. Acccording to Charlotte Canning, one of the Queen's ladies-in-waiting, and a splendidly spirited girl, 'not a grouse was to be had for the Queen's luncheon & Ld Glenlyon went out to get a few for dinner. He has recovered his sight very much but his shooting must be fearfully dangerous to those who go with him.'

Albert himself went out after grouse on Friday 13th, and returned at lunchtime with four and a half brace. Next day he stalked, and in the course of the afternoon killed three stags. 'He said he saw one herd of more than 1,000 & another 3 of 400,' wrote Lady Canning in her diary. 'He had a great deal of running & a little creeping & came home excessively pleased; Ld Glenlyon was the only person besides keepers who went with him.'

Early the next week, however, the Prince showed a regrettably un-British lack of discrimination over the kind of target he was prepared to engage. In the park at Blair were several half-tame, more or less domesticated stags, and in her journal (which is often a great deal livelier than the Queen's) Lady Canning left a graphic account of how he mowed one down out of the dining room window:

The Prince was to shoot a fat stag from the window. A few of these were caught when young & put into a sort of park – the others came to them & there is a spot they jump down & cannot get back from, & the park now has a very good herd in it. They are in peace there, no one ventures amongst them, & they bellow all night in a variety of sounds like bulls and roar sometimes almost like a lion.

The rifle was brought into the dining-room & the fat stag chosen. The Queen went to a window of another room & looked out. I saw the poor beast catch up his legs for an instant & then look round surprised & walk a few steps and then die—they say it was well shot thro' the heart.

The other stags walked quietly away very little startled & the dead hart was brought round to the door on a horse for the Queen to look at him. It was quite a Landseer picture, all the tents [of the troops] & the Highlanders on guard for a background & the dead deer & the pony standing by him, a number of picturesque kilted keepers ... The poor little Princess was dreadfully distressed at the stag's death ... She burst out crying and could not be consoled. Seeing the deer lifted up shocked her; she said 'his head fell & his neck was no more strong.'

According to Lady Canning, the incident made the Queen 'shake and be very uncomfortable'; and so when the Prince proposed to repeat the performance the next day, Victoria sent for her lady-in-waiting to be with her while Albert gratified his blood-lust. 'He wanted her very much not to see it,' Lady Canning recorded, but 'of course I could not keep her away from the window & she was looking on when the stag was killed. He dropped down dead the instant he was struck.'

Significantly enough, no mention of these distressing scenes occurs in the Queen's own journal. Whenever Albert missed a stag on the hill, she reported the event cheerfully enough, evidently believing that the failures were due more to bad luck than to incompetence, and often remarking on the good nature with which the Prince bore misfortune. But when his conduct became in any way less than admirable, she preferred not to remember it at all.

One beast which escaped the royal fusillade was Tilt, a stag with particularly fine antlers which was brought into the park at Blair as a calf in the year of Albert's visit, and spent a luxurious existence there, dining on hay, oats, powdered horn and other delicacies. As a result he grew a series of magnificent heads, all of which were collected and kept when he cast his antlers in the spring. When he died at the age of thirteen in 1857, his whole body was stuffed, and it still reclines in the great hall at Blair, looking faintly ridiculous among all the weapons and armour.

Victoria's keenest pleasure came in accompanying the men to the hill, even though her role was only that of a spectator, and usually a distant one. While she waited, she and Lady Canning would amuse themselves by sketching—and nowhere could have been better suited to their favourite pastime, for the views in every direction were

magnificent. On several occasions large-scale deer-drives were held
in Glen Tilt, and the Queen was taken to a suitable point from which to
observe the proceedings. Of one such day she reported:

> We sat down on the ground, Lady Canning and I sketching, and
> Sandy and Mr Oswald ... lying on the grass and looking through
> glasses. After waiting again some time, we were told in a mysterious
> whisper that 'they were coming,' and indeed a great herd *did* appear
> on the brow of the hill, and came running down a good way, when
> most provokingly two men who were walking on the road – which
> they had no business to have done – suddenly came in sight, and then
> the herd all ran back again and the sport was spoilt ... My poor
> Albert had not even fired one shot for fear of spoiling the whole
> thing, but had been running about a good deal. The group of
> keepers and dogs was very pretty.

On September 21st the Queen became much more closely involved.
'It was a long hard day's work,' she wrote afterwards, 'though extremely delightful and enjoyable, and unlike anything I had ever
done before.' She would have enjoyed it even more, she reported, had
she been able to stay with Albert all day; as it was, she set out with
him and came home with him, but was left behind when the real
excitement began – the fate of many a hanger-on before and since.
Having driven up Glen Tilt in carriages, they got out and took to
ponies:

> Albert and I walked about a bit, and then Lady Canning and we
> mounted our ponies and set off on our journey, Lord Glenlyon
> leading my pony the whole way, Peter Fraser, the head keeper (a
> wonderfully active man), leading the way; Sandy and six other
> Highlanders carrying rifles and leading dogs, and the rear brought up
> by two ponies with our luncheon-box. Lawley, Albert's Jäger, was
> also there, carrying one of Albert's rifles; the other Albert slung
> over his right shoulder to relieve Lawley. So we set off and wound
> round and round the hill, which had the most picturesque effect
> imaginable ... As we ascended we had to speak in a whisper, as
> indeed we did almost all day, for fear of coming upon deer un-
> awares. The wind was, however, right, which is everything here
> for the deer. I wish we could have had Landseer with us to sketch
> our party, with the background.

It was left to Lady Canning – a much more accurate and objective reporter – to record that the Queen's pony was grey, that the monarch herself had 'her long shepherd's Plaid apron tied round her instead of a habit', that on the ponies at the back were 'piles of cloaks & the great luncheon box', and that when the Queen wrote that they 'wound round and round the hill', she meant in fact they ascended a zig-zag path cut from the face of the hill for the former Duke of Atholl when he was eighty years old.

While Albert went after some stags that had been sighted in the distance, the ladies reclined on the mossy summit of Cairn Chlamain, sketching and admiring the view into Mar Forest. 'The Queen was quite delighted with the wild scenery,' her lady-in-waiting noted, 'and the Prince was in ecstasies' – even though he missed with the only shot of the morning.

After a heavy picnic (the luncheon box, wrote Lady Canning, was 'just like a dressing case, and all the bottles & cruets & Plates are in one place where they can be used without unpacking') Albert again set forth, and looked, according to the Queen, 'like a little speck creeping about on an opposite hill'. Owing to a misunderstanding, both parties waited a long time for the other to move on, so that the whole expedition was still high on the hill when the sun went down, and the Queen became alarmed lest they should all be benighted. But the ponies picked their way safely down in the twilight, and the Queen was rewarded by a magnificent sunset:

> As the sun went down the scenery became more and more beautiful, the sky crimson, golden-red and blue, and the hills looking purple and lilac, most exquisite, till at length it set, and the hues grew softer in the sky and the outlines of the hill sharper. I never saw anything finer. It soon, however, grew very dark.

The onset of night in no way worried Lady Canning, who wrote:

> Nothing could be more beautiful than the blue evening hush over those distant ranges of hills at sunset; seen from the height it might have been Greece.

In the days that followed, many similar expeditions took place, all of them enjoyed by the Queen; and the stay at Blair was on the whole a success. The only flaw was the friction that developed between Lord

Glenlyon and Lady Canning as the lady-in-waiting sought to protect her mistress from the excessive rigours of the hill. In her diary she summed the situation up with her usual forthright vigour:

Ld Glenlyon & I again had a sort of dispute in few words for he always wants to keep the Queen out as long as possible & I to get her home. She, out of civility, will do anything proposed & only throws out hints that she wants to be back before dark, & avoid steep places. He understands no hints & I have got a reputation for great fuss & fidgets. All this goes on whenever the Prince is not there.

On another occasion, after the laird's plans for the afternoon had been frustrated, she wrote:

Ld Glenlyon's temper cannot stand these reverses. I am his *bête noire* & somehow he thinks me a complete spoil sport & the incarnation of fuss, & the Queen is amused beyond anything & she & the Prince laughed the whole evening at various little anecdotes Car [Caroline Cocks, another lady-in-waiting] told of his complaints against me. Ly Glenlyon is quite delightful & I am very glad to see so much of her.

Excessive zeal was the cause of Lord Glenlyon's temper: of course he wanted Albert to have the best possible sport, and went to some trouble to get the Prince shots at stags. Drive after drive was arranged, and although most of the manœuvres failed, Albert in the end had plenty of shooting. The Glenlyons were ill-rewarded for all their efforts, for on the night of September 26th a fire broke out in the castle and gutted the kitchen and stable. But then on their final afternoon – September 30th – the Queen and her party had a grandstand view of Albert in action:

I was told of an immense herd [wrote Lady Canning] & saw at a distance a hill that looked as if covered with brown fern, but the brown hill-side seemed to move, & the herd came on for nearly two miles. The hill-side was alive with them & we could hear their bellowing & the sound of their feet, with a glass we could see them beautifully. From our bird's eye view we could see both Prince & deer at once when they could not see each other & it was interesting beyond anything to watch their stalking – how near he got sometimes without knowing it.

Some stags got into the wood & the whole herd was quite low down when they took a panic and turned, flying in columns like strong streams which took a great while to *defiler*. The Prince ran up to get 5 shots but too far to take effect. There were more than 2,000 deer. The herd rushed by the drivers but nothing would turn them then. The Prince killed a fine hart in the wood just before dark.

As the Queen sailed home for London and Windsor, after so long in the hills, the 'coast of England appeared terribly flat', and members of the Government soon heard about the enchantments of the far north:

Lord Aberdeen [the Foreign Secretary] was quite touched when I told him I was so much attached to the dear, dear *Highlands* and missed the fine hills so much. There is a great peculiarity about the *Highlands* and Highlanders; and they are such a chivalrous, fine, active people. Our stay among them was so delightful. Independently of the beautiful scenery, there was a quiet, a wildness, a liberty and a solitude that had such a charm for us.

Presents of venison, sent south by the lairds with whom the royal couple had stayed, kept them in touch with the north. But the ostentatious practice of sending stags whole meant that sometimes the meat arrived in less than perfect condition. 'My Dear Breadalbane,' wrote an official in a slightly pained letter sent one October from Windsor Castle,

Two fine haunches have arrived from your Forest in prime order, which shall be duly reported and served to Her Majesty; I may as well waive all false delicacy in this matter and tell you how much better it is, when you send venison here, to send the Haunches cut, than the Hart entire with horns and skin: two that came entire last year were *entirely* spoilt so that not a morsel could be sent to table, and the carriage on them amounted to upwards of £15.

The royal couple's next Scottish visit came in 1847, when they sailed round Wales and up the west coast of Scotland to stay with the Duke and Duchess of Argyll at Inveraray. As usual, Albert discerned frequent resemblances to the scenery of Europe (the mountains of Caernarvonshire, the Queen wrote 'reminded him much of *Ischia*'). When they landed, they were received 'in true Highland fashion', by a posse of nobles, by representatives of the Celtic Society, by Highland soldiers and by pipers, who preceded their carriage for the last stretch to the house.

The visit was marred by relentlessly wet weather: day after day the rain poured down, and the Queen's excursions were severely curtailed. She did, however, go on to stay at Ardverikie, a fine shooting-lodge on the shore of Loch Laggan, and when she drove along the loch the meadows by the road 'reminded us much of *Thüringen*.'

In comparison with earlier years, the visit was a disappointment. 'There is little to say of our stay at Ardverikie,' wrote the Queen. 'The country is fine, but the weather was most dreadful.' And yet, provoking though it was at the time, the rain had a long-reaching and beneficial effect on the future of the royal family in Scotland. In 1848 the royal physician, Sir James Clark, urged the Queen to take a lease of a small castle called Balmoral which stood in the broad valley of the Dee, some eight miles from Braemar, in the eastern half of the Highlands, where the climate was much better than in the sodden west. According to Sir Theodore Martin, the official biographer of Albert, 'the dry, bracing quality of the air [was] precisely what, in Sir James Clark's opinion, was most essential for the peculiar constitutions of the Queen and the Prince.' Victoria and Albert accepted the doctor's advice, and after careful inquiries took a twenty-seven-year lease of the castle and estate from the Earl of Aberdeen, whose late brother had rented the place from its owner, the Earl of Fife.

The site of Balmoral is a lovely one: as Ivor Brown aptly remarked in his book about the house and the estate, the Dee valley at that point combines the best of Highland and Lowland. The floor of the glen is spacious and level, fertile enough to grow good crops and outstanding trees; but all round this gentle little plain the mountains stand guard· the skyline is full of summits, and whether the peak of Lochnagar is in sight or the mist is down upon it, one is constantly aware of the barren wilderness round about.

The Queen's first sight of it was on September 6th, 1848. 'We arrived at *Balmoral* at a quarter to three,' she wrote. 'It is a pretty little castle in the old Scottish style.' Looking down over the house from the hill behind, the Queen and her husband instantly felt at home: the glen of the Dee 'reminded us much of *Thüringen*.'

Albert began his holiday in characteristic fashion – by rushing out immediately after some stags which had been reported close by – and failing to get one; and he spent most of the next three weeks either stalking or having the deer driven to him. The Queen, as usual in the Highlands, accompanied his expeditions with her own retinue, keeping as close to him as she could, and sketching the splendid views.

But soon the royal couple began to develop a far more proprietorial attitude to their surroundings than before: hitherto on their Highland visits they had been guests, entertained for their pleasure, with no responsibility to the local community. Now at Balmoral they were in a place of their own (albeit only rented); immediately in love with it, they soon conceived a great loyalty both to the estate itself and to the staff who served them in the hills.

Lord Malmesbury, who stayed in the old castle one September, left a delightful picture of the royal family on holiday:

> Nothing can exceed the good nature with which I am treated both by Her Majesty and by the Prince. Balmoral is an old country house in bad repair, and totally unfit for royal personages ... The rooms are so small that I was obliged to write my dispatches on my bed, and to keep the window open constantly to admit the necessary quantity of air ...
>
> We played at billiards every evening, the Queen and the Duchess [of Kent] being constantly obliged to get up from their chairs to be out of the way of the cues. Nothing could be more cheerful and evidently perfectly happy than the Queen and the Prince, or more kind to everybody around them ... They evidently enjoyed to the utmost the beauty and tonic climate of the Highlands.

The old house *was* inconvenient: nobody denied that. But the fact mattered little to the Queen or to Albert, both of whom were immediately sure that they had found a perfect holiday home. Not only were they eager to return the following year: as soon as possible they set about buying the whole estate. Negotiations began in the autumn of 1849 for Balmoral itself, and for the estates of Birkhall and Abergeldie, which marched with it on either side. Birkhall was bought in the name of the Prince of Wales, who was then aged seven, and Albert took a long lease of Abergeldie. The acquisition of Balmoral proved more difficult, but at last agreement was reached with the trustees of the Earl of Fife, and Albert bought the fee simple in June 1852.

At once he began planning a new house, more in keeping with the place's new status, and as his architect he chose William Smith, the city architect of Aberdeen. Together the two men planned the new castle, which was to go up on a site about a hundred yards north of the old building – a point which gave a better view into the surrounding hills. But before the new house had been started, the Queen and her husband had a cairn erected on a nearby hill, Craig Gowan, to commemorate (Victoria wrote) 'our taking possession of this dear place.' Her journal reported:

All the servants and tenants, with their wives and children and old relations assembled on the summit. Some merry reels were danced during the ceremony. Albert placed the last stone, after which three cheers were given. It was a gay, pretty and touching sight, and I felt almost inclined to cry. The view was so beautiful over the dear hills; the day so fine, the whole so gemütlich. May God bless this place, and allow us yet to see it and enjoy it many a long year!

Work on the new house began in 1853, and by the time the royal couple arrived for their usual autumn visit the building had already reached the first storey. The Queen laid the foundation stone on September 28th; but not until two years later was the castle ready for occupation. In September 1855, with the tower and one of the wings still unfinished, the royal family moved in, an old shoe being thrown into the hall behind them for good luck, as they entered for the first time. By an agreeable coincidence news of the fall of Sebastopol arrived only three days later, thereby providing the excuse for a fine celebration:

In a few minutes Albert and all the Gentlemen, in every species of attire, sallied forth, followed by all the servants, and gradually the whole population of the village ... to the top of Craig Gowan, where the cairn stands. We watched, and saw the bonfire (prepared the previous year after a false report of the fall of the town) lit, accompanied by cheers. It blazed forth brilliantly, and one could see the many figures surrounding it, some dancing, all shouting, and Ross playing the pipes, Grant and Macdonald [two of the keepers] continually firing off guns. Albert ... said the scene had been wild and exciting beyond everything. Healths had been drunk amidst great enthusiasm.

The Queen was delighted with her new home, which she found spacious and comfortable; and outside, on the estate, Albert wrought a great number of improvements. The place had been much run down when he bought it, and he soon showed himself a model landlord, laying out new plantations, building stables, game larders, a venison larder, and even a new bridge across the Dee. Every autumn when the time came to go south, the Queen recorded how sad she was to leave 'this dear place', which she and Albert had done so much to transform: 'Every year my heart becomes more fixed in this dear paradise.'

Devoted as they were to the house and to the land, they became no less attached to the servants who looked after them in their Highland retreat. Prominent among the estate staff was John Grant, the head keeper, who was thirty-eight when Victoria and Albert first arrived, and according to the Queen, 'an excellent man, most trustworthy, of singular shrewdness and discretion, and most devotedly attached to the Prince and myself. He has a fine intelligent countenance.'

Another outstandingly goodlooking man was John Macdonald, described by the Queen as 'a Jäger of the Prince's ... remarkably tall and handsome.' Macdonald came from Fort William, where Albert had happened to see him in 1847: wanting a personal stalker, he had engaged him on the spot, being 'greatly struck by his good looks', as the Queen reported.

In 1849 the man who proved the most faithful of all the Queen's retainers joined the royal staff: John Brown. He was originally employed as a part-time gillie; but in 1851, when for the first time he led the Queen's pony, he entered her service full-time, and 'advanced step by step by his good conduct and intelligence' until he became her 'permanent personal attendant'.

With all these men – whom they greatly liked and admired – Victoria and Albert formed an easy and relatively informal relationship. Albert had Macdonald teach him Gaelic on their long marches to and from the hill, and once, as they ascended Ben Muich Dhui, in Balmoral forest, with 'Albert talking so gaily with Grant', John Brown observed to the Queen: 'It's very pleasant to walk with a person who is always "content".' 'Yesterday,' wrote Victoria, 'in speaking of dear Albert's sport, when I observed he was never cross after bad luck, Brown said, "Everyone on the estate says there was never so kind a master. I am sure our only wish is to give satisfaction." I said they certainly did.' In 1850, when Edwin Landseer stayed for the first time at Balmoral, the Queen had him draw all her favourite servants, and to this day their portraits, done in crayon, hang in the drawing room of the castle.

From the start Albert took a keen interest in the deer forest, and was

17 Coulin Lodge in the 1970s. The pointed windows were those of the chapel.

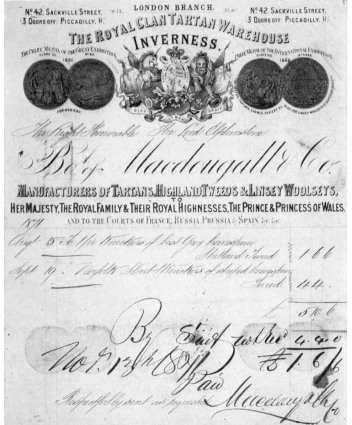

18 Victorian tradesmen speak out: an invoice of 1867.

19 'A Bad End'.　20 'Hero and Leander'.
Original sketches by General Crealock in the Braemore visitors' book.

21 Tilt, the famous stag at Blair Atholl, and all his heads.

22 'The Titan Breaks Bay': from a drawing by Crealock.

23 'A Downhill Shot': from Grimble's *The Deer Forests of Scotland*.

24 Heavy Victorians: the twelfth Duke of Hamilton with his daughter, guests and keepers at Dougarie, Isle of Arran.

out on the hills almost every day of his autumn holidays. Yet he never became either a very good shot or a very discriminating stalker. On one famous occasion, on the Muckle Pap of Lochnagar, he shot five stags and a hind with six shots, which caused the Queen to write in her journal: 'Albert ... killed with six shots five stags and a hind out of one lot, which is quite wonderful and almost unheard of.' More often, however, her diary is full of his misses; often he wounded beasts, which he rarely bothered to follow up himself, but left to the keepers and gillies with their dogs. On many occasions he merely thought he had hit a stag, and the hill men must have spent hundreds of hours on fruitless searches. 'Albert returned much vexed at having failed to get the finest stag in the forest after an excellent chance,' she wrote ... 'Albert much vexed to have shot a fine stag and lost it again' ... 'Albert had a shot at the big stag and thinks it was wounded, but so far no traces of it, which is very vexing.'

This erratic marksmanship was due at least in part to the inefficiency of the Prince's rifles, which were clumsy and inaccurate. But a study of his game-book reveals, in an oblique fashion, how unreliable a shot he was. In this magnificently bound tome, with deep blue calf covers and heavy gold tooling, lined inside with white silk, are recorded all the deer that the Prince shot; and although many of his Highland stags were of decent size—thirteen or fourteen stone—included among them are also some beasts of only five or six stone. These can only have been calves or knobbers—second-year stags—and their presence in the game-record has only two possible explanations: either Albert made such a bad shot that he hit a beast at which he was not aiming, or he ignored the advice of his stalker (who would have been pointing out the best stag to shoot) and blazed away at anything he could see. Neither explanation does the Prince much credit. Nor does the fact that he had all these runts solemnly entered in his game-book. Was he *proud* to have shot a beast of five stone six pounds?

One odd feature of his record is that it includes no details of stags' heads, not even giving the number of points; only the weights are listed. Nor, usually, is anything written in the 'Remarks' column. Almost the only comment is the occasional 'Shot in the presence of the Queen and H.R.H. the Prince of Wales', or 'Shot in the Presence of Her Majesty the Queen and H.R.H. the Princess Alice'.

Just as Albert could shoot a tame stag from the dining room at Blair, so at Balmoral he did not greatly mind how he got the stags, as long as he caught up with them somehow. Although he did a great deal of

I

stalking proper, he also held frequent drives, particularly of the Ballochbuie Woods, and he constructed one entirely artificial aid in the form of The Ditch—a gully some four or five feet deep and over half a mile long which he had cut across the mouth of Glen Gelder—a large, flat expanse on the fringe of the forest, near the castle, which until then had presented a difficult obstacle to stalkers, as they had hardly been able to cross it unobserved. Today, although the trench has been partially filled in by the weather, its straight line, lancing across the tussocks and peat hags of the corrie's floor, still bears witness to Albert's predilection for walking rather than crawling.

That he managed to climb the mountains at all is a matter for some surprise, considering the clothes that he seems habitually to have worn. Paintings of him on the hill show him in high, stiff white collar with a choker outside it, light grey, tight-waisted frock-coat, close-fitting check trousers and spats—an ensemble (completed by a deerstalker, white walking stick and gloves) which could scarcely be more restricting or uncomfortable. Whether or not he dressed in this regalia simply for the benefit of the artist, and on other occasions wore something more practical, it is impossible to say; but the pictures certainly seem designed to represent real stalking incidents, for in one, by Landseer, Albert is seen standing puffed up like a cock grouse beside a freshly killed stag which John Grant is gralloching, while Victoria comes up behind on her pony, led by John Brown; and in another, by Carl Haag, he is leading the way up a hill-path followed by a chain of stalkers and ponies, on one of which a dead stag is already loaded. The artists show Albert dressed to kill in the middle of stalking expeditions, not merely on the way out or back.

The Queen accompanied Albert to the hill whenever she could, and often became closely involved in his manoeuvres, particularly when he was holding a drive, during which the rifles remained stationary and spectators could be concealed with relative ease. In her journal she wrote a vivid account of one such operation in the Ballochbuie Woods during their first autumn at Balmoral:

We scrambled up an almost perpendicular place to where there was a little *box*, made of hurdles and interwoven with branches of fir and heather, about five feet in height. There we seated ourselves with Bertie [her son, the Prince of Wales], Macdonald lying in the heather near us, watching and quite concealed; some had gone round to beat, and others again were at a little distance. We sat quite still, and sketched a little; I doing the landscape and some trees, Albert drawing Macdonald as he lay there.

This lasted for nearly an hour, when Albert fancied he heard a distant sound, and, in a few minutes, Macdonald whispered that he saw stags, and that Albert should wait and take a steady aim. We then heard them coming past. Albert did not look over the box, but through it, and fired through the branches, and then again over the box. The deer retreated; but Albert felt certain he had hit a stag. He ran up to the keepers, and at that moment they called from below that they 'had got him', and Albert ran on to see. I waited for a bit, but soon scrambled on with Bertie's and Macdonald's help; and Albert joined us directly, and we all went down and saw a magnificent stag, a 'royal', which had dropped, soon after Albert had hit him, at one of the men's feet. The sport was successful and everyone was delighted – Macdonald and the keepers in particular; the former saying, 'that it was Her Majesty's coming out that had brought the good luck.' I was supposed to have 'a lucky foot,' of which the Highlanders 'think a great deal.'

Another September, when a drive was held in Corrie Buie, and snow lay on the tops of the hills, the Queen became so caught up in the general excitement that she went for a flying tumble in the heather:

At last the deer came out and straight upon us. It was the finest sight imaginable; there were about thirty or forty hinds with four or five stags, one, in particular a magnificent one with fine horns. Albert aimed and got him. We went to look at him, and meanwhile Albert ran back to shoot another, which Duncan came to say was wounded. In running back after Albert, which I did very fast, I got such a tumble, falling my whole length on the heather, and I think on a stone, for I hurt my knee a good deal.

It is hard to determine what the Queen's feelings were when she witnessed the deaths of so many fine deer. Although she had been greatly distressed when Albert shot the tame stags at Blair Castle, she seems to have found the killing of deer on the open hills less traumatic; and indeed all her feelings appear to have been subordinated to her blind adoration of Albert. If he shot badly, and was greatly vexed or provoked, she too was upset; if, on the other hand, he got his stag – even though he may have had to enlist the help of Solomon, the deerhound, to bring the wounded beast to bay—she was thrilled at his success.

Once, as they drove home together in a horse-carriage after a day on the hill, Albert killed a stag by leaning across the Queen and firing out of the window. Victoria recorded the scene with an extraordinary lack of emotion:

> On our way back when it was nearly quite dark, we saw some deer near the road, and Grant said one was a large stag and told Albert to fire, which he did, across me. Almost immediately the animal was seen to fall—they jumped out and ran up, to find a very fine stag with nine points, quite dead. It was dragged down for me to see. What luck!

The Queen gives no idea of how violent the incident must have been. To have had a large-bore rifle go off in her face, within the close confines of a carriage, must have been a shattering experience. The noise must have been deafening. The carriage must have filled with gunpowder smoke. The horses, though doubtless well restrained by their driver, must have done their best to bolt. Yet of all this commotion the Queen writes not a word: 'What luck!' is all she says. Nothing was memorable to her beyond the fact that beloved Albert had scored again.

In the evenings the stags which he and his guests had shot were exhibited outside the castle after dinner, and often (as the Queen herself wrote) the scene was a stirring one:

> Bertie shot a stag—a great delight—which was shown by torchlight after dinner, and then the men danced a wild Reel, shouting, carrying the torches in their hands.

Such was the pattern of their Highland holidays: stalking and grouse-shooting for Albert; excursions into the hills for the Queen, and many walks in the environs of the castle. In 1856 Albert had a bothy built near the shore of Loch Muick, and there, right out in the wilderness, he and Victoria several times spent the night. Then, in 1860 and 1861, they made two major expeditions to explore the mountains that lay beyond their own marches, travelling by carriage and on horseback. On both these occasions they rode westwards up the Geldie burn and then down Glenfeshie, to the north-west. For the Queen to stay incognito in an ordinary inn was a thrilling adventure; and for everyone involved the journeys must have demanded strenuous physical efforts. During the expedition of 1861 they covered sixty miles on the first day, and sixty-nine on the second.

That autumn proved Albert's last; and his Highland stalking career ended in characteristic fashion with his missing a stag during a drive of the Abergeldie Woods on his final day at Balmoral, October 21st. 'Albert returned soon after,' the Queen recorded, 'having got nothing, which was too vexatious.'

A month later, at Windsor Castle, he fell ill with typhoid, and in three weeks he was dead. Although the stricken Queen returned to Balmoral the next year, and never ceased to love the place dearly, she did not recapture the gaiety she had felt there when Albert was alive. Never again was her enjoyment so uninhibited. In the autumn of 1862 she had a cairn raised on Craig Lowrigan in memory of the Prince Consort, and, as if to carry out his posthumous wishes, took personal charge of the arrangements for stalking that year. In a memorandum heavily edged with black she ordained:

The Queen wishes that the Prince's Forest should remain perfectly quiet this year. In future (if she lives) it is the Queen's wish that everything should go on as formerly – that Grant should receive his orders from *no one* but the Queen *herself* (as he always did from the Prince) or from someone sent *specially* and *directly to him*, with orders from the Queen – this regards orders of every kind respecting the forest and all connected with it – the stalkers, keepers, dogs, etc. etc.

Respecting the Grouse, the same course as hitherto to be pursued. The Gentlemen were always able to go out, without special reference to the Prince, excepting as regarded the near and best ground. The Queen would also wish none of the nearest grounds to be shot over as, both here and at Windsor, she does not wish any *real* shooting to take place this year – nothing, *in short*, which could be at all considered as the Prince's ground.

Evidently some discussion took place – either among the royal family or among the estate staff – about the possibility of dividing the forest into several different beats; but the Queen resolutely opposed the idea, sensibly maintaining that one large area of ground would be easier to work, especially if a wounded deer had to be followed for any distance. The principle to which she clung was that everything

should carry on as nearly as possible as before; and in her memoranda—
which are a curious mixture of juxtaposed statements about the past
and precepts for the future—she repeated the idea again and again. In
one note, laying down how Grant was to stalk for the Prince of Wales
and the other princes, she wrote:

> Grant would come to the Queen always the evening before to
> receive her orders as to whom was to go out and when and where to,
> and everything to be done *as formerly*. Four times a week to be the
> outside for stalking in *our* Forest. The Queen is anxious that the same
> course should be pursued as in former happy days.

Inside the castle she took the same care to keep things as they had been
in Albert's time. In another note edged with the thick black mourning
border she laid down:

> The Queen wishes none of the stuffed stags' heads, shot by the
> Prince, to be removed from their present places, nor any other shot
> by the other Princes to be added to those put up in the lower and
> upper corridors.
>   In other parts of the house, in the hall, in the ballroom, if it does
> not spoil the appearance of the house, they might be sparingly added,
> but the Queen does not wish any but extraordinarily fine heads
> (something quite peculiar, not ordinary Royal ones) to be stuffed in
> future, if shot by the Princes, unless they wish to take them away
> and place them at houses of their own—merely their horns to be
> retained.

The policy of keeping the forest quiet may have eased the Queen's
nerves, but it also caused practical difficulties, and in a couple of years'
time Dr Andrew Robertson, the factor, was seeking permission to
decimate the grouse:

> Dr Robertson presents his humble duty to Her Majesty the Queen
> and would respectfully bring under Her Majesty's notice the state
> of the Balmoral Forest.
>   The past two years have been very favourable for the breeding of
> Grouse. Last year they were so numerous in the Forest as greatly to
> impede Deer-Stalking. This year they are still more abundant, and
> the chances of any gentlemen being able to approach deer are very
> small.

The object of Dr Robertson in submitting these remarks is with
the view of obtaining Your Majesty's permission to reduce the
number of Grouse, by shooting them down early in the season.

Grant is desirous that this plan should be adopted—he says the
shooting, if done early, will in no way injure the deer—they will go
to the high ground for a few days, but will return to their old haunts
very speedily, after the noise of the shooting is over.

In time both the grouse-shooting and the deer-stalking at Balmoral
settled back into a normal pattern; and during the rest of the Queen's
long life a great many members of the royal family enjoyed themselves
in the forest.

How much Victoria and Albert, by their sheer enthusiasm for the
Highlands, may have influenced the development of stalking in general,
it is impossible to say. By the 1850s, when the Prince's passion for
Scotland was at its height, the vogue for stalking was already well
established, and the fact that the sport received royal assent perhaps did
little to accelerate its development. Yet, by spending every autumn at
Balmoral, the Queen and her husband probably did contribute to the
general romantic enthusiasm of the Victorians for mountains and
far places; and so, in an oblique fashion, they may have increased
still further the drift of well-to-do southerners towards the Scottish
moors.

In a later generation embittered nationalists accused Victoria of
having invented and fostered 'Balmorality'—a term which signified a
patronising attitude, those who held it enjoying Scotland in a condescending way but not being prepared to take the country seriously.
The word was invented in 1932 by George Scott Moncrieff—a writer,
as Ivor Brown remarked, who claimed that Victoria's enjoyment of
Balmoral had somehow influenced Scotland for the bad, and who
'curiously assumed that the occupation of Balmoral by Queen Victoria
was responsible for almost anything bad that happened in Scotland then
or later.'

The term was singularly inept: just because the Queen filled her
castle with tartan, dressed her family in the kilt and adopted Scottish
customs wholeheartedly, it did not mean that her attitude towards the
Scots was in the least condescending. On the contrary, she and Albert
loved the Highlands, and they found at Balmoral a haven which none
of their other homes could rival. The congenial surroundings—and the
activities that took place in them—undoubtedly formed a large part of

the place's attractions; but above all it was the *people* who delighted the royal couple in their mountain retreat.

'We were always in the habit of conversing with the Highlanders,' the Queen once wrote. 'The Prince highly appreciated the good-breeding, simplicity and intelligence, which make it so pleasant and even instructive to talk to them.' With those words Victoria precisely described one of the chief pleasures that stalkers of every social rank have found in the Highlands, in her time and since: the delight of spending long days in the company of men whose strength, self-sufficiency and natural dignity exactly match the hills which are their home.

Chapter Ten

Landseer & Co.

Of all the enthusiasts who gave impetus to the craze for stalking, none proved a more effective advocate than the painter, Edwin Landseer. Scrope had extolled the sheer excitement of the chase; St John had done the same, and had further spiced his books with original observations on the wildlife of the Highlands. Victoria and Albert had given the sport their royal assent and so made it socially desirable. Yet Landseer, in a way, did all these things at once. Not only did his paintings glow with the romance of the deer and their wild background: that he was patronised first by nobility and later by the monarch herself confirmed deer-stalking as the smartest pastime imaginable.

Landseer first visited the Highlands in 1824, as a handsome, soft-faced youth of twenty-two, whose wavy fair hair flopped over his forehead in a manner that ladies found most fetching. Already he was a precociously successful artist, but his reputation so far was mainly that of a painter of dogs. As a recent biographer, Campbell Lennie, remarked, 'he was already beginning to be beset by wealthy ladies waxing lyrical over the virtues of their pets, and begging him to paint them.'

Scotland provided him with a sharp and beneficial change. In the words of another critic, 'Scotland taught him his true power – it freed his imagination: it braced up his loose ability; it elevated and refined his mind; it developed his latent poetry; it completed his education.'

The aim of his first visit was to study deer, and for this purpose he stayed ten days with the Duke of Atholl at Blair. Thence he went on to Bruar, where, as the guest of William Scrope, he was introduced to the pleasures of the hill. Delighted at once by the deer and by their country, he soon became a keen stalker, even though he remained all his life an erratic shot.

His artistic sense was always stronger than his blood-lust, and sometimes, to the intense vexation of his gillies, the second would give

way to the first at the critical moment of a stalk: just as the chance of a
shot presented itself, he would thrust the rifle at one of his retainers and
whip out his sketching materials instead. At first the gillies gave vent
to their irritation in Gaelic, but gradually they realised that their master
knew more of the language than they thought, and as Thormanby put
it, 'it made them very careful of speaking Gaelic in his hearing ever
after.'

The way in which Landseer's sporting and artistic instincts fused
together was once observed at close quarters by Lord Ossulston, later
the Earl of Tankerville, who came upon him stalking alone and crept
up on him, thinking he was a poacher:

> We soon ensconced ourselves behind a heathery knoll within a few
> yards of our poacher, to watch his proceedings before we finally
> pounced upon him. He was a little strong-built man, very like a
> pocket Hercules, or 'Puck' in the 'Midsummer Night's Dream'. He
> was busily employed gralloching his deer. This he did with great
> quickness and dexterity, not omitting to wash the tallow and other
> treasures carefully in the burn and deposit them on the stone beside
> the deer. He next let the head hang over so as to display the horns,
> and then squatting down on a stone opposite took out of his pocket
> what I thought would be his pipe or a whisky flask: but it was a
> sketch book!
>
> Seeing that we had mistaken our man, I came into the open and
> found myself face-to-face with my friend of many years to come—
> Landseer.

Soon the painter began making annual visits to the Highlands, and
one magnet that drew him northwards every autumn was the presence
at The Doune—her holiday home in Rothiemurchus—of Georgiana,
Duchess of Bedford. The second wife of the sixth Duke, Georgiana was
described by the diarist Le Marchant as a 'bold, bad woman with the
remains of her beauty'. She was old enough to have been Landseer's
mother, and his long liaison with her inevitably attracted malicious
attention. Today the Bedford family accepts that he was the father of
at least the last two of her ten children.

According to Sir Walter Scott, the sixth Duke took The Doune 'to
gratify the Duchess's passion for the heather'. He did not care for
Scotland, and so, when she went north in the late summer, she was
often alone. Yet not even The Doune, which stood among the ancient

pines of Rothiemurchus, could satisfy her passion for the wilds, and she
had herself built a kind of sporting encampment in the remoter and
grander setting of Glenfeshie. There, on a small, flat, grassy plain
levelled by the action of ice and water, with mountains towering on
all sides, and the river Feshie debouching from a splendid gorge, she
went to ground every autumn in a tiny village of huts made from wood
and turf on stone foundations.

Landseer followed, setting up house in another group of huts a few
hundred yards away. The accommodation was evidently primitive,
for in the forest's game-book he wrote a poem — 'Glenfeshie Ballad
No. 1' — which contained the following lines:

The boards so green were hung around with skins of cats and
                                                            and foxes.
All sat by day on wooden chairs and slept in wooden boxes.
Two slept together in one room, in huts which let no cold in ...

Soon, however, the walls in both Landseer's and the Duchess's
establishments were decorated with frescoes by the master. On the
plaster above the fireplace in his own main hut Landseer painted a
group of deer whose dominant member was a suspicious hind; and
the walls of Georgiana's main bothy bore several sketches, as did those
of the hut she used as a dining room.

All these works were doomed to a short life. They were executed in
the 1830s, but after the death of the Duchess in 1853 the huts fell into
disrepair, and by the time Queen Victoria descended the glen on her
grand tour of 1860, the buildings were so tumbledown that the frescoes
had already been largely destroyed. Their demise had been hastened by
a border dispute between neighbouring lairds, both Grant of Rothiemurchus and The Mackintosh claiming the land on which the bothies
stood. The Queen found the site — which she called 'the scene of all
Landseer's glory' — both beautiful and melancholy. 'We were quite
enchanted with the beauty of the view,' she wrote. But then 'we met
Lord and Lady Alexander Russell [members of the Bedford family]
and had some talk with them. They feel deeply the ruin of the place
where they formerly lived, as it no longer belongs to them.'

Only one of the Glenfeshie frescoes has survived — and that at one
remove, copied by the distinguished amateur artist, General Henry
Hope Crealock, who visited the place in the 1860s and found 'one large
drawing of a deer in quite good condition still, fresh in colour, a

charming sketch'. Today the spot is still known as 'the Duchess of
Bedford's', but only the stumps of low stone walls and a broken-down
chimney buttress now mark the place where seven modest huts once
stood in that little green plain. No doubt both painter and patron
would be delighted to know that the deer come down every evening
to graze peacefully over the ruins.

The forest of Glenfeshie inspired Landseer to several of his best-
known oil paintings, including 'Stealing a March' and 'Waiting for
the Deer to Rise'. In this last the three burly characters lying on the
hill are taken from life: they are Horatio Ross, the stalker Charles
Mackintosh and Malcolm Clark (also known as Callum Brocair, the
Fox-Hunter), a local character celebrated for his great strength.

The story was told of an occasion on Carn Toul when Ross shot five
stags in quick succession, and was denied further carnage only because,
in the excitement, a bullet was rammed down the rifle barrel before
the powder. On examining the dead stags, Ross found that one was
exceptionally fine, and said to Malcolm that he would give £20 to see
the animal brought home whole, rather than cut in pieces. Malcolm,
replying that 'it should not cost the Captain that sum', hoisted the
eighteen-stone stag on to his shoulders and carried it down to a point
at which the pony could reach it. In due course it was laid out on the
green in front of The Doune, in the presence of the Duchess of Bedford.

Landseer's prowess as both artist and sportsman gave him regular
access to the finest forests in the Highlands, among them Black Mount,
where he often stalked and painted as a guest of the Breadalbane family.
John McLeish, the head stalker in the 1840s, described him as 'a nice
wee mannie' who 'carried a braw rifle', and at least two of Landseer's
major paintings – 'The Stag at Bay' and 'The Deer Drive' – were
based on incidents that he witnessed at Black Mount. The idea for 'The
Stag at Bay' came to him on a day when a beast which had been
wounded on Ben Toig ran down to Loch Tulla, and killed two
deerhounds before being despatched. Landseer was in the lodge when
the action started, but ran out in time to witness the final scene. The
setting for 'The Deer Drive' was the high pass between Altahourn and
Larig Dochart, where Lord Tweedmouth and Lord Dudley once killed
nineteen stags in a single drive.

Another forest in which Landseer always found a welcome was
Ardverikie, and there too he adorned the walls of the lodge with
frescoes. These pictures also were destroyed (by a fire which burned the
old house down on October 11th, 1873 – by a coincidence the day on

which Landseer was buried); but fortunately they had by then been photographed, and to General Crealock these 'original sketches and ideas' of some of the artist's greatest pictures were 'more truthful and lifelike than the finished pictures done later.'

No forest, however, was more important to Landseer than Balmoral. The old Duke of Bedford had died in 1839, and after a decent interval Landseer proposed to Georgiana, only to be rejected—a rebuff which made him increasingly dependent on the patronage of the Queen and Prince Albert. Having already painted various royal portraits, both canine and human, he was first invited to Balmoral in 1850. 'Her Majesty begs that you will come well provided with drawing materials,' wrote the Private Secretary, Sir Charles Phipps. 'The usual evening costume is the kilt, worn by everybody who claims to wear one, but at any rate we are not particular in these mountainous districts, and many of Her Majesty's guests appear in Trousers.'

That autumn Landseer sketched the Balmoral stalkers and gillies, and he later painted several pictures of the Queen in her Highland home. In 1851 he completed his best-known picture of all, which had royal connotations, if no actual royal connections—'The Monarch of the Glen'. This painting—aptly called by one critic Landseer's 'definitive close-up' of a red deer stag—shows a magnificent royal poised majestically against a background of mountain peaks and swirling mist. The picture was originally commissioned by the government to fill one of the panels in the House of Lords Refreshment Room; but before it had been completed, the House of Commons struck from its estimates the £1,500 which would have paid for this painting and two others, and 'The Monarch of the Glen' went instead to Lord Londesborough, by one account for 350 guineas, and by another for 800.

Whatever price he paid, he got a bargain: thirty years later the picture changed hands for £6,510, and then, in another eight years, for £7,245. Other Landseer paintings appreciated at a similar speed: for example, 'A Midsummer Night's Dream' (an illustration from the play) was commissioned by the engineer Isambard Kingdom Brunel in 1851 for 400 guineas and sold by him in 1860 for £2,940. Lady Pringle, who owned 'The Stag at Bay', refused offer after offer for it, one of them of £10,000. Execrated though he may be by twentieth-century critics, Landseer appealed powerfully to the Victorians.

The success of his stalking pictures was due largely to the extraordinary way in which he identified with the deer. He captured the excitement of the sport, from the human point of view, in a manner that has never been surpassed; yet at the same time he saw the whole operation from the deer's side as well. 'Landseer *was* his stags, in a way that he never was his sheepdogs,' wrote one commentator; and, besides the emotions of the hunter, the artist recorded the suffering of the quarry in a manner that some people find stirring, others mawkish.

'The Sanctuary', for instance, shows an exhausted stag which has at last found refuge on an island in Loch Maree, and the animal's distress is clearly portrayed. So is that of the beast in 'The Stag at Bay', its tongue lolling out and its back buckling as it fights off two hounds from its stand on the edge of the stormy loch. To claim (as one modern author has) that Landseer could 'exalt the sport of deer-stalking yet portray its consequences with a savage, debunking irony' is surely rubbish. The fact merely was that he had the honesty, the practical experience and the skill to record both sides of the proceedings; and it so happened that the elements in his stalking pictures—romantic settings, noble animals, suffering and death—together made an irresistible impression on Victorian sensibilities.

Landseer's contemporary success was immense. In 1874, the year after his death, an exhibition of his work at the Royal Academy drew 105,000 paying visitors; a sale of his own art collection in May that year raised £69,000, and his will was proved for £160,000.

It is impossible to measure Landseer's effect on the expansion of stalking: one can only surmise that it was considerable. During his heyday —the 1830s, 1840s and 1850s—the popularity of the sport constantly increased. Nor were the new stalkers by any means all witless young bloods with more money than sense: their numbers included politicians and statesmen of the highest intelligence, not least Lord Malmesbury, who was twice Foreign Secretary, in 1852 and 1858.

In 1844 he took Achnacarry Castle and its surrounding forest on a fifteen-year lease from its owner, Cameron of Lochiel; and, returning there autumn after autumn, he came to love the place with a passionate attachment. Though the pressure of state business sometimes forced him to take secretaries and despatch boxes with him into the Highlands, he conceived a lasting affection for Achnacarry which is memorably recorded in his autobiography, *Memoirs of an Ex-Minister*.

Whether he was observing the pines of the primeval forest, which 'stand like white skeletons that have died in their old age', or watching Lord Edward Thynne kill an eagle 'as it was soaring above him with a rifle and a single ball', or stalking himself, or reporting that Mr Bruce, the brother of Lord Elgin had come back from the hill in a filthy temper because the stalker had ordered him to crawl *up a waterfall*, Malmesbury enjoyed every detail of his Scottish holidays. He himself had some exciting moments, not least one evening towards the end of September 1849:

> I had been out deer-stalking, and as I was returning home alone, and by bright moonlight, I saw a hind on the hill a little above the road, and shot her, but just as I was stooping over her with a knife, she sprang up and struck me with one of her fore feet, hitting me in the forehead just between the eyes. The blow was so violent that it knocked me down and stunned me for a short time, and on recovering my senses I found I was quite blind, but this was only from the blood. Her hoof had cut a deep gash in my forehead and along my nose. The animal was lying quite dead by my side. I walked to the house, which was not far off, and the maid who opened the door was so frightened at my appearance that she fainted forthwith. This laid me up for a week, but with no further consequences.

Malmesbury was an erratic rifle shot, and did not mind admitting it in his book. On the hill, however, his lack of prowess sometimes embarrassed him. When he visited Balmoral in September 1852, Prince Albert organised a deer-drive in some of the woods. The rifles were posted in a line, and, as Malmesbury recorded,

> two fine stags passed me, which I missed; Colonel Phipps [the Private Secretary] fired next, and lastly the Prince, without any effect. The Queen had come out to see the sport, lying down in the heather by the Prince, and witnessed all these fiascos, to our humiliation.

One year, when the whole of the party at Achnacarry was confined to the house for a day by violent wind and rain, it was decided, to pass the time, that each person should tell a story. Malmesbury's own tale concerned a young Highland shepherd who met a pixie, and was granted one wish, which would be fulfilled for the rest of his life.

Since the young man wanted to go to sea, the fairy granted him the favour of a continual fair wind, for ever blowing behind him. At sea the gift proved so bountiful that the man soon made a fortune; and then, returning to the Highlands, he bought a deer-forest and hired 'the best stalker in Scotland'. Alas, his plans for a sporting life were futile:

whenever he went to the hill, the faithful wind, constantly changing, pursued him in every direction he took so that he could never get anywhere near the deer. 'The terrible truth broke upon him that if he lived to a thousand years he never could possibly kill a stag.'

Malmesbury was much interested in the fairies, elves and goblins by whom (the Highlanders supposed) the deer forest was still populated. Besides, there was at hand a more substantial wild creature, in the form of the monster of Loch Arkaig. Well-known in its own area long before the Loch Ness monster ever surfaced, the denizen of Loch Arkaig was the object of intense superstition. John Stuart, the stalker at Achnacarry, had glimpsed it twice: he had seen its equine head and hindquarters as it lay basking, and, because it was hollow-backed, concluded that it could not be any form of fish. Malmesbury recorded:

> The Highlanders are very superstitious about this creature. They are convinced that there is never more than one in existence at the same time, and I believe they think it has something diabolical in its nature, for when I said I wished I could get within shot of it, my stalker observed very gravely: 'Perhaps your Lordship's gun would misfire.'

Another alleged monster, well known at the time, was that of Loch-na-beiste, in the forest of Letterewe, on the west coast. In 1840 the tenants of the proprietor, Mr Meyrick Bankes (a gentleman from Liverpool who used to stalk the forest from his yacht moored in the harbour at Poolewe), called on him begging him to undertake the destruction of the beast, so an attempt was made to draw off the water from the loch. As a result the depth was reduced to only six feet, except at one point, where there was a hole in the bed of the loch, and the water was still some fifteen feet deep. To this hole, it was concluded, the monster must have withdrawn, and into it were poured fourteen barrels of raw lime – a proceeding which caused the death of most of the trout in the loch, but failed to shift the great beast. After this no further attempts were made to molest him.

It is clear that Malmesbury, like Queen Victoria, found the Highland holidays a perfect relaxation from the cares of state. For him – as for thousands of people since – the point of the energetic outdoor life was that it forcibly dislodged all who took part from the ruts along which they normally moved. Malmesbury recorded with delight the experience of Sir James Hudson, who was once obliged to spend a night in a distant bothy in Glen Kamachray:

25   A Victorian stalking party
sets out.

26   Stalking at Ardtornish in
the 1870s.

27 Beasts coming into the larder in 1905: then as now.

28 The Marchioness of Breadalbane with Peter Grant, her head stalker.

29 The Prince of Wales out stalking in the 1890s.

30 F. D. Godman with his family, guests, stalkers and gillies at Inchrory in 1905.

1905
74 STAGS
1800 GROUSE
55 HARES
400 RABBITS
4 FISH

31 Dressed to kill: the American millionaire Walter Winans.

32 Walter Winans and his entourage.

He said there were seven men, five dogs, three women and a cat in two small rooms, more like hencoops than rooms, and only three beds for the whole party. The maid-of-all-work asked him with whom he would like to sleep, and he answered that if he couldn't sleep with her, he would prefer Macoll, the stalker. The latter, however, replied: 'Methinks you had better sleep alone.' So Sir James had a bed to himself, as far as I know.

Malmesbury became so fond of Achnacarry that when his lease ended he left the place with keen regret. On October 2nd, 1859 he saw a flock of wild swans flying south—'a broad hint to me to do the same'—and he wrote a moving description of his final evening, October 25th:

I beat the woods at Achnasoul, and killed six woodcocks, twelve blackcocks, also the stag whose leg I broke two days ago. This good day's sport and luck has closed my connection with Achnacarry, which has lasted for 15 years of the prime of my life.

I rowed home from Moich with a heavy heart. Loch Arkaig was motionless, and the colour of obsidian. The sun, after a bright day, had set behind a heavy mass of clouds, against which the mountains of Scaurnahat and Murligan looked ghostly in their garments of snow, whilst the northern slopes and corries of the Pine Forest retained every flake that had fallen. The stags, as is usual in a hard frost, were roaring with redoubled passion in the wilds of Gusach and Guerraran. The herons were screaming as I disturbed them from their shelter in the islands; and then again the roaring of the harts reechoed through the forest. As I landed at the pier a freezing mist fell over the whole scene, and thus we parted. *Vale!*

By the middle of the century stalking was still regarded as a novel sport. In a practical handbook on shooting published in 1854 the author, Robert Blakey, described stalking in Scotland as 'a comparatively modern shooting amusement, confined chiefly to the higher classes of English sportsmen, ... full of interest and excitement ... a most laborious and excitable amusement, keeping the powers of both mind and body upon the full stretch.'

To illustrate his theme, Blakey quoted several long extracts from a novel called *The Smugglers* by one Mr Cooper, which, he said 'for its truthfulness and veracity' had been approved and quoted by Scrope,

K

among others. Certainly the extracts give a lively and amusing picture not only of the sport itself, but also of the relationship between Glenvallich, the laird, Tresham, his fat and inexperienced guest, and Maccombich, the stalker.

After a spy – during which Tresham of course cannot even see the deer, let alone tell what they are – the party makes so vigorous an ascent that Tresham is first forced to abandon his rifle to the gillie, and then to remove the coat which he insisted (against his host's advice) on wearing:

> Tresham, breathless and reeling, was absolutely forced to make frequent halts. Youth and spirits, and good English bottom themselves, failed at length, and the young man came to a standstill. 'You were right,' said he, 'about this cursed jacket; it is too heavy for such work ... to the devil with the velveteen!' and he threw it from him.

Various manœuvres – all excellently described – bring the party almost within reach of the chosen stag:

> The forester was now sent on to ascertain the means of further progress; and after an absence of more than ten minutes, which to the sportsmen seemed a full hour, he returned creeping like a worm and beckoning the party to follow in the same manner. This they did, and at length, keeping along the peat cracks, got a chasm deep enough to afford cover for the whole body.
>
> 'He's no a hunder' yards from you this moment, Glenvallich,' whispered the forester, in scarcely audible accents, 'and the wind is strong from him. Ye most climb this knoll; if you can get him within eighty yards, dinna seek to get nearer, for he's in a wide green hench, and he's very jealous. I dinna think ye'll mak' muckle better o' it, but achone! Sir, tak' time and be canny – I wudna for ten pounds he got awa!'
>
> 'Never fear me, man; but here's Mr Tresham must take first chance – I'll fire only if he misses. Come along, Harry.'
>
> The forester cast a look of mingled disappointment and remonstrance at his master, but it was disregarded. Tresham, also, who still shook from head to foot with recent exertion and present excitement, would have excused himself from interfering with the anterior rights of his friend in this particular animal; but Glenvallich would not listen to him.

'Have done with debating,' said he, 'we shall lose the deer. Follow me, Tresham.'

Cautiously, like a cat on its prey, foot by foot and inch by inch, did Glenvallich, grovelling in the heather, advance towards the crest of the knoll in front of him; when the deer's antlers moved he was still—when they took their natural position he moved forwards. Tresham followed in his track, stopping or advancing as he did, until they had reached some twenty paces onwards from the ravine. Glenvallich then signed to him to raise his head with caution.

He did so, and saw, with a sensation of eager delight which increased his agitation to a painful pitch, the noble stag lying among some rushy grass, apparently in the most unsuspicious tranquillity, occasionally scratching a part of his hide with a fork of his antlers, and driving away the insects which appeared grievously to torment him.

'Take him as he lies, Harry; aim low, at the shoulder,' whispered Glenvallich. The heart of Tresham beat more audibly than ever it had done on going into action, as he carefully extended and levelled his rifle. Whether it was the slight click of cocking, or some movement made in the heather as he stretched out the piece to take aim, is uncertain; but the stag started and made a movement as if about to rise, just at the moment when Tresham was pressing the trigger. The circumstances probably unsettled his aim, for the rifle exploded but the ball flew over its intended object.

But not thus was the unfortunate animal to escape; for scarce had the report of Tresham's shot made him start from his lair, when the rifle of Glenvallich gave forth its fatal contents and the stag, making one high bound from the earth, tumbled headlong forwards, and lay struggling in the agonies of death ... 'Hurrah! Capital! Grand! By Jove, he's got it!' shouted Tresham, starting up ... so the hunters advanced to break the deer, as it is called, by cutting the throat and disembowelling it; and while Maccombich was performing this sportsman-like duty, it was amusing to watch the rapture to which, when unrestrained by habitual caution, he now gave full way on the glad occasion of a successful shot.

Apostrophising it in Gaelic, he addressed to it every reproachful epithet he could think of, as a villain which had so often baffled their murderous efforts; it was a scoundrel, and a rascal, and a devil, to whom he wished a bad end, and whose soul, heart and liver he gave to the devil; then, changing his tone, he lavished upon it every expression of endearment in which his language is so fruitful; but which, when translated, often sound strangely enough to English ears. It was his dear, his darling, his bonny beast, his cattle, his love. He seemed to abandon himself to the very intoxication of delight; and it was singular to see a man, habitually grave and reserved, acting as if for the time he had actually been deprived of reason.

No sport that England could offer promised anything like such outlandish eccentricity; and the mixture of amusement and awe which stalking aroused at the time is admirably reflected in a series of cartoons by John Leech, published in *Punch* in the early 1860s. They describe the adventures of Mr Briggs, a stout and oafish party who goes to the Highlands for his holiday and blunders perspiring about the hill, connecting only when his rifle goes off by mistake. The captions are splendidly laborious: 'The Royal Hart Mr Briggs did *not* hit', 'After aiming for quarter of an hour, Mr B. fires both his barrels—and—misses!!!!' and so on, but the deer are well drawn, and all the background details are accurate, showing that the cartoonist knew his Highlands, even if Mr Briggs did not.

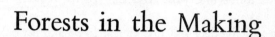

Chapter Eleven

Forests in the Making

To rent a forest, or to stalk as the guest of a friend, was one thing; to make a forest of one's own was something different, and as the demand for stalking grew, rich men began to create sporting estates all over the Highlands. The first of the new proprietors had come in search of profitable farms and a position in society; now they began coming for the grandeur and peace of the Highlands. As Philip Gaskell aptly remarked in his study of Morvern, a Highland deer-forest was 'as remote from their everyday affairs as any desert island, yet not beyond the reach of an English industrialist with a long annual holiday.'

To make a deer-forest was simple enough, provided one had the money. All one had to do was to buy a large piece of hill land, build a suitable house on it, clear the ground of sheep, and wait for the numbers of deer to build up – which they did with surprising speed.

In Morvern the principal landowner was Octavius Smith, a successful industrialist who, according to John Buchan, 'fell so much under the glamour of the West Highlands' that he bought the estate of Achranich in 1854. He got 9,000 acres for £12,000, and to this original purchase he added, in 1859, the larger estate of Ardtornish (22,000 acres got for 36s. an acre) The whole forest, of over 30,000 acres, was from then on known as Ardtornish, and the Smith family became the most enlightened of lairds, building not only a large new house for themselves, but also cottages for the people of the parish, as well as a new school, and in general reconstructing local society, which had been wrecked by the evictions.

At the start of the Smiths' occupation there had been no gamekeeper and no shooting. In the first year that a game-book was kept (1853) only thirty-four grouse were killed, and although red deer were occasionally seen, none was shot. But the amount of sport available increased fast, as successive pieces of ground were cleared of sheep, letting the heather grow up and thereby providing the grouse (which live on heather shoots) with food and cover. Grouse-bags rose steadily to more than 300 birds in 1867 and 1868, and the deer gradually recolonised the entire area. One hind was shot in 1868, and two stags in the following year. By the 1870s regular stalking was possible.

The return of the deer did not appear to be a direct consequence of the sheep's removal, for the deer spread back on to the ground by way of a glen in which sheep were still pastured; but the absence of competitive grazing and the relative lack of disturbance undoubtedly encouraged them to remain and helped increase their numbers. Another factor which probably contributed to their rehabilitation was the substantial reduction in the human population (the result of the evictions and emigration) and the consequent drop in the amount of poaching for food. Then, the sporting potential of the estate became even more highly regarded, and the status of the gamekeeper steadily rose. In the 1860s the head keeper, Thomas Dalgleish, got £54 a year all told (compared with £48 paid to the head shepherd) and shepherds were paid game-money – 6d. for every grouse shot on their hirsel (the ground occupied by their flock) and 5s. for a stag.

The effect of suppressing vermin is well illustrated by some figures from the forest of Langwell, in Caithness. A gamekeeper, Donald Ross, was appointed in 1848, and in that year he killed fifty polecats, twenty-eight wild cats, five foxes, two otters, one marten and 200 weasels, besides a substantial number of hawks, crows and other winged vermin. When the Duke of Portland bought the estate in 1857, the place still offered only modest sport: the bag for 1859 was only four red deer, two roe and seventy grouse. But with full scale keepering and afforestation (including the removal of the sheep) the bags improved spectacularly: in 1871 no fewer than ninety-three stags and 1,115 brace of grouse were shot.

Another striking instance of the power of deer to re-establish themselves is afforded by the island of Rhum. Various old records show that there was a large population of red deer on the island until the seventeenth century, but that thereafter the number steadily fell, until by about 1790 the deer were extinct, almost entirely as a result of human predation. In 1826, however, the whole human population of Rhum emigrated, and the island was given over to sheep farming. Deer were reintroduced when the island was afforested during the 1840s, and by the 1890s the herd was some 800 strong. Today the whole island is a nature reserve run by the Nature Conservancy Council, and, with a careful annual cull being made, the deer population remains steady at about 1,500.

During the nineteenth century the policy of encouraging the shootable wildlife and cutting down domestic grazing stocks gradually spread through the Highlands. In most forests grouse and deer coexisted without trouble, but on some estates the grouse were considered a nuisance (being likely to disturb deer during a stalk) and so were shot by the keepers to stop them becoming too numerous. In some places the keepers even went round smashing their eggs in the spring.

Thanks to the squirrel-like tendencies of the fifteenth Lord Elphinstone, who hoarded letters, receipts, plans, legal documents and even pay slips, it is possible to draw a close-up picture of the formation of one deer-forest – Coulin, in Wester Ross. Lord Elphinstone bought Coulin in 1866, and although he kept the place for only six years, the changes he made there are worth considering in detail, for the story of this one forest represents, in microcosm, what was happening at that time all over the Highlands: the transformation that came over Coulin was repeated in dozens of similar Highland settings.

Coulin had once been part of the vast forest of Applecross, which originally stretched far inland from the west coast peninsula still bearing the name. In the 1840s the whole forest of 144,000 acres had been bought by the Duke of Leeds from the Mackenzie family at under £1 an acre, but since then it had been split up, and the portion bought by Elphinstone – for £66,000 – was known as Achnashellach. Whether he acquired the ground with the intention of dividing it up further, or the idea came to him later, is no longer clear; but in any case he soon disposed of Achnashellach itself, together with its mansion house, to a Yorkshireman called Robert Tennant, at a price of £26,000. He was thus left with the northern portion of the estate – some 16,000 acres of mountain land, with good grazing, a useful number of trees, a small, decrepit lodge and no access road.

In those days, before the Ordnance Survey had reached the far north, no accurate maps existed upon which the marches of Highland properties could be drawn. Surveyors could be hired to prepare individual plans, but these generally proved unreliable, and when a forest changed hands the only practical means of defining its marches was for the solicitors concerned to describe the boundaries in writing. Thus, when Elphinstone bought Achnashellach, the official description of the forest extended to more than eight sides of closely handwritten foolscap:

> The lands of Achnashellach and others with the Mansion House and office belonging thereto, the lands of More-More, or Mone-More, the lands and forest of Coulan, or Coalen, with the shooting lodge and offices, the town and lands of Gortonfruich, the lands of Lair, the town and lands of Balnacarra, or Balnacra, the town and lands of Culags, or Coulags, which lands and others before mentioned comprehend the whole ... [the land] to the southward of the watershed line of the mountain called Coirbreac and a line drawn from its eastern shoulder to the loch called Loch-an-dhu-Derich; as also the tract of land lying on the south side of Loch Dhoull called Craignellan Face, extending upwards to the skyline as seen from the house of Achnashellach ...

The fishing rights, in the various lochs and rivers, were specified with the same exactitude, the stretches of water generally being described as *ex adverso* (opposite) a certain piece of land, or with reference to the *solum* [bed] of a certain loch. And yet, in spite of all this precision in the apportionment of land and water, disputes constantly broke out in the years that followed over border areas.

In the first winter of his occupation Elphinstone was naturally anxious to know how many deer his new forest held, and in November he wrote to the head stalker, Finlay Finlayson, asking for a report. Finlayson was illiterate, signing his pay chits with a cross, while someone else wrote 'Finlay Finlayson, his mark'; and from the surviving receipts one can see that it was Alex Matheson, the second stalker, who did the writing. Thus, when Finlayson answered the new laird's request for information, the letter purported to have been signed by him, but in fact was in Matheson's elegant hand throughout. Between them, on November 23rd, 1866, the two men concocted a report which made up what it lacked in the way of punctuation by keeping admirably to the point:

> My Lord
> I received your Lordships letter dated 20th wishing to know several questions which I will answer as far as I know
> about the number of deer in Coulin will average about four hundred sometimes two hundred will be seen in one lot of stags

between thirty and forty stags can be shot every year if the place is kept properly   twenty four stags was shot this season

about thirty hinds to be killed this season as there are good many on the ground

about the venison   the Keepers used to get two Hinds each the shepherds used to get one hind each   I mean the shepherds on the estate and the rest to be distributed among the Tenants on the Estate and some to his Lordship favourites the Minister Postmaster Dr Welsh

about the Market   there is a career [carrier] too and from Dingwall weekly and an agent that takes it [venison] but I suppose that he will only take the Hanches

There can be some salmon got with the net in March but very little with the rod sooner than April except sea trout ...

I was speaking to the House Keeper and she said to me that the Lodge requires nothing

We used to destroy all the vermin as much as we could   the grouse are increasing   we did not destroy any grouse eggs in the forest but I used to shoot some in the forest later end of the season and none on the sheeps pasture

there are fourteen Families and one pauper on your portion of the Estate

I am oblidge to your Lordship for Kepperin [the Keeper's] House

I beg to inform your Lordship that there are a number of sheep in the forest about 300 and a man Herding lodging in Coulin

I beg your Lordship to let you [me] know if you want any Hinds to be killed this year   I [have] no Riffle and no Licens to shoot any game

I am your Lordship most humble Servant

Finlay Finlayson

Elphinstone must soon have furnished Finlayson with a weapon, for two months later, at the beginning of February, the stalker wrote again, in snow and ice, to say that 'the Rifle are good' and that he could 'prove it in bad weather like in good weather.' By then he had shot twelve hinds, which had been distributed as follows: two to each of the stalkers, a half each to the shepherds and the gardener, a quarter each to the pauper at Coulags, the herdsman, Captain Ferguson of the Volunteers, the Reverend Mr McKenzie, the post master and Dr Welsh; and half a beast to the dogs.

The ice on the river, Finlayson wrote, had swept away the bridge above the loch, but in spite of the snow the deer were still in fair condition: 'There was not a day but they would get some food the time of the storm as they gathered into the woods and to the low ground.'

Meanwhile, word had evidently gone round that new jobs might be available at Coulin, and in December a stalker called James Campbell wrote — with studied formality — from Alness:

My Lord,

Having Heard a letter from Lord Selkirk on the 24th October last stating that your Lordship bought the estate of Achnashellach and at the same time his Lordship stated that he was to make application to your Lordship on my behalf for to get into your Lordship's employ as a head stalker in which capacity I have served his Lordship from my youth until the year 1864 at which time his Lordship gave up Geldermory Forest — I need not make any mention of my capabilities as a Stalker and Forester as likely his Lordship would have mentioned all this at the time of making the application on my behalf to your Lordship. I had another letter yesterday about the forementioned situation of the situation of a forester on your Lordship's estate of Achnashellach if not already filled up it would be conferring a great favour by appointing me to the situation. I have always made it a rule to give every satisfaction in my power to my employer or to any nobleman or gentleman on whom my employer wished me to attend.

An answer would greatly oblige your Lordship's most Humble and Obedient Servant

James Campbell

P.S. I beg leave for encroaching on your Lordship's goodness, if your Lordship should know or hear of any other place being open if your Lordship's place is filled it would be bestowing a favour by letting me know.   J.C.

Whether or not Campbell's obsequious inquiries brought him any employment, the records do not reveal: apparently not, for Finlayson remained the head stalker at Coulin for the time being, and Campbell's name does not appear in any of the pay slips. Whenever a man was taken on to the staff, he was made to sign a small, handwritten contract; for instance, when Duncan Mackenzie took service as an under-keeper, he signed a little note:

I hereby agree to accept service as Under Keeper with Lord Elphin-stone upon the following terms — Wages to be at the rate of £30 (thirty pounds) a year ... also grazing for one Cow but without any follower — and grazing for one Pony, it being at the option of Lord Elphinstone to pay me the value of the pony's grass in money should he at any time find it inconvenient to allow the pony to graze in the forest.

Elphinstone himself, living at Musselburgh, kept in touch by means of frequent letters, giving his orders and soliciting information by post. His men not only carried out his instructions but also tried to keep him posted as to the sporting possibilities of his estate. Archibald McDonnell, one of the keepers, wrote on March 6th, 1867:

My Lord,
I have received your Lordship's of the 2nd and according to your Lordship's request I have opened the box and found the guns quite dry and safe; the gun cases will be put on shelves in the gun room but all the other things I have returned into the box again.

The river here is very low at the moment ... It would be quite useless your Lordship coming here at present in expectation of sport while the River is so low but whenever there is a change in the weather I will let your Lordship know at once. I am tying some flies for your Lordship which I hope will prove well.

Another letter, written in March 1867, reported that McDonnell had been to Skye to inspect some pointers, but that both the dogs on offer had mange. The owner wanted £36 for the pair, but McDonnell wrote disgustedly that they were not worth *six* pounds. 'I have tried the river today,' he went on, 'it is in good order. I rose two clean salmons ... if it should continue as it is I think there might be some sport got.'

The proprietor, meanwhile, was projecting large-scale improve-ments. First he cleared off the remaining sheep, so as to give the deer better feeding and less disturbance. Then he began to lay plans for a new lodge on a fine site between Loch Clair and Loch Coulin, about a mile and a half north of the point at which the old house stood.

Before the lodge could be built, Elphinstone had to construct a road to the proposed site, and for this he needed the permission of his neighbour, Sir Kenneth Mackenzie, who owned the forest of

Kinlochewe, part of which lay to the north. When Elphinstone wrote in September 1867, Sir Kenneth granted his request at once, airily brushing aside the offer of a look at the plan:

My Dear Elphinstone,

I don't the least want to see the plan of your road, so you are very welcome to set to work on it whenever you like. The only thing I would suggest is that you should *bridge* at a place or in a manner that will not interfere with the fishing.

In another note, written four days later, Mackenzie confirmed the permission, and also gave Elphinstone the right to quarry stone from anywhere he liked on Kinlochewe territory. But at the same time he repeated his condition that the fishing pools should not be spoilt by new bridges, and he added another quaintly undemocratic requirement, 'binding you to prevent the public from acquiring a right of way along your new road'.

Luckily for Elphinstone, the approach to his site, from the Kinlochewe road to the north and round the eastern shore of Loch Clair, was relatively short. The line was surveyed by William Paterson, a civil engineer from Inverness, and the length proved to be only 1 mile, 517 yards. Paterson advertised in the local newspapers for contractors, and two men put in estimates which varied widely: Kenneth Bain of Beauly worked out that the road would cost £1,360 7s. 6d., while John Ross of Fearn said he could build it for only £568 3s. 11½d. Not only was Ross far cheaper: he also had an excellent reputation, and even when he demanded £3 expenses to come and look at the proposed job, Paterson thought it worth writing to Lord Elphinstone to suggest that he should be taken on:

He has made many miles of roads in the Highlands ... and I can recommend him as an active, skilful and honest contractor ... It is not at all usual to pay the expenses of a contractor in offering for work, but under the circumstances your Lordship will see that it would be desirable to secure a good man at the expense of £3.

Ross got the job; and separate tenders were invited for the task of bridging the two small rivers that lay on the route. This work was secured by Charles Mackay, a carpenter from Inverness, who bid £230 apiece for each of the bridges, one of them a forty-nine-foot span and the other fifty feet. Paterson reported that the use of iron girders would increase the price of each bridge by £85, and Elphinstone, who never parted with money unless he had to, decided to economise by building entirely in wood. Luckily he had plenty of timber close at hand, for Coulin was still well wooded on the lower ground.

Work on the road and bridges began in the autumn of 1867. Kenneth Murchison, Elphinstone's factor, marked the trees that were to be cut, and sawyers, working in pairs, felled and prepared them. Whenever the ground allowed it, horses dragged the trunks down to the bridge sites; but in some places, where the hill was too difficult for horses to work, the men themselves had to do the dragging.

Some forty trees were cut from the high ground above Loch Coulin, but these proved not enough, 'I have been marking more wood at the west end of Loch Clair out of sight of the loch at the black burn,' reported Murchison in December 1867. 'The ground is very rough so that the horses cannot work, therefore I employed men to drag the trees to the saw pit.' For this – a back-breaking job – the men were paid the same wage as the sawyers – 2s. 6d. a day. In all, twenty-four piles were needed, and as they had to be between seventeen and twenty-one feet long, each one used the whole trunk of a Scots pine.

When all the piles had been driven, work was held up by a shortage of sawyers – caused, apparently, by the laird's parsimony. 'Perhaps your Lordship will give orders for at least an additional pair of sawyers to prevent any claim by the Contractor,' pleaded Paterson, in one of many letters couched in similar terms.

As the bridges took shape, and work on the road went forward, there were even more mundane matters to be attended to. 'Please let me know what price your Lordship paid Lord Hill for the manure per yard so that I may charge Mr Tennant the same,' wrote Murchison at the end of 1867; and during that autumn also two samples of water, from burns that might make sources for the supply in the new house, were sent to a specialist at Edinburgh University for analysis. That designated 'No. 1 Achnashellach,' the chemist reported, 'is good as far as the organic constituents are concerned. It, however, contains a very objectionable quantity of *albuminoid ammonia*; which would induce me to condemn it ... for drinking and for culinary purposes.'

Luckily the second specimen, which came from Coulin itself, proved more suitable. Although it had 'a distinct but not powerful chalybeate taste', it contained 'an average quantity of organic matter, and no objectionable amounts of inorganic constituents.' This water, the specialist concluded, would answer well.

Elphinstone himself, besides visiting the place from time to time, kept closely in touch by letter, writing two or three times a week and busying himself with the smallest detail. He prescribed, for instance, that the rails on the bridge nearest the lodge were to be made rustic— that is, they were not to be squared off, but were to be left rounded, with the bark on.

The lodge to which the road and bridges led proved, by the standards prevailing at the time, a modest affair; yet, even if it was no mansion, it was no cottage either. Since the whole Elphinstone family and their guests were likely to be there at once, and since a reasonable force of servants had also to be accommodated, the number of rooms was considerable. Moreover, as there was no other place at hand in that upland wilderness where the spiritual welfare of the family and its retainers might be maintained, the building incorporated a small chapel, twenty-three feet by fourteen.

On the ground floor, besides the chapel, were the drawing room, dining room, gun room, drying room, servants' hall, butler's pantry, butler's bedroom and housekeeper's room; and, also on the ground floor, but ranged round a courtyard at the back, were the kitchen, cook's pantry, scullery, wash-house, laundry, beer cellar, coal cellar, separate larders for meat, fish and game, and two small bedrooms. Upstairs were nine further bedrooms, and different nurseries for day and night. There was one lavatory downstairs and two upstairs, and only one bathroom.

The neat stone house, with its steeply pointed gables, cost Elphinstone £5,062, and he spent a further £485 on furnishing it. The bill for roads, bridges and paths was £1,455, and he laid out several hundred pounds on draining, fencing, and planting new trees. Altogether, it cost him £8,002 to put his deer-forest in order.

Almost every penny of this sum was spent locally: some went as far afield as Inverness, to the engineers and contractors based there; but even they employed mainly local men, and the great bulk of Elphinstone's outlay must have found its way into the pockets of people living in the immediate vicinity of Coulin. The setting-up of the forest thus greatly benefited the local community. Had the deer not been present on the hill in enticing numbers, the lodge would probably never have been built; and had it never been built, all that money would have gone elsewhere. Besides, if the local people had not found employment in the building and running of Coulin – and other forests of its kind – they would almost certainly have found no employment at all, since there was no other work for them to do.

A wide variety of tradesmen, craftsmen and shopkeepers benefited from the deer-forest economy. Besides the labourers directly employed at Coulin by Ross and Mackay, a number of individuals won particular contracts for building paths or fences. One such was John Macdonald, who in March 1869 signed a typical handwritten undertaking:

> I hereby bind myself to make and finish a Bridle Road which is to be made between the River Coulin and the west end of Loch Tarlich, and the aforesaid road I will make at one penny halfpenny per lineal yard four feet wide with side drains where necessary. And also I bind myself to finish the aforesaid road to the satisfaction of the Right Honble Lord Elphinstone or any person whom his Lordship may appoint to inspect the same.

Macdonald must have been a hard and resolute worker, for his income can hardly have been less than that of a sawyer, who got 2s. 6d. a day – and to earn this amount at the rate he proposed, he would have had to complete twenty yards of the path every day, besides walking to and fro between the site and his place of lodging. (It is hard to convert the money of the 1860s into modern financial equivalents, but one useful guide is the price of food: a dozen eggs cost 6d., or about one-twentieth of their price a hundred years later. At this rate a labourer's daily wage of 2s. would now be worth £2·00.)

Even when the main building programme had been completed, there was a good deal of casual work for locals. Donald Beaton, a surfaceman, who maintained the road, charged 2s. 8d. a day. John Marchison, a gardener, got 2s. a day, and John McLean of Balnacra earned 16s. for 'eight days cutting firewood, one day of the above repairing fence at the loch side at 2/- per day.'

No matter how modest the amount earned, everyone had to sign a receipt for what he or she was paid:

> Work for Lord Elphinstone by Widow McLean, Balnacra, two days at Achnashellach pulling heather or moss for stable 1/- per day
> Widow McLean

By far the most expensive of the tradesmen were the carriers, who were obliged to charge high rates to feed and shoe their horses and keep their carts in good repair. In May 1869 Farquhar McLennan and Alexander McLean charged 24s. 'for carrying McDonnell's [a keeper's] lodggage from Achnashellach to Coulin with our carts.' For using his horse and cart on the hill, that same year, to carry stones to the drains, Donald Maclean charged 5s. a day; and coal, which cost only one guinea a ton in the first place, cost another 10s. a ton for transport from the railway station to Achnasheen.

Weight was evidently the governing factor, for whereas Alex MacLean of Coulags got 2s. 6d. for 'one day spent carrying her Ladyship to Coulin', he charged double that for 'one day spent carrying home a stag from Coulin forest to Achnashellach', the beast presumably being twice as heavy as Lady Elphinstone. Another commodity which attracted heavy carriage charges was beer; although its normal price was only 6d. a pint, the carriers exacted a toll of 10s. for every cask that they took up to Coulin.

Among other tradesmen who derived benefit from the forest, the blacksmith was perhaps in the most regular demand, since all local transport was by horse and cart, and the hill-ponies used for bringing in the deer also needed shoeing. Donald McKenzie of Kinlochewe charged 3s. for fitting 'eight made shoes', and 4s. for four new shoes that he had fashioned specially. Besides this bread-and-butter work, there were occasional odd jobs such as '1 handle in a frying pan', for which he earned 1s.

It is not clear from the records when the new lodge was first occupied. The Elphinstone family were at Coulin in the autumn of 1868, but they must have camped in the old house, for at that stage the new one had not even been fully planned. Judging from the shopkeepers' invoices, however, and from the sudden spurt of buying which they record, the new lodge must have been finished and furnished late in the summer of 1869.

Andrew Fraser & Coy, Cabinet Makers & Upholsterers, of Inverness, suddenly found themselves doing brisk business: the goods they supplied that autumn included eighteen iron beds, fifty-two chairs (various), Venetian blinds, carpets, four 'best basons', ten 'basons for servants', matting for the green room, thirty-six hassocks (at 2s. each), two dozen egg-spoons, a great many 'Chambers' (pots), hearth-rugs, candlesticks, eight 'strong tumblers', soap dishes, ewers, brush-trays, water-bottles and coal scuttles. The Elphinstones' total bill for 1869 amounted to £351 1s. 7½d., on which the shop magnanimously allowed a discount of £1 1s. 7½d., leaving his Lordship £350 to pay.

In that year and the ones that followed, tradesmen in Dingwall and Inverness supplied an astonishing variety of goods. Food, naturally, was the most regular requirement, and from James Ferguson of Dingwall came innumerable consignments of cheese, prunes, sultanas, mustard, Carolina rice, tea, ground coffee and digestive biscuits, besides other basic domestic necessities such as balls of twine, paraffin, 'one cast iron kettle to hold one Gallon (4/-)', and bottles of 'King of Oudh's sauce'. From Mackenzie & Fraser of Inverness ('Glass, China & Fancy Goods Merchants: Accounts Rendered Half Yearly') came 'two dozen cut tumblers, one and a half dozen cut champagnes, two China Creams', ewers, basins and soap dishes – the bill amounting to more than £15.

Mrs Macrae of Kinlochewe supplied whisky at 3s. a bottle, and beer at 8s. a dozen; Howden Bros, seedsmen of Inverness, sent 200 'strong transplanted Scotch fir', evergreen rye grass, whin seed, hybrid rhododendrons, one hundred willows (3s. 6d.) and one twenty-inch pruning saw. From Donald McRitchie the chemist came Finest English Oil of Lavender, a box of Hamilton Pills at 1s. 4d., a packet of Iceland Moss Cocoa at 9d., and a packet of Sea Moss Farina at 1s. Frasers, the upholsterers, followed their huge initial order with others for birch towel-rails, blankets, looking-glasses, counterpanes, one five-foot-by-three-foot iron cot, cane chairs, floor cloths, mattresses, bolsters, door-studs, and 1⅛ yards of Crimson Utricht Velvet (11s. 3d.), together with three yards of crimson fringe.

But by far the grandest suppliers were Macdougall & Co., of The Royal Tartan Warehouse, Inverness, who modestly styled themselves 'Manufacturers of Tartans, Highland Tweeds and Linsey Woolseys to Her Majesty, the Royal Family and their Royal Highnesses, the Prince and Princess of Wales, and to the Courts of France, Russia, Prussia, & Spain, &c, &c.', embellishing their writing paper with the royal crest and representations of the medallions which the firm had won. From these exotic premises came such essentials as 'one pair of Knickers [breeches] of best Grey homespun Shetland Tweed' at £1 6s. 6d., and 'Norfolk Shirt & Knickers of striped homespun Tweed' at 4 guineas.

For some things the Elphinstones were obliged to send farther afield. For example from Walter Carson & Sons, 'Sole Manufacturers of the Original Anti-Corrosion Paint', of La Belle Sauvage Yard, Ludgate Hill, London EC, came a twelve-inch 'Archimedean' lawn mower (at £4), together with 2s. worth of emery for sharpening it.

L

But almost all the lodge's needs could be satisfied from near at hand. Duncan Cameron of Dingwall – 'Maker of Every Description of Boots and Shoes' – would build shoes to measure at about 16s. the pair. Charles Keith, Bookseller and Stationer of Inverness, supplied Sandwich paper and Kitchen paper by the quire, and packets of 'curl paper' at 2s. apiece. A photographer who came out from Kinlochewe charged 10s. for one day spent photographing at Coulin, a further 7s. 6d. apiece for 'two different negatives of Coulin', and 3s. 6d. each for twelve prints seven inches by five.

But few Highland establishments can have been busier than William A. McLeay, of 80 Church Street, Inverness, who styled himself 'Bird Stuffer &c', and besides selling cartridges, fishing tackle and other sporting equipment, dressed deer-skins and mounted an amazing variety of animals and birds. McLeay, it seems, would stuff anything, whether it was a stag's head (at 14s. 6d.), an otter at 12s., a brace of ptarmigan at 9s., a golden eagle at 18s., a wild cat at 15s., or what the invoice described as a 'Blk Thd Diver' at 7s. 6d. Through the services of McLeay and other taxidermists, the Highland lodges gradually became crammed with glass cases full of birds, and stags' heads sprouting gloomily from the walls.

Even the local solicitor found extra business. The account sent in 1869 by Andrew Smith of Dingwall was modest enough, but no doubt helped to keep his office ticking over:

Oct. 29   To meeting you tonight with reference to trespassers
          in your forest 10/–
Nov. 3   Writing John Macdonald Balnacra and Duncan
          McLennan Coulags threatening them with Interdict
          if they or any of their families are found trespassing in
          your forest
          1 @ 3/4 & 1 @1/– 4/4

The trade which all these outsiders picked up was strictly seasonal: almost all their business came between August and October, during the grouse-shooting and stalking seasons. But for the men and women actually employed on the estate, the deer-forest brought full-time employment. In May 1869 McKinnon, the factor, wrote to tell Elphinstone that he had taken on a grieve, or bailiff, at a salary of £45 a year and 'the usual allowance' of meal. For this, the letter went on, 'you are to have his own services for all works, & those of his wife as

Dairymaid ... he thinks it [the grazing] will keep a dozen of milch cows all the year round and a lot of young cattle during the summer.' In another letter McKinnon confirmed that the grieve 'is to be entirely your Lordship's servant. He will supply the produce of any cows your Lordship puts on the ground, while you are in the Country, and when you are away he will sell it on your account.'

Apart from the grieve, at least three stalkers (also known as game-keepers) were permanently employed. Finlayson, the head stalker, was paid £40 a year, and the under-stalkers such as Alex Matheson received £30. There was always a chance of supplementing their wages with vermin money, and bounties paid were handsome—£1 for a fox, 10s. for an otter, 7s. 6d. for a wild cat, 5s. for a polecat and 1s. apiece for winged vermin such as crows and hawks. The skins of all animals and birds had to be handed in as proof that they had been killed, and in one year—with a bag of two foxes, three otters, two polecats, two wild cats and twenty-seven winged vermin—Matheson earned himself an extra £6 12s., thus boosting his entire annual salary by twenty per cent.

Apart from their keepering work, the job of the stalkers was to look after the lodge and outbuildings during the absence of the laird, to see that the paths and bridges were in good repair, and generally to keep an eye on the forest. Another task—then as now—was to tidy up after the family had gone south in the autumn and to send on the things they had left behind. Matheson wrote from Coulin on November 12th, 1869:

My Lord,
I received your Lordship's two letters—I sent the rifle and gun with Mr Bishop and the Knickerbockers but your Shirt could not be found in any part of the Lodge ... the weather are very wet and stormy since you have left and very little work done since ... There is not a stone of the wire fence bored or gathered yet ... my chimney are not much better I will keep a list of all the leaks ... I only killed two Hinds yet.

I am your Lordship's most
obdt Humble servt
Alex Matheson

please turn over
My Lord, there was a very high flood here last night and it Brock

away the Base in the burn and Brock away part of the lead pipe leading to the cistern an the water are completely stopped we cannot light fire in the Kitchen for fear of the Boiler bursting until the plumber will get it mended.

It is not clear how much Lord Elphinstone himself enjoyed the forest which he created. The records suggest he was a cantankerous fellow, who often engaged in fiddling disputes with his neighbours about the fishing rights in the lochs or the exact line of the march. The fishing was certainly worth arguing about, for in one controversy about the rights in a particular loch it was recalled that the 'Duke of Leeds had trawled it and caught a cart-full of sea trout and salmon, besides some [fish] distributed among the people present.' The boundary disputes, on the other hand, seem to have been largely a waste of time; nor did Elphinstone have any luck when he tried to let off one awkward bit of land to a neighbour, Mr Scott. Offered the grazing at Mone-More, Mr Scott declined to take it, remarking that 'times are changed now. Cattle bring a grand price, and sheep are ruination.'

Elphinstone also antagonised another neighbour, to the south-east, Mr Shaw of Glencarron, by proposing to run a wire fence between Glencarron and Coulin forests, the aim being both to stop the Coulin deer wandering too far afield, and to deny the Glencarron sheep access to the deer-forest proper. His scheme drew from Shaw an agitated protest, in which many of the anxieties which beset recently established Highland lairds are clearly apparent:

My Lord,
    Resuming my slight acquaintance with you, I write on a subject of almost vital importance to myself and this property. It is respecting a report I have heard that a wire fence between Coulin-Achnashellach and Glencarron is contemplated.
    The late owner of Achnashellach was the first to introduce them — and between ourselves it was a great breach of faith. I gave that gentleman a large price for this piece of land in consequence of the deer which were always on the ground, and the first thing he did was to entirely exclude them — but with this of course you have nothing to do.
    I really think between gentlemen and adjoining proprietors this exclusiveness and unsportmanlike proceeding ought to be avoided ... If however, you still feel it necessary to put up a fence, I hope it will

be of such a nature as to stop deer as little as possible—a low fence with a wooden top bar. I am sure of one thing, if these wire fences are made in all directions they must eventually ruin the breed of deer—no Achnashellach deer can ever again set foot in Coulin. Besides, if instead of animals in a state of nature ranging about, they are to be confined in paddocks, where can be the sport in killing them?

I trust you will take these remarks as they are intended, in good faith ...

Yours faithfully,

G. Shaw

Elphinstone forwarded this letter to another neighbour, Sir Ivor Guest, who by then had taken over Achnashellach. A day or two later Guest replied:

I quite agree ... that it is unfair that Shaw should get a large rent for the sheep-farm and expect to kill your deer too, and if he will not clear his ground, he must expect to lose his sport. I think from the general tenor of his letter that if called upon to pay half the cost of a fence he will insist on its being a stone or turf dyke according to the Old Act of Parliament.

Elphinstone sought legal advice about this old act, which, he found, did lay down that a proprietor could compel a neighbour to bear half the expense of putting up a march fence, provided the barrier was made of stone or peat. But he can never have pursued the matter of the Glencarron fence very far, for he was already talking about turning Coulin back into a sheep-walk, or even selling the entire estate. Sir Ivor Guest soon got wind of his idea, and wrote to him on September 30th, 1872:

My Dear Lord Elphinstone,

I am sorry to hear that you have thoughts of disforesting Coulin—it seems such a pity now that deer have taken so well to the ground ... I heard ... that rather than spoil an old forest you would dispose of the estate if you found another purchaser and buy another place already under sheep.

If this is the case, I should be glad to discuss the question of taking over Coulin, as it would suit me very well to have room for another rifle, and as you know the forest could be very well worked from here.

In due course Guest bought the estate for £75,000, and thus the Coulin ground was reunited with that of Achnashellach, the two forming a single forest, as they had before. Elphinstone, it turned out, had made a shrewd investment: having bought the place for £40,000, and having spent some £8,200 on building and road-making, he made a profit on it of nearly £27,000 in only six years.

Many other rich men were active in the Highlands at the same time; but no one built more spectacularly than did Sir John Fowler, the engineer and designer of the Forth Bridge, whose eyrie called Braemore, overlooking Loch Broom in Wester Ross, thrilled everyone who saw it. 'Fowler is doing wonders at Loch Broom,' wrote Sir Kenneth Mackenzie in 1867, in one of his letters to Lord Elphinstone,

> but only such wonders as anyone may do whose circumstances allow [him] to squander money at pleasure. Any owner of a rough Highland property who can afford to spend £50,000 on furbishing it up may vastly increase its value and its amenity and possibly improve its appearance. Unfortunately those £50,000 are generally missing.

Fowler's project was vividly described by A. E. Gathorne-Hardy, who saw it as a young man:

> No one but the great engineer ... could have planned and constructed the sportsman's paradise ... When he bought his estate in Ross-shire, and considered where to build his house, he determined that it should stand sufficiently high to counteract the somewhat relaxing character of the climate, and should command a view of the strath and of the sea.
>
> At once he was assured that no such site existed. But with the giants of his calling there are no such things as impossibilities, and he simply marked on the ordnance map a spot on the side of the hill of the required altitude and situation. As the point selected was on a very steep braeside, 500 feet above the river and the road to Ullapool, it was not desirable to excavate a very large site, and Sir John contented himself with space for his house above, constructing the stables, garden and offices five hundred feet below, with a beautiful

winding road of three miles with an easy gradient to connect the two buildings, from the upper of which a stone could almost be dropped upon the other.

An unfailing water supply, perfect sanitary arrangements, and power for working machinery and making electric light were provided by damming the burn above and making a little lake close above the house, just below the sanctuary in the heart of the forest below the peaks of Ben Dearig and Ben Lear.

To this celebrated lodge came many distinguished stalkers, and the visitors' book in which they left their various marks is now a collector's piece, embellished with sketches by Landseer, J. E. Millais, General Crealock, and several lesser hands, as well as with the comments of enthusiastic guests, many of whom burst into verse in attempts to express their gratitude. Most of the poems now seem embarrassingly fulsome; but one early visitor, William Russell, paid a nicely turned compliment to the splendour of the site:

> As Eagles soar on high with tow'ring flight
> To plant their Eyries on some lofty height,
> Whilst lesser birds with unambitious quest
> In humbler places seek to weave their nest —
> So at Braemore with wond'ring eyes we find
> This bold conception of a mighty mind —
> And looking downward to the lowly glen
> Where crouch the dwellings of less daring men,
> Admire at once the genius of the man
> And now the perfect working of his plan.

Quotations in Latin were no rarity. An excerpt from Ovid's 'Hero and Leander' was inscribed by General Crealock opposite one of his own typically dark, powerful and romantic pencil-and-ink sketches, which shows a stag swimming out into a loch towards a hind, improbably silhouetted against the moon, on a crag rising from the farther shore. The most celebrated comment, however, was that made in 1874 by Lord Cairns, the Lord Chancellor of the day.

One evening at the end of September he returned from the hill at about six o'clock with two good stags, and was met by his host, who himself had shot five stags, with the news that a government official had that moment arrived from London bearing the Great Seal, which had to be affixed to some state documents. The business was conducted there and then: in the courtyard, surrounded by dead deer, the Lord High Chancellor attached the insignia of his office to the parchments; and afterwards in the visitors' book he recorded:

> About this date a Great Seal was, for the first time, seen on this part of the coast: and allowed to depart, not only unmolested, but thankful and happy, carrying away impressions of Braemore more lasting than any which it made while there.

The life of the lodge at Braemore was short. In the 1930s the Fowler family sold the house and forest to a brewer named John Calder, who first lived in the lodge but later left it empty and allowed it to deteriorate so far that eventually, during the 1950s, the roof fell in. Calder then offered the lodge to the Scottish Youth Hostels Association but they, not unreasonably, decided that the cost of maintaining the house would be far beyond their means, and declined to take it – whereupon Calder was so angry that he had the place blown up. Some of the stone was used for building road bridges, and the rest was pushed over the side of the hill. Today only a shelf marks the spot where the great turreted mansion, known locally as 'The Castle', once perched high above the glen.

Braemore thus came to an inglorious end. But many other examples survive to show the immense solidity with which the Victorians built their sporting lodges, and probably none is more striking for sheer quality of workmanship than Wyvis, in Ross-shire.

This house was built by Walter Shoolbred, the third son of James Shoolbred, who had founded the firm of James Shoolbred & Co., makers of high-class reproduction furniture. Not only did Walter inherit money from the family business: he also originated the Guildford Stage Coach – and somehow these two disparate elements in his background gave him a taste for deer-stalking. In 1882 he rented a forest called Corriehallie, and then in 1884 he bought the forest of Wyvis from Horatio Ross. Soon afterwards he bought a second forest, Kildermorie, which marched with Wyvis to the north, and for some years he ran the two as a single unit.

There was already a lodge at Wyvis, but it was old, and Shoolbred, having demolished it, set about building a modern house more in keeping with his social status. The site was at the western end of Loch

Glass, and since there was no satisfactory road to it, his first action was to build a steamer at the eastern end of the loch. This vessel, plying up and down the four-mile stretch of water, carried in all the stone, slate, wood and other materials for the new building.

Shoolbred spared no expense in making the lodge as solid as the rock on which it stood. An exceedingly meticulous man, he took the closest personal interest in every detail, and his own professional knowledge of woodwork evidently put the builders and carpenters on their mettle, for the craftsmanship is of the highest order. The house is built of unevened stone, with a red slate roof, and is panelled throughout, mainly in oak, with some pine. The heavy doors would not disgrace a stately home in England, and every one of them still shuts with a heavy, satisfying clunk. The carving on doors and mantelpieces is outstanding, and every room is meticulously finished. Most of the cupboards are recessed and hidden; and even one of the bell-pushes is concealed behind a small sliding panel so that the decorative pattern is not spoilt. On the back of almost every window-shutter a mirror is mounted so that at night, when the shutters are closed, every source of artificial light is redoubled and thrown back into the room.

The outbuildings – keeper's house, dog-kennels, game-larders – were finished to the same exacting standards. The keeper was no less snugly empanelled than the laird, and even the dogs were luxuriously housed, their quarters being lined with pine panelling and their runs furnished with cast iron posts (made by a firm called Bayliss) on which the gentlemen might cock their legs. Separate larders were built for grouse and deer, the latter being crowned by the bronze statue of a stag (a royal, inevitably). So well was the timber for all these structures seasoned and chosen, and so skilfully were they built, that ninety years of Highland wind, rain and snow have scarcely warped or shifted a single plank.

The great fascination of Wyvis today is that it has remained exactly as it was when Walter Shoolbred first devised it. Each time the house has changed hands the contents have gone with it, so that the place is now a living museum in which not only the furniture and pictures but also the blankets and the cutlery are original. The decorative contents of the lodge would make a conservationist's hair stand on end – the stuffed golden eagle in the hall, the peregrine in the dining room, the wild cat on the landing, to say nothing of many magnificent red deer heads. Yet as an example of the surroundings in which the Victorian sportsman felt at home the place is unique.

Shoolbred opened up his forest with the same thoroughness as that with which he tackled the house. He laid out twenty-five miles of hill-paths, all of them properly built, with bridges and culverts which survive to this day. The men who built the paths were hired in Evanton, and since there was no means of transport to and from work save their own legs, they often had to walk five miles to the forest gates, where a horse and cart would meet them and take them up the glen.

Another long and arduous job was the construction of a deer-fence along the forest's south march, from the entrance to the property to the top of Ben Wyvis. Whenever the iron stakes could no longer be driven into the ground, they were leaded into holes bored in the living rock. (The melting of lead must itself have been a formidable task in such remote and difficult country.) One mile of the march was marked by a stone wall, which was built at an altitude of about 2,500 feet. The farthest point of the wall was fifteen miles from the workmen's home, and it seems likely that here, as elsewhere, they lived out during the summer in a camp near the site.

This kind of forest-building was repeated with slight variations in one place after another, and gradually an immense area took on very much the face it wears today—bare mountains and empty glens, the different properties divided (if at all) by only the occasional fence or wall. In some of the glens poor stumps of stone walls were still to be seen, showing where human beings had once scratched a living; but in most of the hills there was no sign of human habitation.

A hundred years later, the wire in the fences has rusted away; but the iron stakes still march with wonderfully Victorian confidence straight up and down precipitous faces, and boundary walls scale impossibly steep ridges. Above all it is the paths—beautifully engineered and fitted into the contours—which bear witness to the skill and thoroughness of the builders. When one crosses a burn by means of a shod ford, with the stones all neatly cut and laid together like outsize cobbles, it is agreeable to reflect that, come spate or drought, a century of Highland weather has made no impression on this humble artefact, built so simply and yet with such care.

By no means all the lodges have survived. Indeed, a surprising number were destroyed by fire. Ardverikie was burnt down on the day Landseer was buried; Meoble, on South Morar, was burnt; and at Corrour, in Inverness-shire, both old and new lodges (on different sites) in turn succumbed to blazes. Several others also went

up in smoke, and the reasons for the lodges' vulnerability are not hard
to discover: most were lined with wood, so that once a fire had started,
it burnt furiously; and all were so remote that there was no chance
of help being summoned, still less of it arriving, in time to bring
salvation.

Chapter Twelve

Victorian Heyday

The period between 1880 and 1910 was the heyday of Highland stalking, and the deer-forest as a whole extended farther than ever before. Part of the reason was social pressure, in the form of a demand for sport; but the main causes were economic. In the 1870s the price of wool fell sharply, and in the 1880s the price of mutton did the same, so that the rents of sheep farms were forced down to less than half what they had been twenty years before. Even at these reduced rates, many proprietors could find no one to take their land, particularly the higher grazings.

Sporting leases, by contrast, were in ever-growing demand – with the inevitable result that a second round of clearances took place, this time of sheep rather than of men, and the amount of land reserved for deer went up and up. By 1890 the number of forests had risen to 130, and they covered 2½ million acres. Twenty years later yet another million acres had been afforested.

Most of this vast tract was still in the hands of traditional owners. The Duke of Sutherland held far more than anyone else, with 1,326,000 acres. Next came the Earl of Breadalbane, with 438,000, then the Earl of Seafield (305,000), then the Duke of Richmond and Gordon (269,000), the Earl of Fife at 249,000 and the Duke of Atholl at 201,000. (In comparison with these giant preserves the Queen's holding at Balmoral – then about 25,000 acres—was tiny.)

Yet if a relatively small amount of land had been bought by southerners, the great majority of the deer forests were rented by them – and at astronomical cost. By 1885 a dozen forests in Argyll and Inverness were let for an annual rent of at least £2,000 apiece. Since the stalking season lasted only about ten weeks, each tenant was paying £200 a week, or nearly £40 for every day on the hill – and that before he had hired all the extra servants needed or paid for his house-party's food and drink.

The sportsmen, in consequence, were mostly well-to-do Englishmen, and many came from aristocratic families. Stalking was an almost exclusively upper-class sport, and the social tensions which it engendered became all-too apparent whenever it was threatened by some proposal for egalitarian reform such as the 'Access to Mountains' Bill of 1885, brought before Parliament by the distinguished Member, James Bryce. The Bill excited Highland lairds and their tenants to rage and apprehension: the naked snobbery which seethed beneath the surface came boiling up in an outburst from another M.P., W. Bromley-Davenport:

Now a strange Bill with a strange title is presented to Parliament, called the 'Access to Mountains' Bill, but which might with more accuracy of definition have been termed the 'Destruction to Deer-stalking', 'Ebullition of Envy', 'Indulgence of Ill-nature', 'Irritation of Owners', or 'Spoiling of Sport' Bill, which has no pretence or outward visible sign of benefit to anybody, not even a possible political end to serve; but is simply an open and undisguised attempt to injure Highland proprietors, and so reduce the value of their estates as to make them almost worthless.

For who would hire a deer forest or a grouse moor if he were liable at any time, at the conclusion of a long stalk, perhaps, to see the hideous apparition of ''Arry' in appalling checks on the sky-line in full view of the deer ... ? And what redress has he? Says the Bill: 'In case of any action of interdict, etc. etc., founded on alleged trespass, it shall be a sufficient defence that the lands referred to were uncultivated mountain or moor lands, and that the respondent entered thereon only for the purposes of recreation, or of scientific or artistic study.'

So ''Arry', when challenged as to his business on the sky-line of the deer-forest, has only to pull out an old betting book, which for the nonce he turns into a sketchbook, and proudly proclaim himself to be a 'Hartis' ... eventually, after resorting to the weak and futile expedient of bribing this particular ''Arry' to go away and pursue his scientific researches, or study art, elsewhere, with the only effect of multiplying the artistic or scientific breed to an alarming extent in that district, the wretched proprietor or lessee will have to give up, the one his profit, the other his pleasure, at the bidding of the

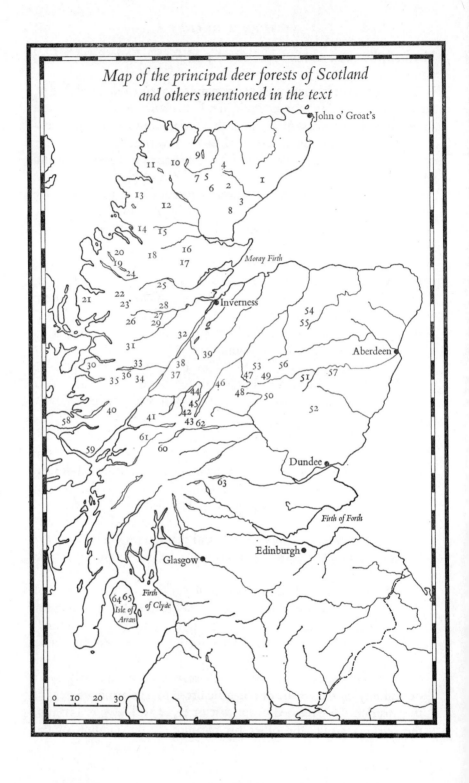

Map of the principal deer forests of Scotland
and others mentioned in the text

John o' Groat's

9 1
11 10
7 5 4
6 2 1
13
12 8 3
14 15
16
20 18 17
19 24 Moray Firth
25
22
21 23 28 Inverness
26 27 54
29 55
32
31
39
38 53 56 Aberdeen
30 37 47 49
35 36 34 46 51 57
44 48 50
45
40 42 52
41 43 62
58 61
59 60

Dundee

63

Firth of Forth

Glasgow Edinburgh

64 65 Firth
Isle of of Clyde
Arran

0 10 20 30

senseless sentimentality of fanatical socialism, and at the sacrifice of hundreds of honest thousands of pounds sterling which Scotland now annually receives from English sporting enterprise.

Fortunately for the stalkers, Bromley-Davenport's fears were as exaggerated as his language. The dreaded Bill was never made law, and the march of fanatical socialism was for the moment checked.

Such, by then, was the annual migration to the north that authors began producing books devoted entirely to Scottish field-sports. In 1880, for instance, Alexander Macrae, late forester to Lord Henry Bentinck, published *A Handbook of Deer-Stalking*, an excellent little manual of practical advice, with a brief foreword by Horatio Ross (then aged seventy-nine) who confessed that for some fifty years he had contemplated writing just such a volume, but had been prevented by 'indolence and procrastination'. Among many admirable precepts, Macrae laid down that 'if a young stalker is leading a gentleman' in a difficult stalk 'he must consider whether the gentleman is tractable enough', that is, whether or not he is likely to crawl properly.

In 1882 there appeared Robert Hall's *The Highland Sportsman: A*

---

*Key to map of the principal deer forests of Scotland
and others mentioned in the text*

1	Langwell and Braemore	22	Coulin	44	Ardverikie
2	Borrobol	23	Achnashellach	45	Benalder
3	Kildonan	24	Kinlochewe	46	Gaick
4	Badanloch	25	Strathconon	47	Glenfeshie
5	Loch Choire	26	Killilan	48	Atholl
6	Ben Armine	27	Glencannich	49	Mar
7	Klibreck	28	Glenstrathfarrar	50	Fealar
8	Dunrobin	29	Fasnakyle	51	Balmoral
9	Ben Loyal	30	Knoydart	52	Glenclova
10	Gobernuisgach	31	Glenaffric	53	Rothiemurchus
11	Reay	32	Balmacaan	54	Glenfiddich
12	Benmore	33	Glenquoich	55	Blackwater
13	Glencanisp	34	Achnacarry	56	Glenavon
14	Rhidorroch	35	Glendessary	57	Glentanar
15	Corriemulzie	36	Glenkingie	58	Ardnamurchan
16	Kildermorie	37	Culachy	59	Ardtornish
17	Wyvis	38	Glendoe	60	Black Mount
18	Braemore	39	Coignafearn	61	Glenetive
19	Letterewe	40	Conaglen	62	Corrievarkie
20	Fisherfield	41	Mamore	63	Glenartney
21	Applecross	42	Corrour	64	Dougarie
		43	Rannoch	65	Brodick

compendious Sporting Guide to the Highlands of Scotland, which was in effect a gazetteer of sporting properties, listing the principal deer-forests and giving – among a mass of other facts – the lengths of the main lochs and rivers and the heights of the biggest hills.

The variety of information offered by the book was astonishing: not only did the author give remedies for canine diseases, the close seasons for birds and fish, details of postal services and a table of the number of trees needed to plant one acre of land; he also included formulae for estimating the weight of a stack of hay, ascertaining the contents of rectangular vessels, and – a *sine qua non* for all travellers – judging the weight of cattle ('multiply the square of the girth in feet and inches by the length in feet, and multiply the product by ·23, ·24, ·26, ·28 or ·30 according to the fatness of the animal, and the result will give the weight in imperial stones').

A similar volume, *Outdoor Sports in Scotland*, appeared later in the 1880s. Its author, who styled himself 'Ellangowan', was J. G. Bertram, and he, like Hall, collected facts about deer-forests and grouse-moors with the enthusiasm of a magpie. For real *aficionados*, however, neither of these compared with Augustus Grimble's *Deer-Stalking*, which came out in 1886. Written by an expert who himself had experience of many of the forests involved, this short book was a form of latter-day Scrope, devoted exclusively to the practicalities of stalking and spiced by a few anecdotes from the author's own experience. 'This most fascinating of sports', he called it; and though he had 'met those who ridicule it, and have protested they would derive as much pleasure in shooting a donkey on Hampstead Heath as in pursuing the wild red deer across the Border', his own enthusiasm was limitless.

Whether intentionally or not, Grimble concentrated in this volume on the deer, methods of stalking, equipment and so on, writing very little about the forests themselves. But ten years later, in *The Deer Forests of Scotland*, he made handsome amends: this second book, which described all the forests county by county and gave something of the history of each, was beautifully produced, with sketches by Archibald Thorburn, and is a collector's item to this day.

An even more lavish production was *Deer-Stalking in the Highlands of Scotland* by General Henry Hope Crealock, whose enthusiasm for the chase and skill as an amateur artist had made him welcome in many a forest. He also rented several forests himself, among them Fannich and Glendole. Like Landseer he was plagued by the conflict between his hunting and artistic inclinations, and often exasperated his stalker by scrutinising a stag through his glass far longer than was necessary for sporting purposes. He also had a habit of holding a sprig of heather in front of his face while crawling – although he scarcely needed camouflage, as most of his face was hidden anyway by a great bushy beard.

Crealock died before he had finished the book, but it was tidied up by his brother, John, and published in 1892 – an amalgam of advice and personal experience rendered unique by its many large reproductions of the author's pen-and-ink sketches. Dark, powerful, extravagantly romantic, the pictures show stags silhouetted against water, or distant hills, or the moon; yet if the backgrounds are exotic, the animals themselves are drawn with rugged strength and grandeur.

In attempting to capture the romance and drama of their subject, some amateur writers were driven into verse – with awful results. It would be unnecessarily cruel either to name the author, or to quote more than one verse, of 'The Death of the Red Stag':

> ''Twas a gran' shot whatever!' 'And sport meet for kings
>   Is the stalk to a king in the land of his rule;
> And deep is the craft that successfully brings
>   Twenty stone within reach of this trusty old tool!'
> And the sportsman, delighted, looks lovingly down
> On the steely-blue barrels in wood of nut-brown.

In 1904 there appeared *Stalking Sketches* by Captain H. V. Hart-Davis, a slight but handsome volume of reminiscences mixed with advice, also embellished by the author's own drawings; and 1907 saw the publication of a minor classic, *The High Tops of Black Mount*, by that formidable stalker Alma G. Breadalbane. Spurred on by her evident belief that the higher one climbed the hill the closer one came to God, Lady Breadalbane stalked Black Mount with more energy and skill than most of her male contemporaries, and she set down her recollections in unashamedly purple prose, which was enhanced by the numerous photographs taken by her friend, Olive Mackenzie.

From these books, and from references in other works, one can gain a clear view of the late-Victorian stalking scene. The sportsman would leave London in the evening by sleeper train: fifty years earlier the journey to Inverness would have cost him £20 or more, but by the

M

1880s, thanks to the completion of the railways, he could cover the same distance for only £5. Borne northwards through the night by the Limited Mail, fortified by 'a big cigar, a sound sleep, one whisky and soda at Carlisle, more sleep, Perth, a wash and a hearty breakfast', (wrote Grimble), he would change trains and find himself, a few hours later, 'in mortal combat with a very tough chop in a Highland inn'. Then he would be collected by a dog-cart sent down by his Highland host and driven the twenty-odd miles to the lodge.

Next morning the start would be an early one: he would be up at 6 a.m., breakfast at half-past, and away by 7.30 on a twelve-mile pony-ride to the furthest march of the forest, in the company of one stalker and a couple of pony men, with a small packed lunch in his pocket. Once on the ground, he would spend the rest of the day alone with his stalker, and by the time he returned to the lodge at dusk, in triumph or despair, he would have covered at least another dozen miles on his own feet. After a hot bath, a heavy dinner served by a small army of butlers and footmen, and the inevitable cigars in the smoking room, he would sleep like the dead until it was time to take to the hill again.

A life of such violent exercise provided the ideal excuse for eating on a gargantuan scale—a pastime at which the Victorians were in any case not backward. One of Ellangowan's sources described to him the ideal base from which to launch operations:

Happily I started on the best of all foundations, a capital breakfast. Attend and envy me: *item* first, a steak of broiled salmon; *item* second, a helping from a pie composed of jellied sheep's head nicely seasoned and palatable; *item* third, a savoury omelet piping hot; *item* fourth, one half of a rizzard haddock; add to these home-baked bread in the form of scones and oatcakes, as well as honey, marmalade at discretion, plenty of cream and real good coffee, and you will give me credit for having breakfasted. There was a dram after, but that is never counted, although the whisky is well disguised in several tablespoonsful of heather honey. We started for the seat of war about seven o'clock mounted on ponies.

So gross an intake at breakfast could be defended to some extent on the grounds that the stalker would have very little in the way of lunch—no more than half a cold grouse, a sandwich or a piece of cake, which could be eaten in a quiet moment and washed down with a dram

of whisky from his flask. By no means all Highland sportsmen, however were condemned to such midday frugality. For a typical royal
shooting luncheon, sent out to the rifles from Balmoral during a deer-
drive in the Abergeldie woods, the menu was as follows:

> Homard Naturel, Sauce Rémoulade
> Ragoût de Mouton Provençal
> Poulet et Langue à l'Anglaise
> Salade Vosigienne
> Épinards au Beurre
> Pommes de Terre Mâitre d'Hôtel
> Tarte aux Framboises et Groseilles
> Compote de Pêches
> Pouding au Riz
> Apple Dumpling

This scanty picnic was served to sixteen rifles, but besides them some
fifty loaders and beaters had also to be re-stoked, on less exotic fare.

In those days, as now, part of the point of a stalking holiday was to
escape from the routine of everyday life. But the idea of the Victorians
escaping from routine is almost a contradiction in terms, and many of
the Highland lodges were run on routines of their own, no less rigid
than those which prevailed in the south. At the establishments owned or
rented by the Ellice family, for instance, all clocks were put forward
two hours and kept there throughout the party's stay, so as to make the
most of the hours available for sport. Thus, while it seemed to the
occupants of the lodge that they were breakfasting at nine, they were
in fact breakfasting at seven – and so on throughout the day. The system
must have caused fearful confusion among tradesmen, and among
people arriving and departing, who had to be collected from, or
dropped at, stations and other places. Yet it does not seem to have
occurred to the Ellices to breakfast at seven without changing the
clocks. Breakfast was at nine, and that was that.

Highland evenings were evidently formal enough to strike dread
into the heart of any guest none too sure of himself. 'The entrance into
the dining room of a stalking house is a critical moment in a day's
sport,' wrote General Crealock:

> Mortification and vexation of spirit await the unlucky wight who
> has missed a good chance or, blundering his shot, has wounded and

lost his beast ... Chaff is no name for what he may expect, and woe
betide him if he tries to stammer lame excuses ...

As the stalker of the day walks into the dining room all eyes are
turned on him, and he is saluted with a general query from all:
'Well, what have you done?' But the question need not be asked:
you can generally tell by the way he comes into the room what has
taken place on the hill.

If he has blood, triumph is in his eye, his gait is brisk and joyous,
and he is full of chaff; while if he has failed, he has not a word to
say for himself, looking very meek and ''umble.' ... The bachelor
seems to me to have much the best time of it when he misses; for
he has not to undergo a certain lecture and chaff besides from the
wife of his heart, and beyond his own mortification there is nothing
to follow.

But the poor married man has, I suspect, a rough time of it ... for
I notice the wife is as jealous of her husband's reputation and as keen
for blood as her lord. How often has one watched the lady's manner
on entering the drawing room! If her husband has missed, she comes
in very quietly and is civil to everyone; but if he has killed a good
stag, she enters the room with her nose *en l'air*, and an expression on
her face of 'Thank God I am not as other women are—my man
don't miss.' Then follows the smoking-room ordeal, when you
have to stalk your beasts over again and give all the details.

Apart from keeping their husbands up to the mark, there was not a
great deal for the ladies to do. They might walk and sketch, go boating
on the loch (if there was one) and even fish a little, but for them to go
stalking, even in the role of spectator, was most unusual. Still rarer was
it for a lady to shoot, and apart from a single reference in Lord
Malmesbury's memoirs to Lady Seymour stalking in 1845 at Achnacarry, the Marchioness of Breadalbane stands on her own as the
only lady who regularly took a rifle to the hill in the nineteenth
century.

Alma Graham, a daughter of the fourth Duke of Montrose, was
introduced to shooting at an early age, and she soon made herself
expert, in spite of the formidable handicap of a squint so pronounced
that people could not tell whether she was looking at them or at some
object in the vicinity. In 1872 she married Gavin, the seventh Earl of
Breadalbane (for whom, in 1885, the marquessate was revived). The
couple had no children, but by her marriage Alma became mistress of

immense sporting estates, of which the 100,000-acre Black Mount was only one.

She was by nature a very humble woman, whose delight it was to visit her tenants. Most of them spoke only Gaelic, and – much to her credit – she learnt enough to make herself understood. In her memoirs she left a charming account of how, after a hard day on the hill, she came down in the evening to one such modest dwelling – her stalker's home:

> What a bright welcome met us there! The cheerful homely kitchen, furnished with a row of happy-looking little girls, standing large-eyed, like a flight of steps in age, and Johnnie, the one laddie, showing signs already of becoming a strong and active man for any kind of hill-work. In the parlour was spread such a tea as only Clais-gobhair could produce – the home-made scones, butter and jam, milk which stood all cream in the jug, and Mrs. Grant flitting round in her gentle care of every want. I am ashamed to say I drank seven cups of tea.

Who could possibly guess, from reading such innocent memoirs, that the author was a compulsive gambler, and by her wild extravagance brought the Breadalbane family – powerful as it was – to the verge of ruin? No hint of this emerges from her book. Yet a punter she was, and a disastrously unfortunate one at that: it was quite normal for her to put several thousand pounds on a horse in a single bet, and almost always she lost.

As Lady Breadalbane admitted, she was often asked by her friends what she found so fascinating about struggling up the hills of Black Mount 'just at the end to shoot a defenceless stag'. Her answer, couched in characteristically extravagant terms, was that 'the stag is the least part of it all,' and that

> the real enjoyment and pleasure consist in the close intercourse with nature – the solitude, the apartness, the constant variation of light and shade, the mystic vagaries of the fleecy clouds, the grandeur of the passing storms, the tender sadness of the setting sun leaving his last rosy kiss on the brows of the peaks, and the quiet peace of evening as we turn towards home.

She conceded that it was often a battle to reach the 'utmost purple rim' of the forest's high hills; but once there, she asked,

can anything be more delicious than the sense of accomplished will?
All trifling cares and troubles left far below, life seems altogether on
a higher, nobler plateau; and the almost awe-striking realisation of
the immensity of nature among the eternal hills fills the mind with
solemn rest. Here in these grand surroundings we may consciously
feel God walks with man.

Close though the Almighty might be, His proximity in no way
inhibited Lady Breadalbane from slaughtering His creatures, and by
dint of hard practice and long experience she became an excellent shot.
Clad in square-heeled boots, a voluminous, ankle-length grey skirt, a
short jacket and a flat cap shaped like an enormous muffin, she would
set off up the glen at seven in the morning on her 'merry little grey
pony' to meet her favourite stalker, Peter Grant (who, by the time her
book appeared, had 'passed to higher things than even the eternal
hills'). With him she would ascend to the high tops and stalk as long
and tenaciously as any man. Her resistance to wind and weather must
have been extraordinary, for she scorned any outer cape or coat,
remarking that by far the best thing to take was a woollen jersey,
which could be slipped into the stalker's pocket.

Her accounts of scenery were lyrical and extensive; but when she
came to describe the action itself— the final crawl-in and the shot— she
either shied away from giving details or thought them of no interest
to others. One of her triumphs, for instance, when she shot six stags
with six shots on September 30th, 1897, got only the most perfunctory
account in her book.

She and one of the stalkers, McInnes, made for the top of Aonach-
more, having arranged that the other men would move the deer up
to them. She gives a good idea of how the excitement built up as a
great mass of deer climbed towards the ambush, but only a flat and
stilted description of the actual shooting:

Slowly I raise the rifle and cover him as he steps along. He stops a
moment to look back at his neighbours and gets the shot in the right
place. He is quickly followed by a fine ten-pointer a few yards
further back. Two barrels have now accounted for two stags, and
the rifle is quickly reloaded ...

Nowhere in her memoirs does Lady Breadalbane mention venison,
or say what was done with all the meat that came out of the forest. But

it is clear from other records that none was sold: there was no market for it close to the sources of supply, and no means of transport fast or reliable enough to ensure that it reached a suitable market in good condition. During the stalking season many haunches, individually wrapped and boxed, were sent away to friends, and a great deal of venison was eaten in the deer-forests themselves, by the shooting parties, by the servants, and (not least) by the dogs. Lady Breadalbane's own bill-of-fare books, giving her menus during the shooting seasons of the 1890s, show that venison was constantly on the table, in the form of whole roast haunches, collops, hot-pots or merely 'hashes'. (*Hachis de venaison* was a favourite standby for breakfast, along with mutton cutlets, steaks viennoise, smoked salmon *en papillottes*, devilled chicken and macaroni.)

Whether the stalkers put on or lost weight during their holidays, no records relate; but their physical fitness (or lack of it) was a subject of some concern to contemporary commentators. Inevitably most sportsmen arrived in the Highlands (as they do today) soft after a life in the City. 'With regard to your personal condition,' wrote Grimble,

if plenty of lawn tennis be played, and hansoms and 'pints' eschewed and hill-walking is not an unaccustomed exercise, the shooter will be fairly fit at the commencement of the season, and each day out will make him more so. The great thing in going up a long steep hill is to stop and *admire the view*, the moment nature warns that too great a strain is being placed on the pumping powers of the heart.

Do not mind who is in front, or how far; do not struggle on until the heart is bumping against the ribs; do not be ashamed to sit down and rest. Many a good man out of condition has seriously injured that organ by trying to 'live' with a practised walker up a severe hill ... There are times when it is a matter of shot or no shot to reach a certain point before the deer get past it: then you must make the best dash up-hill you can, and the heart must take its chance of hurt if the deer are to take theirs.

Grimble offered sound advice on every aspect of the hill, not least the problem of stag fever – the febrile trembling that comes over many a rifleman as the moment of the shot approaches. He wrote:

The disease must run its course. Advice will not cure it, *neither will whiskey*; but after a course of downright bad misses the foresight of your rifle will by degrees cease to wobble round and round. The eye will see clearly that there *is* a stag within a hundred yards, and the brain begin to tell that it will be better to keep the sight steady if you wish to taste one of his haunches instead of sending him off to give a treat to a neighbour.

For another ticklish problem – that of being overcome by a desire to cough or sneeze while lying in wait for a stag to rise – Grimble had an equally practical solution:

A sup of water may put matters right if there is any handy, if not, then bury nose and mouth in the peat and explode therein; no matter if you come up looking like a Christy minstrel, it will wash or dry off very quickly.

Few, if any, gentlemen ever gralloched the beasts they shot, and most of them would probably have been physically incapable of disembowelling the stag. Grimble did it once, but it sounds as if Captain Hart-Davis never managed it:

Recollect that the operation of gralloching is not a savoury one for the olfactory nerves, and that it is therefore prudent to sit to wind-ward [while the stalker gets on with it], and if you are a smoker to light a pipe. You will then, in comfort, have full leisure to contemplate the head and horns of the stag you have secured.

The energy of the Victorian stalkers was phenomenal. In her memoir of her father Henry Chaplin, Lady Londonderry recorded how, by the beginning of the 1880s, he was renting more than 70,000 acres every year in Sutherland. Not content with Ben Hope and Melness forests, he also took Ben Armine, Loch Choire, Clebrig, and later, Gobernuisgach. All this land was still exceedingly wild: there were no roads or even bridle paths, and at Loch Choire there was no accommodation except a shepherd's hut. As Lady Londonderry remarked, 'the faces of the present generation of gillies would be long indeed if they were bidden to take a stag fourteen miles across the hill without any sort of track.' Duncan MacRae, a stalker who first went to Loch Choire in 1881, recalled how beasts were brought home:

I often think of the old times when the deer had to be taken to the larder without a path on the place. Just think of taking stags to Ben

Armine from Corrie-na-Fhearn, Corrie-na-Seillich and round above Loch Choire and Halmadarie and the floes east of Creag Mhor. The men and ponies nowadays would not do it, but in the old days it was all done in the best of spirits, and I never knew of a stag not being brought home. Of course, then the deer were almost all taken home the following day in daylight, but a few that were got near the Lodge were taken the same night. The way it was done was the pony had to be led out to where the stag was lying, and when it was balanced on the pony's back and strapped on the deer saddle, the pony was allowed to find his own way home, and with a little practice the pony would get quite good at following his own track home and when it came to a bad place it would snort and smell the ground and would go round and shun all the doubtful places.

It was the ambition of many stalkers to achieve 'the triple' – bag of fur, feather and fish in a single day. As Grimble reported:

In forests where there are grouse-shootings attached, and a salmon river also, it is by no means a difficult feat to bring off the 'swagger' performance, as my young friends at Eton would call it, and kill flesh, fowl and fish all in the same day. The first two – the stag and the grouse – are nearly certainties, and it is Mr Salmon, with his capricious appetite, who usually stops the way to the achievement of the triple event.

As the craze for stalking built up towards its peak, the development of sporting rifles proceeded apace – and indeed it seems likely that the passion for the Highlands itself contributed to the speed at which innovations were brought in. During the 1840s many experiments had been made with different types of rifling and different shapes of bullet in attempts to overcome the fundamental problem of the muzzle-loading rifle – that the bullet had to be smaller than the bore. Charles Lancaster, for instance, produced an oval bore and a correspondingly oval bullet, while another gunmaker, W. W. Greener, devised a principle known as the Minié, whereby the bullet was made with a hollow base so that it expanded into the rifling as it was forced up the barrel.

The Purdey family were always in the forefront of rifle development, and it was James Purdey the younger who, during the 1850s, perfected the rifles to which he gave the name 'Express Train', later shortened to 'Express'. These weapons were of 40-bore and 50-bore (about ·500 and ·450 respectively), and fired a much larger charge, to give a higher velocity and flatter trajectory: so efficient was the Express formula that nearly half a century passed before it was superseded.

Competition between rival gunmakers was keen, to say the least, and claims of superior performance by somebody else's rifle evidently raised blood pressures to a dangerous height. Competitive trials were held regularly before an independent judge, generally the editor of the *Field*; and in the absence of elaborate machinery for timing or measuring impact, the trials had perforce to be somewhat empirical. Penetration tests, for instance, were held at the London Field Rifle Trial, staged in Putney during the first week of October 1883, and the competing weapons were fired from a range of forty yards into a bank of pine boards one inch thick and one foot square. A Martini-Henry ·450 bore, loaded with eighty-five grains of government powder and a conical, hardened bullet of 480 grains, penetrated twenty-two and a half boards, but a ·500 Express with a solid bullet weighing 381 grains penetrated twenty-seven and a half.

This trial was clearly an elaborate affair, yet it entirely failed to satisfy W. W. Greener, who nearly choked with rage when he came to describe it in his book *The Gun*:

> There were but six competitors – Messrs. Adams, Bland, Holland, Jeffries, Tranter and Watson ... The trial resulted in Messrs. Holland being declared winners of every class; but to the gun trade and to sportsmen in general the trial cannot be considered to have been fully satisfactory ... The best grooving or system of rifling has not been proved, the merits of rival systems still remain undecided ...
>
> The Great (?) London Rifle Trial of 1883 has failed to prove to gunmakers the best kind of rifling adapted for Express or other rifles ... The winning rifles, Messrs. Holland state, 'were all rifled on our new non-fouling principle.' This may mean everything or it may mean nothing – more probably the latter.

While the gunmakers quarrelled in London, Express rifles held the field unchallenged in the Highlands, the main dispute among stalkers being about whether one needed the extra punch of the ·500, or whether the ·450 was powerful enough, and whether one should use solid or expanding bullets – these last being designed to flatten on impact and so to minimise the chance of passing straight through an animal without delivering an immediately fatal blow.

With a ·500, declared Grimble, 'the expanding bullet should be discarded *entirely*' because it did so much damage to the meat. The same author had witnessed an awesome demonstration of the power of a ·500 solid: the stag fired at was killed outright, 'the bullet passing right through the heart and body; another stag in the line of fire was shot through the neck, and a third one beyond received a broken hind leg, and all three were put into the larder.'

According to Grimble, the double-barrelled, breech-loading ·450 was the rifle most used in Scotland during the 1880s. Such a weapon could be bought for as little as £20, although if a 'Mr Longpurse' must needs go to Rigby, Grant or Purdey, he might pay as much as £70. Assuming that the first shot at least would be unhurried, Grimble advocated that the right barrel should be loaded with a solid bullet, and the left with an expanding one; but that if the shot looked like being rushed or difficult, the stalker should have hollow bullets in both barrels.

In this desire to use a solid bullet if possible, one can catch a revealing glimpse of the Victorian sporting code. Because the rifleman had to be more accurate with the solid bullet, and there was less chance of getting away with it if the shot was bungled, the solid bullet was more sportsmanlike than (and therefore preferable to) the hollow.

In this context the telescopic sight, which was then just coming into use, gave rise to agitated controversy. Although a few stalkers welcomed it as a useful innovation, the majority condemned it as grossly unsporting, in that it made shooting much too easy. A telescopic sight might be permissible in some foreign countries, where a stalker might get only one chance in a day, declared Grimble; but in Scotland, where chances were frequent, rifles so equipped 'seem a mistake'.

> If the quarry will only keep still, it is apparently brought up almost within touch of the muzzle of the rifle, and missing becomes nearly impossible. All the difficulties of judging distance, all the nicety of taking the sight in bad light, all the pleasure in fact of making a brilliant shot with an ordinary rifle is done away with.

In these controversies, no consideration was given, needless to say, to the animals being shot. The fact that an expanding bullet and a telescopic sight were more humane – in that they greatly minimised the chance of a stag being wounded – seems never to have occurred to the Victorians. Nor were they particularly discriminating in their choice of targets. Exhorting his readers to improve their marksmanship, Grimble wrote:

> Practise! Practise! Practise! if you want to become a dead shot – at a mark on the level, as sea-birds on a smooth sea, at rocks and stones, uphill and downhill, and across valleys – and by degrees a perfect knowledge will be gained as to what sort of sight should be taken.

Such practice-shooting was more comfortably described than carried out, for the Express rifles produced formidable report and recoil, and a few shots were enough to give the marksman both a headache and a sore shoulder. Lady Breadalbane left a vivid account of her first experience with an old-fashioned Express in the 1880s:

> A rifle was taken at haphazard from the gun-room ... In those days I had eyes to see through a stone wall, and fortunately a pair of arms long enough to get over most of the other difficulties. That rifle did not hide its light under a bushel ... It bumped me on the nose, and kicked me in the shoulder till I was black and blue, and four or five shots at the target sent me home with a headache for the rest of the day. Its report was like a peal of thunder.

Then, at the end of the century, the long reign of the Express rifles quite suddenly came to an end. With the invention of the far more efficient cordite powder, a ·303, or even a ·256, was powerful enough for the Highland deer, and the new rifles – though derisively known as pea-shooters – soon put the old cannons out of business. In 1900 Lady Breadalbane bought a ·303 made by Purdey, and considered it 'for lightness, quickness in handling, and noiseless report, unsurpassed'. It was also, she wrote, an incentive to practise at the target, 'for there is no recoil and no concussion to give headaches.'

The use of the old-fashioned deerhounds gradually died out in the 1880s in most forests, for individual proprietors or lessees no longer had space in which they could easily be deployed. In Scrope's day, when he had had nearly 150,000 acres over which to range, he could afford to let the dogs chase a stag for several miles; but once the

Highlands had been divided up into smaller properties, such tactics were no longer advisable, for a single run might clear an entire forest of deer and frighten them so badly that they stayed off the ground for days. In place of the deerhounds, whose assets had been speed and brute strength, collies, beagles and even terriers were used to follow up deer that had been wounded.

In a few forests, however, the deerhounds were kept on. The Duke of Sutherland, for instance, still had hundreds of square miles in which to run them; another keen dog-man was Cameron of Lochiel, who used hounds regularly at Achnacarry. A spectacular accident occurred there in the autumn of 1874, when Lochiel wounded a big eight-pointer and a dog called Cruachan was slipped at it. As the beast went forward to cross a burn, both it and the dog were swept over a waterfall. Through the first drop Cruachan kept his grip of the stag's throat, but he was swept away in the whirlpool below, and was later found dead in the burn. The body of the stag was also recovered from the water, at a point some 300 yards downstream, and the beast was found to weigh twenty stone – the largest ever shot in the forest.

The sheer brutality to which some of the Victorian sportsmen could happily descend is evident in Sir Samuel Baker's own account of how he knifed a stag to death in Glen Tilt. A formidable big-game hunter, Baker fell into discussion with the Duke of Atholl about whether the deerhounds at Blair would actually seize a stag rather than merely bay it and wait for the rifle to arrive, as was their normal practice. Baker felt sure they would, and to prove his point he volunteered to take on a stag with his knife only.

A 'large party', including a number of ladies, drove up Glen Tilt in carriages to watch the sport. 'Certainly the presence of many ladies brought us luck,' wrote Baker – for soon he spied a single stag in an excellent position for a course. Leaving the admiring spectators on the road in the bottom of the valley, he took to the hill with two keepers in attendance:

We were not many minutes in suspense: there was no doubt that the stag was lying down, as he suddenly sprang up from the heather and the broken surface of the hill face.

This must have been a lovely sight from the carriages, although rather far for the unassisted eye. For a few seconds the stag took up the hill, but the hounds ran cunning and cut him off: he then took a straight course along the face towards the direction where the carriages were waiting below. The hounds were going madly, and were gaining on him. I now felt certain that he could not breast the hill at such a pace, therefore, ... we made all speed for the bottom to gain the level road.

It did not take us long to reach the welcome solid footing, and away we went, as hard as we could go, along the road towards the direction of the carriages. As we drew near, we could see the hunt. The deer had passed the spot where our party was in waiting, but he now turned down the hill towards the river with the two dogs within a few yards of his heels. Presently we lost sight of everything: we rushed forward, passing the carriages, which were empty, as everybody had joined in the hunt, and after running about quarter of a mile down the road we heard the bay and shortly arrived at the spot where the stag was standing in the middle of a rapid and the hounds were baying from the bank.

No doubt the hounds expected to hear the crack of a rifle, and to see the gallant stag totter and fall in the foaming river, according to their old experiences. However, they were not long in doubt. Patting both the excited hounds upon the back, and giving them a loud halloo, I jumped into the water, which was hardly more than hip deep, but the stream was very rapid.

The stag, upon seeing my advance, ran down the bed of the river and halted again after a short run of 50–60 yards. The two keepers had followed me, and Oscar and his companion no longer thought of baying from the bank, but, being carried forward by the torrent, together with ourselves, were met by the stag with lowered antlers. I never saw dogs behave better, although for a moment one was beneath the water. Oscar was hanging to the ear, I caught hold of the horn to assist the dog, and at the same moment the other hound was holding by the throat. The knife had made its thrust, behind the shoulder, and the two gillies were holding fast, by the horns, to prevent the torrent from carrying away the dying animal.

This had been a pretty course which did not last long, but it was properly managed, and, in my opinion, ten times better sport than shooting a deer at bay.

As Baker remarked, to him the affair 'appeared exceedingly simple,' as he had been 'accustomed to this kind of hunting for many years in the mountains of Ceylon.' Most of his contemporaries, however, were lily-livered enough to prefer more conventional methods of getting their deer: to them the rifle and spy-glass were more important than the knife.

Yet their clothes, also, were a matter for concern, and contemporary authors were lavish in their advice as to what sportsmen should wear. In several forests the proprietors or tenants invented special patterns of tweed which were thought to correspond with (and so blend into) the local colours of the hill. At Glenforsa, for instance, on the Isle of Mull, the check of brown, blue and white introduced by Colonel Greenhill Gardyne was said to be 'hardly discernible from a rock'. In Glenfeshie Mr Ellice created 'the Glenfeshie mixture', with a large red check running through it, and one author (Captain Hart-Davis) discerned a particular advantage, for many forests, 'in the Harris tweeds of the peculiar red colour known as "Crottal".' Once a particular mixture had been introduced to a forest, it was worn by all the stalkers as a kind of uniform. Only at Blair Atholl did the professional stalkers continue to wear kilts when on the hill: elsewhere, including Balmoral, plus-four suits were ubiquitous.

Apart from his suit, the stalker was warned against the dangers of wearing the wrong fabric near the skin. 'Discard linen shirts of any sort,' wrote Grimble, 'and wear the best flannel ... '. 'Nothing but flannel or wool should be worn,' said Hart-Davis; and both he and Grimble agreed that boots advertised as waterproof were best left at home.

> Whether wearing boots or shoes, on no account use those that are waterproof, for in the course of a day it will be certain that a sea is shipped, and then if waterproofed the moisture stays in all day ...
>
> Do not wear knickerbocker breeches which are the fashion at present, for in going uphill they pull on the knee, and, however slightly, it will tell at the end of the day or in a long run. The pockets of the coat should all be made to button — this little precaution will save the loss of many a cigar-case, pipe or flask ... Of course, if your attendants consist of a pony and man, a gillie and a stalker, short of a hot bath you can carry pretty well what you please.

Had the stalkers devoted as much thought to the lives of their quarry as they did to their rifles and their wardrobe, they might have found out more about the animals they pursued with such enthusiasm. As it was, ignorance about the deer's ecology was still widespread. Many people, for instance, were still puzzled to hear that although the stags cast their antlers every spring, very few of the shed antlers were ever found. Various absurd theories were advanced to explain this enigma, among them the idea that the stags were so embarrassed by the evidence of their frailty that, when they sensed the casting of their antlers was imminent, they repaired to some secret place (reminiscent of an elephants' graveyard) where no one could see them. It was also claimed that, to cover the traces of their humiliation, the stags deliberately trampled the fallen antlers into soft bogs. So strongly were fanciful notions of this kind entrenched that when experienced stalkers began to put forward the correct explanation – that the antlers are eagerly *eaten* by both hinds and stags, and furnish them with much-needed calcium – their claim was greeted with derision.

Nor does anyone seem to have realised that it was lack of shelter and food, more than any other factor, which prevented the deer from growing larger. Captain Hart-Davis did remark that 'woodland deer have stronger antlers than their hill brethren', but neither he nor any of his contemporaries advocated the planting of trees as a means of increasing the deer's stature.

Hardly any of the proprietors or their tenants made much effort to conserve their stocks and improve their herds by culling the old stags, or those with bad heads. On the contrary, the Victorians were trophy hunters almost to a man: they pursued the beasts with the best heads and the biggest bodies, and there was often rivalry between neighbouring forests to secure the best trophies of the season. (At one stage the lodge at Dougarie, on the Isle of Arran, was adorned with over 200 pairs of antlers.) The depth of wanton destructiveness was reached one year in Atholl, when a particularly fine ten-pointer had been seen about the forest for several seasons, but had persistently eluded the stalking parties. Instead of leaving the animal to breed for another year, the laird gave orders, after the season had ended, that the keepers were to shoot it, and in due course its antlers were hung in a place of honour in Blair Castle. In the second half of the nineteenth century more than 700 pairs of horns graced the castle, 200 of them in the long gallery alone.

The exercise of self-control was so unusual as to be worth recording individually – and if a good stag was spared, it was generally for some special reason. Thus when Lord Lovat was visiting Old Murdoch, a retired stalker, at his bothy in the forest of Glendoe, he spared a beast because it was so well known to the old man. Grimble reported the incident as follows:

33 Victorian poacher: John
Farquharson.

34 Lloyd George tormented by a
fiendish Duke of Sutherland: a cartoon
from the *Bystander* of 1913. The caption
reads: 'Inteet it is a long wa-a-ay. Phew!
I had no idea of the dis-tance. I'm afraid
it is rather inaccessible. Yes, yes, yes!
I am afraid so. My leg feels almost as if
it had been pu-ulled, look-you! To
gootness, yes!'

35 Enter the motor car: hinds shot at Glencarron in the 1920s.

36 King Alfonso of Spain dressed for the hill, with the Duke of Sutherland (left), at Dunrobin in the 1920s.

37 Wyvis Lodge, Evanton.

38 Typical Highland stag in velvet. (Lea MacNally)

39   Stags boxing in the spring. (Lea MacNally)

40   A stag roaring in the rut. (Lea MacNally)

As he sat at the open door a very fine stag appeared feeding over the skyline not three hundred yards off. Lord Lovat sprang to his feet to seize his rifle whilst saying to Murdoch, 'Look at that splendid stag. It is more than a royal.' To this the veteran replied, 'Yes, my Lord; he is just a grand fourteen-pointer, and o'er yon knoll he comes most days about this hour until at last I've learned to look for him and treat him as a friend.'

On hearing these words Lord Lovat at once laid aside his rifle, simply saying, 'Well, Murdoch, it will never be levelled against any friend of yours'; and thus, to please his old servant he denied himself a chance such as few stalkers would have been able to resist.

Examples of such heroic self-restraint were all too rare; there were constant complaints that the quality of the deer was declining, and several proprietors tried to improve matters by importing park stags from England and, after a period of acclimatisation, letting them loose on the hill. One of the first to do so was the Duke of Portland, who brought some stags from Welbeck Abbey, his home in Nottingham-shire, and put them out at Langwell in Caithness. Lord Burton, who hired the forest of Glenquoich on a long lease and fenced in a park round the lodge, brought in a stag and a hind from Raby, as well as hinds from Stoke Park and Woburn. At Balmacaan, on the shore of Loch Ness, the Earl of Seafield became concerned at the steady dimi-nution in the size of the deer, so he established a stud of park stags whose champion was a mighty royal from Windsor. When the Duke of Hamilton cleared the sheep from the forest of Dougarie, on Arran, in 1859, his first action was to bring in fourteen hinds-in-calf and six young stags from the park at Knowsley, near Liverpool. Several lairds benefited when the Duke of Marlborough decided to disperse the herd at Blenheim.

To transport a highly nervous wild animal 400 or 500 miles in days when no efficient tranquillising drugs were available must have been a matter of some difficulty. The park stags were taken bound, blind-folded and with their horns cut off, by horse and cart to the nearest railway station, then by train to Perth or Inverness and finally by horse and car again to their Highland destinations. Many must have died from stress on the way; and of those that arrived in good health some survived only a short time, for their size proved too fierce a temptation for the stalkers on land neighbouring the forest to which they had been imported, and as soon as they had grown a new set of

N

antlers, they were mown down in quick time, even though they were distinguished — and in theory protected — by coloured collars or ear-tags. A few, however, enjoyed prolonged Highland careers: at Apple-cross, for instance, General Crealock recorded that 'two enormous stags from Sir John Thorold's famous herd were masters ... for several years ... splendid fellows weighing nearly thirty stone each.'

Another means by which stocks were increased was the sale and transfer of calves from one forest to another. Whenever a new forest was made out of sheep ground, the deer moved in of their own accord and began to colonise the empty hills; but this natural process was slow, and could be accelerated by the importation of calves from established forests, where they were caught in June when only a few hours old and reared by hand before being turned out into their new environment.

The power of the sporting lairds was far reaching. When the railway companies wanted to build their Highland line through part of Corrour Forest in Inverness-shire, the owner, Sir John Stirling Maxwell, gave permission on two conditions: the first that a station be provided at which his guests might get on and off the train, and the second, that the station would never close for as long as his family remained at Corrour. Furnished thus with their own private railway halt, visitors to the lodge were able to approach their destination in some style. A pony and trap would convey them to the western end of Loch Ossian, and there they would embark on a steam yacht for the three-mile voyage to the doors of the house, so saving themselves a long and uncomfortable drive along the gravel track that skirted the water.

By these various processes some 5,500 square miles of the Highlands were gradually converted into a gigantic deer-ranch. Apart from the social repercussions (which are discussed in Chapter Fourteen) the effect on the environment was profoundly damaging. The deer, which are lethally efficient grazers and browsers, carried on in harness with the sheep that remained, and together the two species finally finished off any chance there might have been that the remnants of the primeval forests would regenerate themselves naturally. With so many animals constantly scrounging food, no seedling survived for long, and no new trees could grow. The result was that the hills became even barer, and the soil even poorer, and the deer were left with less shelter than ever.

Chapter Thirteen

—————— ❀ ——————

Sportsmen and Others

The Victorian stalkers were plagued by questions about what was and was not sporting. Telescopic sights, as we have seen, were considered totally unsportsmanlike by many; the use of expanding bullets was on the whole to be regretted. According to General Crealock, however, the meanest crime a stalker could commit was to give his wind deliberately to beasts over the march, so as to move them upwind and bring them on his side of the boundary.

Also high on the list of irritations in this context were the march fences with which some owners insisted on bounding their property. Most of the fences, or walls, were designed to contain or exclude sheep, and were low enough for the deer to jump over. Some proprietors, however, sought to protect their deer from bloodthisty neighbours by erecting barriers seven feet high. This, needless to say, was thought highly unsporting. 'I'd as lief stalk a deer in a sheep-fank [a gathering enclosure built of stone]' one old stalker said to Grimble—and indeed purists such as W. Bromley Davenport considered that the whole of Scotland had already been ruined by this kind of partitioning: to them Scottish stalking was artificial, and for natural stalking one was obliged to seek out some primeval wilderness abroad (not that such considerations prevented the purists slaughtering a great many Scottish stags).

No doubt there were many stalkers who, deliberately or otherwise, transgressed the strict confines of the Victorian sporting code. But there was one man who persistently excited more derision and hatred than all the rest of the malefactors put together—the American millionaire Walter Winans.

The reason for his spectacular unpopularity was simple: besides being a fanatically keen deer-stalker, he had a passion for deer-*driving*, which he indulged on a gigantic scale; and driving the deer was in

many people's eyes the grossest of sporting solecisms, since it reduced
the noble animals to the status of rabbits or other inconsiderable
quarry.

The mainspring of Winans's passion was clearly his own brilliance
as a rifle shot. He could – and frequently did – kill stags galloping at
200 yards, and his prowess was of an altogether different order from
that of the normal Highland marksman, for whom a stationary target
at one hundred yards presented quite enough of a challenge. Obviously,
for someone capable of shooting deer on the run, driving provided
the ultimate excitement. 'How can a man learn to hit game encountered
unexpectedly or in rapid motion if he never shoots a rifle except with
both elbows resting on the ground?' he asked scornfully; and he had
nothing but contempt for those boastful shots who engaged standing
targets only:

> Few men who go deer-stalking have ever killed a deer moving,
> even at a walk, while fewer still are those who can kill a right and
> left when the stags are running past at the speed of a racehorse and
> bounding into the air.

A Vice-President of the National Rifle Association of Great Britain,
and a Chevalier of the Imperial Order of St Stanislaus of Russia,
Winans expounded his theories in a series of books, beginning with
Revolver Shooting (published in 1901) and ending with *The Sporting
Rifle* (1908). To him it was not merely foolish, but positively dangerous,
that rifle shooting was 'being reduced to a mere game'. In his first book,
he remarked,

> I drew attention to the dangerous consequences to a nation through
> excessive devotion to games, such as cricket, golf and football. Many
> partisans of these games were indignant at my remarks, but public
> opinion now endorses my doctrine of the absolute necessity that
> every able-bodied man should be able to handle a rifle.

His fanatical enthusiasm recalled the days of Henry VIII, when every
adult male in the country had been obliged by law to practise daily
with bow and arrow. Constant practice, Winans recommended,
should still be the order of the day; and since he considered that 'the
final stage in this practice shooting is to fire at marks flung in the air',
he called upon manufacturers to produce a machine which would

'throw balls of about cricket-ball size, or perhaps a trifle larger, straight up to a height of about twelve feet.' His books contained minutely detailed plans of the running deer targets in use at Wimbledon and Bisley (for which the original cartoon had been drawn by Landseer), and he suggested that an outline of 'a mounted cavalryman at two hundred or three hundred yards' range' would also make a useful practice mark.

Obsessed as he was with shooting, he was no less keen on camouflage, and once went so far as to dye a horse so that it became less conspicuous on the hill. The mare was an exceptionally good one, her only disadvantage being that she was white. Winans first tried putting a black net over her, but this made her too hot, so from a West End hairdresser he procured 'two colourless liquids'. His instructions were to wash the mare with soda, to get the grease out of her coat, and then to sponge her all over with the first fluid, which smelt of ammonia. The next liquid Winans put on with a set of hogshair oil-painting brushes:

In order to make an artistic job of it I used a four-year-old iron-grey pony as a model, and copied him, putting on the dapples, painting the joints black, the tail black with the bottom left white, the muzzle and round the eyes left lighter, etc. At first no colour appeared, but when I had finished a shoulder and began on the quarter, the shoulder began turning a violet colour, which gradually became black, and a couple of hours after I had finished painting the old mare, she looked like the four-year-old.

The disguise was so effective that when the mare was turned into her paddock, the other ponies did not seem to recognise her, and kicked her – although their antipathy may have been stirred up by the chemicals' awful smell. According to Winans,

this painting was a great success, as it lasted the ten weeks of the stalking season; at the end she began turning all sorts of queer colours, but still she was not so conspicuous as she was when her natural white colour, and whilst the chemical smell lasted it kept the midges off.

Winans went all out to camouflage himself as well. He advocated the wearing not only of different-coloured jackets and trousers, but also of different-coloured stockings, 'if you do not mind the oddity.'

Big checks, he thought, were useful in any forest (even though not 'good form' in a town), and he liked to vary his clothes according to the 'prevailing tint of the season, getting more yellow and red in it as the autumn advances.' He must have been quite a sight as he took to the hill, for most of his clothes were embellished with particular additions which he himself had devised.

His shoes, for instance, were made with a loop at the back, through which he passed the laces before fastening them, 'so as to prevent them slipping up round the ankles.' His waistcoat buttoned high up to the throat, and on his right shoulder he had 'a sort of epaulette strap, which buttons on, under which my telescope strap goes, so that the strap does not slip when I am crawling.' His jacket was made 'hanging straight down', and his sleeves had a 'turnover cuff, which cuff can be turned over the hands if cold.' For trousers, he preferred 'breeches cut off just above the knee, as worn by Swiss peasants, leaving the knee bare.' These, he thought were 'less apt to give rheumatism, as the knee dries as soon as it gets wet, instead of having a clammy bit of cloth against it all day.'

Altogether Winans was intensely practical in stalking matters, and he was not above rearranging details of the hill itself, should he see an advantage in doing so. After a stalk across difficult ground, for example, he suggested that one should

> examine the spot carefully and see if it cannot be made easier by placing sods of turf, stones etc. in a natural way as a screen, so that in a future stalk that piece of ground may be passed unobserved by deer. A short piece so arranged diagonally over a skyline is very useful.

He cannot have been an easy taskmaster, for he did not suffer fools at all. Whenever he got within crawling distance of a stag he left his stalker behind, claiming (quite rightly) that 'you can get closer by yourself'. Also, he pointed out, 'there is no use having the stalker near you, and he will only flurry you by whispering all sorts of distracting things just as you need all your attention.'

Being himself immensely energetic, Winans could not stand idleness, and warned readers to:

> be suspicious of too long a 'spy' for deer on the part of a stalker; it may only be his lazy way of passing the time ... Once I caught two

stalkers (who did not think I understood any Gaelic) 'spying' the
oats in each others' crofts, and comparing their ripeness, when they
were supposed to be spying for deer.

From his many remarks on the subject, it is clear that Winans stalked
a great deal in Scotland; yet his first love was deer-driving, and this
by no means endeared him to his sporting contemporaries. 'Driving is
not deer-stalking,' wrote Ellangowan:

> Driving is fitting sport for feather-bed sportsmen only; it is quite
> pitiful to think that it has now become the fashion for deer to be
> forced up to the gun, just as partridges or pheasants are driven upon
> those assembled to shoot them.

This was the standard late-Victorian attitude to the subject, and
Winans was often reviled, directly and by innuendo, in the sporting
magazines. But one or two less hide-bound people were prepared to
support him, among them Grimble, who recalled that he had had 'a few
chats at Brighton with the much-abused Mr Winans,' and that:

> that gentleman on one occasion frankly told him that he was
> physically not strong enough to undergo the fatigue and hardships
> of stalking; that his hobby was shooting driven deer, and in order
> to indulge in this *five or six days a week for six weeks in succession*, it
> was clearly necessary to have an extent of ground so vast that virtu-
> ally the deer could not be driven off it. Looking at the matter in this
> light, the writer sees no reason why Mr Winans should not be left in
> peace to enjoy himself in his own way – and he certainly pays very
> liberally for all the ground he rents.

Winans conducted his operations on an immense scale. By the early
1880s he held the sporting rights over a far larger area of Scotland than
any other tenant: his ground covered 200,000 acres and stretched from
sea to sea, including the forests of Craskie, Fasnakyle, Glen Cannich,
Glenstrathfarrar, Glomach, Killilan, Luibnadamph, Patt and Kintail.
His rent was said to be close on £20,000 a year, but his annual expenses
must have been at least half as much again, for he needed an army of
servants to put his grandiose schemes into action (one photograph,
'After a Deer Drive', shows seventeen ponies, thirty-five persons and
nearly twenty dead stags).

His drives were planned and executed with the thoroughness of military operations. In *The Sporting Rifle* he included plans of two specimen drives, the larger of which called for eight separate butts, or 'bothies', as he called them. One such manœuvre, he recalled, yielded no fewer than thirty-one stags. He himself preferred to walk with the beaters, so that he could get really fast running shots at any stags which broke back; and he controlled everything with his own system of flag signals and bugle calls. There were prearranged signals for 'Bring a tracker', 'Two ponies wanted', and so on, and if something went wrong he could alter a drive or bring it to a halt.

Winans had strict ideas of his own about what was and was not sporting. For instance, when culling the herd of fallow deer which he kept in his own park, he considered it wrong to shoot the bucks anywhere except in the head or neck, partly because a heart shot would spoil some of the meat, but mainly because 'the poor beast is in a confined space, and cannot ultimately refuse to be shot at, however long he may elude your attempt. It is only sportsmanlike to give him a sporting chance'. Deer-driving on the other hand, seemed to him in no way reprehensible, and he defended the practice vigorously:

> This is an unfortunate combination of words to describe moving deer towards the shooters. It has led to the 'driving deer into a narrow place where they have no escape' style of abusing those who indulge in this form of sport. If the writers of such nonsense themselves tried to *drive* deer, they would find how impossible it is. Deer will not be *driven*; if they think they are being forced, they will break back, however thick the beaters are ... Instead of being called deer-driving, it ought to be called (coining a word in the German manner) deceiving-the-deer-into-going-where-you-want-them-to.

No doubt it was jealousy that goaded many of Winans's critics into print: they must have been bitterly envious of the immense amount of sbort which he secured for himself by means of his money and his doundless enthusiasm. Nor can the opposition have been comforted by the fact that he was no mean artist. 'We have never seen more truly inspiring shooting pictures', said the *Shooting Times* of one collection. 'One breathes the mountain air ... and Mr Winans must be congratulated for the striking lifelike scenes he has created. "They're Away" is simpy marvellously good—a remark which fully applies to "A Running Shot", possibly the best illustration of deer we have ever seen.'

Oddly enough, one of the few sportsmen in that era who enjoyed something like Winans's freedom of movement about the Highlands was a man with almost no money at all – the celebrated poacher, John Farquharson. Even though more and more forests were being carefully preserved, he nevertheless managed to range – uninvited – with enviable liberty.

Born during the 1820s in Glenfernate, north-east of Blairgowrie, Farquharson was the son of a smallholder who rented grazings from the Duke of Atholl, and he traced his own descent to Finla Mor, the first great chief of the Farquharsons of Braemar. The family's land went right up to the march of the deer forest; and so desolate was the ground that when young John first went down the glen and saw a tree, he took it for some sort of outsize kale plant.

Farquharson was far from stupid: a sparely built man of medium height, with very clear, keen grey eyes, he was fond of reading and could talk intelligently on many subjects. Like his predecessor, Alexander Davidson, he was a keeper *manqué*, having worked first for Lord Abercrombie and then, for nine years, in the service of the Earl of Rosebery. During this time he became a champion rifle-shot, and he invented (among other things) the 'Farquharson position', in which a marksman fired his rifle lying flat on his back, with his left arm passed round his head to his right shoulder, and the rifle laid across his body. Farquharson is said to have discovered the advantages of this position by chance when, out in the deer-forest one day, he was surprised by a stag coming suddenly over the ridge while he was lying on his back, and since he was in full view, he had to shoot it without moving.

In 1863 he won the Scottish rifle championship, and in 1869 the Belgian Gold Medal, which in effect made him the champion shot in Europe. In the years that followed he made some outstanding scores in the rapid-fire competitions at Wimbledon. He was also something of an inventor, and in 1870 took out a patent on a new form of cartridge extractor. Unfortunately an Edinburgh gun-maker, Alexander Henry, did almost the same thing at the same moment, and Farquharson had to take out a law suit against him, which eventually he won. Altogether, he was such an expert in all matters to do with the rifle that many of his friends in high places pressed for him to be given a government job, as they felt he would be of great service to the army.

Far from becoming a civil servant, however, he turned poacher, having left Lord Rosebery and gone as head-keeper to a Mr Dalgleish, who owned land in Argyllshire. Because this gentleman would not give him time off to attend rifle meetings, he left after two years, and thereafter devoted himself to the hill, 'making up lost time', as he put it, by constantly shooting among the mountains. Though offered many first-class jobs, he never worked again.

What he did for money, it is not clear, but his poaching certainly yielded a modest income during the season, for the heads of stags could by then be sold for trophies, and the venison must also have fetched a certain amount. He was sometimes accused of shooting stags for their heads only, but his supporters defended him vigorously against this charge, maintaining that Farquharson never killed deer which he did not intend to carry off, and that if he did sometimes leave a carcase behind, it was only because he was too closely pressed by the representatives of law and order to get the body away.

His normal method was to start out into the forest in the middle of the night, so that by daybreak he would be at some promising point in the heart of the deer country. As soon as it was light he would proceed to stalk, keeping on or about the marches, where different forests joined, and he would carry on until he saw someone coming to challenge him. When that happened, he would withdraw at speed. If he shot a beast, he would cut off its head and carry it away to some separate hiding place, leaving the body, cleaned out, cut in half and also hidden, until he could return with an accomplice and remove it under cover of darkness, either the same night, or if that were no use, the next. Each evening he would have a pony and trap drive out to meet him at some prearranged rendezvous, to cart away any spoils there might be, but he himself would often spend the night in the open.

Although not a particularly robust man, he had immense powers of endurance, and if necessary could rough it as well as anybody. During one autumn he heard that a stag of exceptional size had often been seen alone in the wilds between Braemar and Atholl, and after an exacting stalk he killed it, only to find himself trapped on the hill by mist and a blizzard. Having cut off the head, he skinned the beast, sliced himself a fillet of meat from the haunch, and spent the night in the ruins of an old hut, where he lit a fire by the ingenious expedient of emptying the powder from one cartridge on to the ground, and firing another, loaded with some bits of rag taken from his shirt-tails, into it.

Over the fire he grilled the venison, and then settled down to sleep wrapped in the newly flayed skin. Next day the mist was still down, and he was forced to spend a second night in the same wretched hovel, with nothing to eat but the stag's tongue, which he boiled in a kettle. At least he was well compensated for his discomfort, for the stag's head was later sold, after stuffing for twelve guineas, to the owner of a stately home in England.

The vigour and relish with which Farquharson addressed himself to the hill are well caught in *The Romance of Poaching in the Highlands*. The book's jaunty tone suggests that Farquharson was always fortunate in his forays; but in fact he was often hard pressed by gamekeepers, and once or twice was convicted of poaching and fined. It was during one of his narrow escapes in the forest of Atholl that he stumbled on the cave which the old-time poacher, Lonavey, was said to have frequented. He was being chased by three men round a rocky face when he found an opening beneath an overhanging ledge, and from it a series of natural passages that led to a chamber some fourteen feet by twelve. On a natural shelf at the back, some three feet off the floor, lay the decomposing remains of a gun and a dagger, thought to be Lonavey's (see Chapter Five). The long single barrel was eaten through by rust in several places, and the lock, 'from having been composed of smaller pieces, was much more decayed ... What had been the wood of the stock was merely dust.' A little way behind the lock lay the brass butt-plate 'in tolerable preservation', but the dirk was little more than flakes of rust.

Much moved by finding these relics—which could have been deposited there by no one except his celebrated predecessor — Farquharson sat tight in the cave until his baffled pursuers had gone on their way.

Eventually he married and settled down to live a normal life; but his health had been undermined by all the hardships to which he had subjected himself, and he died in 1893 of heart disease and dropsy.

Nowhere does the Highlander's passion for the hill shine out more brightly than in the autobiography—hitherto unpublished—of Robert Campbell, who was a gamekeeper by profession but a poacher by nature, and managed to combine the two pursuits with extraordinary finesse. His memoirs are all too short: written with humour, precision and rare narrative skill, they give a particularly good idea of how the continuous struggle between the gamekeepers and the free-foresters was conducted.

Campbell was born in 1846, the son of a shepherd at Malm, in Glen Cannich. 'I danced, I shouted, I hurrahed', he wrote of the occasion on which, at the age of twelve, he illicitly shot his first stag; and for the rest of his life the deer drew him irresistibly into the hills, no matter what he was supposed to be doing. Aided and abetted by local shepherds, whose daughters he was sometimes courting, he would set out at two or three in the morning to be on the tops before daybreak — and certainly long before the gentlemen who had rented the forest were stirring forth from their lodge. Whenever he shot a stag he would hide it carefully until the evening, and then return under cover of darkness, often with an accomplice, to cut the beast up and carry the pieces home. The venison generally went to helpful shepherds, especially those with attractive daughters.

To help escape detection, Campbell used to carry his gun dismantled inside his clothes and pretend to be going on nature rambles. This vivid account describes a typical excursion in the forest of Kintail, which was then rented by Walter Winans and in consequence alive with watchers:

One evening I could not resist it [the temptation] any longer, so I put the little rifle in my pocket, the barrel in my trouser pocket and up under my waistcoat, and the stock in a large inside pocket in my jacket, made specially for the purpose, and I stole away up Sgurr-na-Morvich as if I were taking a walk. Winans had a great number of watchers taking care of his ground. There were three at Morvich, two at Inchroe, two at Glenleish, four on the Dorusduan ground, one at Camban and three on the Glenshiel side — viz. fifteen in all, with the depot at Kintail, so you may understand how difficult it was to do much poaching, as the watchers were kept continually on the move, counting their deer every fortnight and sending a report of the number to Winans.

So, this evening, which was the first of August, I managed to crawl up to nearly the top of Sgurr-na-Morvich without being seen, as my clothes were exactly the colour of the ground. I kept up the ridge of the mountain in view of Glenleish called Ben-nan-Each, and stalked the herd of fifteen stags which had tempted me from home ... About 8 p.m. I got within about one hundred yards of them, but, unfortunately for me, this was a report day, which occurred on the first and fifteenth of every month, so the watchers were counting their deer and coming with their report to Ross, the head man, who was at Dorusduan.

Straight down below me at the foot of the hill, and standing on the road, were five or six of the watchers, having been to Dorusduan with their report. I could not fire at the deer even with my little rifle, as the mountain was so steep and close to them that they would be sure to hear the crack. At last they went into a sheebeen to have a dram, so they were out of my way – so far – but by this time my stags had fled some distance away ...

Having stalked the herd again, Campbell killed a beast just before dark, and was faced with an unnerving descent:

I was still very much afraid that some of the watchers might have heard the crack of my rifle, if they were by the door of Jessie's, which was the name by which the woman who kept the sheebeen was known. Also, I was afraid that if they were suspicious of me, they would watch the back of my father-in-law's house, which was right at the bottom of Sgurr-na-Morvich. So I kept down through some very bad rocks above Carngorm called Craigan Fundernach, and very nearly lost my life, as at that time I was not very well acquainted with this particular place. If I had been, I should not have tried there at all – but, as I evidently had longer to live, I managed to get beyond the rocks somehow and came to the main road and thence home.

Having looked round the house to see that all was safe, I wakened my father-in-law, who had gone to bed, in order to go and fetch home the stag, which we succeeded in doing about 3 o'clock in the morning, just before daylight.

Campbell evidently delighted in this kind of cat-and-mouse manœuvre, and practised it constantly, to the great vexation of the keepers. Once, however, while stalking some hinds above the Erchless wood in Glen Cannich, he escaped capture only by a hair's breadth:

I stalked to nearly within shot of them, but did not take my rifle out of my pocket – which I never did on any occasion until I was just about to fire. This time, as at all other times, I looked around in every direction to see if I were being observed, when I just saw something like a bird disappear and then appear again on the top of a knoll about 300 yards away. I never let on, but kept looking around and round in a cool, careless way, and sat down to spy at the deer so that it would appear to the keeper – if it were he – that I was amusing myself by looking at the deer.

I was not even sure that it was a person—it might have been a grouse or something—but I dared not look at it directly in case it was the keeper. After spying all round in a casual sort of way, I just took a sweep round with my glass at the knoll where this object was, and discovered it was a man's bonnet, which was enough for me. I did not keep the glass on it for two seconds, but looked round in other directions, then shut it up and began looking over the hillock at the hinds, which were still feeding within 100 yards of me. Swirling my walking stick round and round, I then walked quietly away, cool as a cucumber, until I got to the big wood, where I ran to an opposite point, took out my glass and very cautiously peeped through the trees to get a full view of the person or persons who were watching me.

There was Gold, the Erchless keeper, just rising up from the ground and walking away quietly. He never suspected me of anything, but thought I was taking a walk. . . . Poor Gold, little did he know to whom he was speaking [when the author met him a week later]. If I had not seen the top of his head, he would soon have seen me in to my elbows in the gralloch of a hind. This incident did me a lot of good, as I had had such an uninterrupted run of good luck that I was in danger of becoming too careless, but this sharpened me up a good deal.

So far as can be ascertained from his memoirs, Campbell never *was* caught: his career shows clearly that the professional stalker who turns poacher is the most effective of all human predators on the hill, for his knowledge of the ground and the deer are unrivalled.

Chapter Fourteen

———— ❦ ————

The Stalker's View

Naturally enough, almost all accounts of Highland sport are written by the gentlemen-amateurs; very few professional stalkers have either the inclination or the command of the written word to set down their memories. Yet whenever one of them does commit himself to paper, the result is a vivid and strikingly different picture of life on the hill.

The most telling account of this kind is the diary (hitherto unpublished) kept between 1872 and 1905 by George Ross, the stalker at Corriemulzie, a forest in Ross-shire, and said by his daughter to have been written with a quill pen made from an eagle's feather. The original was unfortunately lost in a fire.

From the measured periods of Grimble's *Deer Forests* one can learn that Corriemulzie had a reputation for 'roughness and inaccessibility', that the approach from Bridge of Oykell could 'hardly be called' a road, and that the lodge was so decrepit that 'a sportsman of the new school who went to inspect the place came away declaring he would not put his servants in such a hole!' One can also discover that 'the ground always yields some heavy stags and good heads.'

What one cannot discover from Grimble—and what springs from every page of Ross's diary—is the sheer incompetence of the sportsmen: stag after stag was missed; often a young stag or a hind was shot by mistake, and beast after beast went away wounded, with no proper attempt being made to follow it up. No doubt the inaccuracy of the Express rifles was largely to blame for the fact that so many fiascos took place, but most of the gentlemen whom Ross took to the hill seem to have been rotten shots, and it is a wonder that in his diary he did not more often give vent to irritation. It is true that his entries sometimes take on a wry note, but he is never scathing or sarcastic: he must have been an exceedingly patient man.

At the start of his time there were evidently not many stags on the

ground, and the stalking parties were often reduced to shooting hares
and grouse with the deer-rifles. Nor were they above having a shot at
hinds, even though it was much too early in the season (if a hind is shot
in August, its calf will almost certainly die, for it is still too young to
feed itself). Ross recorded entirely without comment some typical
expeditions in September 1872:

> *Sept. 24th.* Same party, today being very cold and wet, with east
> wind, we went stalking round the south side of Corriebuie followed
> stags and heinds from there to the rocks above Keas wood, stalked
> them there they both having a good chance, fired four shots each, &
> missed both, followed that lot from there to Ault-na-caorach march,
> stalked them there, Mr Eddie fired three shots & killed one Heind,
> Mr Davys had four shots all at stags and them being within fifty
> yards of him, & missed.

> *Sept. 30th.* Mr Eddie came from Amat walked up Creigloisg
> towards Mealan-da-mohr and had a stalk there and fired two shots
> at a stag, missed, we came from there to the north side of Mealan-da-
> mohr and had another stalk there at a lot of heinds and a beautiful
> stag, fired two shots at him, missed, but accidentally killed another.

Sometimes the gentlemen did not even get as far as missing. One day
in September 1873, for instance, Ross got his two stalkers 'a good
chance of the best stags' in some flats by the march, 'but owing to some
misunderstanding between them, either of them did not fire.' This
habit of hunting in pairs was common, the idea clearly being that
volleys had more chance than single shots of bringing something down.

The shepherds' dogs were sometimes used for tracking wounded
animals, but more often than not the stalking party had no dog in
attendance, so that if a stag was only wounded, the odds were that it
would escape. Thus on September 19th, 1873 'Mr Eddie' went out
round the back of Mealan-da-mohr, killed one stag at two hundred
yards, missed another twice, and later stalked another lot at which he
fired three times, wounding two of them. Undeterred, he tried again
next day, fired at a stag lying, missed it, shot at one running, wounded
it, and lost that too.

Almost all Ross's entries are perfectly straightforward, sounding
exactly as if he had spoken them ('The day was the stormiest day I ever
stood on a Hill', 'It was awful stormy with west wind and rain') and

41 Spying for deer. (Lea MacNally)

42 Stalking sequence (Lea MacNally): a shootable stag is spotted.

43   The approach.

44   The final crawl.

45   The shot.

46   Coming home.

47 Winter mortality: calf and two hinds killed by cold and starvation. (Lea MacNally)

48 Weighing a calf. (Lea MacNally)

ending with the comfortable refrain: 'We then came home.' But in 1874 – for reasons that can no longer be determined – he suddenly went into an altogether higher literary gear. Perhaps he had got married and had an audience to whom he might show off his diary: in any case, his entries were transformed, taking wing on some splendidly high-flown images: on September 14th, for example, he wrote:

We then went up at Craig-na-gobhair, and an awful pull it was, as it was uncommon stormy with wind and rain, we then went to Corriebuie, and spied some Heinds and a small stag; we stalked them, but by that time the stag was over the marsh [march] Mr Dykes then let bang with the Martini, this putting them all to a pace not easy judged, but about thirty miles an hour at any rate. Mr Alfred now aimed, and Mr Dykes too, they both fired at once, not well known who took the best aim, but a heind rolled over stone dead, after warming ourselves with Glenleishs admirable scented dew and making the beast more fit for the pad [gralloching it before it went on the deer-saddle] we then steered our course for home.

Two days later he was again in lyrical mood:

Mr Dykes fired the first shot, missed, Mr Alfred had another shot at a stag, but a heind was running at his side, and it was to her it proved fatal, as she quickly rolled over and lay quiet, as if she would be in that position a month ago. Mr Dykes now whized the wind again with more lead, which made the whole lot to pace the ground with more speed. We then spied another lot on Mealan-da-beig, we stalked them, and after Mr Dykes making the rocks to answer the voice of his rifle well, and not doing much more, we then turned home.

A week later he took the unprecedented step of describing an event that had taken place not on Corriemulzie at all, but in the neighbouring forest of Rhidorroch. The Corriemulzie party itself had a trying day, for, just as one of the gentlemen was about to shoot,

a cock grouse got up and said, quee, querr, as loud as he could, which quickly made the red cavalry to join in one strip, up the hill side. Mr Wilfred, now aiming at the stag, fired a volley or two after him, which made the red band to pace the bray with more speed than they had before ...

o

After this disappointment, however, the party's luck turned, and they got a stag and a hind out of a large lot of deer which came in over the march, obviously having been shot at earlier. It was the cause of this welcome invasion that Ross recorded:

> A gentleman came to Rhidorroch, for a few days stalking; and this being his first day out, himself and McLae observed this lot, with this nice eight-pointer stag among them, and they began to stalk them, when coming nigh to the deer McLae gave him the rifle, as soon as the gentleman came in sight the first deer, he let bang his rifle, which made a white belly to turn over no doubt, they both ran to their prey, but to their great surprise found no horns, on turning round they saw the horney chap near the sky line among the rest at full speed. He now let more lead to whiz about him, which put the whole lot to their last effort to play their fours ... this being about the time we first saw them.

As the season went on, Ross's tone became ever more jaunty and picturesque:

> *Sept. 24th.* Directly on the sky line on the east end of the Cory, we had to take the knee walking, for fully a mile distance, and in some places we had to belly sledge it, for hundreds of yards, till we passed the most of the heinds ... then there was not much time to loose, in a second bang goes the martinni from the gentleman's shoulder and after going a few paces this beautiful animal fell full length sideways on the ground, after re-scenting our breaths with real mountain dew and as usual making the animal lighter for the homeward journey, we then steered our course for home, which we reached at a rather late hour.

> *Sept. 30th.* This morning, the tops was white with snow, for the first time this season, Mr Wilfred and I ... stalked a lot on the face of the hill, and spoke to them once or twice, something louder than speech, which made them to separate our company very quick, but doing nothing more we then went to Corriebuie ...

> *Oct. 5th.* ... We were close to them when we first saw them, they observing us, made off at once, a heind was running along side the best stag, and it was to her it proved unlucky, as she quickly rolled over as dead as a boot tacket.

Oct. 9th. We came now to the back of Mealan-da-beig, and stalked a few there with a stag among them, the martinni getting permission to speak to him, and after hearing her voice, he bowed flat sideways to the ground, after visiting him and colouring the grass a bit, and tasting Glenleish's scented dew once more, we took up our course for home.

Whatever it was that gave Ross his inspiration during 1874, he never again recaptured such form, and the diary in later years is pedestrian by comparison. All the same, it contains some excellent expressions (for instance 'friliching' for gralloching), and gives a clear picture of a forest developing during the last quarter of the nineteenth century. In the 1870s only ten or a dozen stags were killed in a season at Corriemulzie (partly due to the poor marksmanship), but by the 1890s the annual bag had risen to thirty stags, as well as a few hinds. No doubt it was because no more hinds were killed that the numbers of deer built up so fast.

The gentlemen's shooting remained erratic, to say the least. In 1883 only one stag and one hind were killed during the entire season, but on October 10th alone the rifle missed three chances, and another two the next day. Often the party seems to have gone out armed only with a 'pea rifle', and in consequence even more beasts went away wounded. Several times, however, wounded stags came in from other forests, and were either shot or brought to bay by dogs (usually collies), which were used with increasing efficiency. Yet even the experience of the professional stalker could not prevent occasional lapses by people new to the sport. In 1895, when the estate had been sold and let to Sir Arthur Chichester, the new tenant perpetrated a fiasco on his third day out:

> *Sept. 2* This morning being fine, Sir Arthur went up Keas, we stalked four small stags, he fired at one with a 12-bore gun with sights, struck him on the shoulder he went off wounded, he fired at another and struck him five times, and at last I killed him with the stones, the gun was condemned right out there.

Ross clearly had a fine sense of humour. He once remarked that, as they were descending a face towards a magnificent stag, a cock grouse took off at the critical moment 'like Friday' and put the deer away. On other occasions he and his gentleman amused themselves by firing

down the loch to test the trajectory of their rifles, and exploring a cave
by candlelight. Hardly ever did he betray a hint of irritation at all the
disappointments and frustrations which he must have endured. At the
end of one season, when only four stags had been shot, he did write
'Mr Wigson missed fully twenty stags', and in 1902 he was constrained
to remark that the new tenant, Mr Pease, was 'the hardest miser I ever
met'; but otherwise he was optimism itself.

Not so David Taylor, who in 1926 used the pseudonym 'An Old
Stalker' to publish his book *Days on the Hill*, which recalled the high-
lights of his career as second stalker at Glenisla. Perhaps there is a clue
to his character in the fact that he was only a second stalker, for all
through his book, beneath the studied politeness, runs an undercurrent
of bitterness, and the reader is left with the feeling that the author
harboured a thousand grudges, no matter how effectively he concealed
them from his clients. Clearly he was not a natural leader, but a
permanent – and faintly resentful – Number Two.

It must be said in his defence that he had some absurd gentlemen to
deal with. Of one rifle, who always argued with him, particularly
when a stag had been missed, he recorded:

> There were times when he became altogether unreasonable. On
> such occasions I considered it prudent to walk away and leave him
> to follow, accompanied by the man who attended us. The latter then
> had to listen to a detailed account of all my faults and shortcomings,
> but this did not disturb me in the least. When I thought the gentleman
> had recovered his equanimity, I allowed him to overtake me. As a
> rule he never referred again to stalk or excuses, but inquired as to
> what was to be done next.

Sometimes, to keep up their scores and to bolster their reputations,
the gentlemen got their stalkers to take the shot – and then, when they
returned to the lodge, claimed the stag as their own. An even shiftier
trick was used by one man who came in announcing that he had hit a
stag (which in fact he had missed) and then sent Taylor out next day to
get the 'wounded beast'. Realising that the man meant him to shoot a
fresh stag, Taylor spent the whole day hunting for one that more or
less matched the animal they had fired at the day before. Not until last
light did he find a suitable eight-pointer, and then he took two shots to
kill it. He recalled:

I was heartily congratulated, and the other gentlemen in the lodge were brought into the larder to see the stag. Addressing them, he said, 'I knew he was hard hit and could not go far, but I can't understand how I hit him quite so far back, elevation all right, too.'

This same gentleman proved one of Taylor's trickiest customers. He later repeated the process outlined above, but this time, the stalker noticed, he was careful not to say too much about the number of points on the particular animal he claimed he had wounded. Still later he got Taylor to bring his own rifle in the first instance – but even then his behaviour was highly devious:

> The gentleman fired, and I saw him hit a calf immediately over the stag's back. As I expected he [the stag] ran clear, affording plenty of time for a good aim, and I saw my missile take him in a vital part. Just at that moment the stricken calf fell. 'You've got a calf,' said my companion. 'Looks rather like it,' I replied. The stag ran for about twenty yards and also dropped. 'He's down. I knew he couldn't possibly go far,' was the next remark addressed to me.
> On going up to the dead stag the bullet hole had to be found. After it was located he said: 'Isn't it wonderful how far an animal will travel with a bullet through the heart?' Matters now assumed a very pleasant aspect, which they certainly would not have done had I declared the real state of affairs. I have since wondered if he really thought he hit that stag, or if it was only make-believe. Or did he think he had outwitted me?

This sort of self-deception was carried to ridiculous lengths. Another of Taylor's gentlemen persistently over-estimated the weight of the beasts he had shot, and on one occasion the head stalker, knowing this man's weakness, added on about half the difference between the stag's real and estimated weight. But even this was not enough. No sooner had the card with the weight on it been sent in to the lodge than the man himself appeared in the larder, declaring that a mistake had been made, and insisting on weighing the carcase himself. 'The result,' wrote Taylor, 'was little to his satisfaction and it was difficult to determine whether he or the head stalker bore the greater appearance of humili-ation.'

It is hardly surprising that, after a lifetime spent humouring such clients, Taylor became a little jaundiced. Yet it is a pity that he soured his book with his tone of needling self-righteousness, for he also included much excellent observation of wildlife, and he was particularly good at transmitting the eerie loneliness of the hill. 'Town-dwellers ridicule Highlanders for being superstitious,' he wrote. 'Placed under the same conditions, would they be one whit better themselves?'

> My personal experience has convinced me that the superstition of the Highlanders is a natural sequence of their surroundings. Put a man, as I have often been, after dark and alone on the broken hillside, or amidst beetling precipices, hundreds of feet high, with not a human being or habitation within a radius of five miles, and a feeling of awe ... will assuredly assail him ... On quiet nights a deathly stillness reigns. Suddenly a strange sound like what one could imagine to be the half-sigh, half-groan of some colossal giant breaks upon the ears.

Such noises, Taylor knew quite well, were caused by sudden eddies of wind; but even if one did know the true explanation for phenomena of this kind, the knowledge scarcely made the hill a less mysterious place:

> Returning from hind-shooting one night after dark, I happened to cross a patch of soft peaty surface. In doing so I thought I noticed a light among my feet. Looking down, I found my boots to be all aglow with a soft bluish flame. Passing my hand over my boots, the flame adhered to my fingers, but it was absolutely devoid of heat. I walked on, and fresh flame burst from the soil at every step I took.

In spite of all his complaints, Taylor must surely have struck up genuine friendships with some of his gentlemen, for—from the sportsmen's point of view—half the enjoyment of a Highland holiday came from the taciturn yet close relationship, based on mutual respect, which one could form with one's stalker. Ever since the days of Scrope, all but the most boorish of Highland sportsmen have sensed and admired the special qualities of the men who lead them about the mountains; but the relationship has always been a curious one, for the two parties in it are utterly different. The stalker's main assets are fitness, endurance, resistance to weather, knowledge of the deer, and long experience of the hill. The more the gentleman has of these qualities, the more the stalker is likely to respect him; but often he has none, and all he can offer are money, a good rifle, enthusiasm, and an ability to shoot straight. Nevertheless, different though the two men are, they must work together in the closest co-operation if they are to succeed, and it is this necessity for hard physical effort in unison by the two-man team that gives the relationship its peculiar flavour.

The sheer isolation of their homes meant that most stalkers had little or no education; some, however, taught themselves a prodigious amount—and perhaps none more than old Robert Colquhoun, described by his namesake John Colquhoun as 'the finest specimen I ever met with of a Highlander of the old school'.

His words, like his shooting, were slow, but sure to tell. When addressing his superiors, his manner was marked by the greatest courtesy, without the least approach to servility. He was well-read in ancient history, knew all about the siege of Troy, and talked with the greatest interest of Hannibal's passage over the Alps. On one occasion when several gentlemen were talking on a disputed point of history, he stepped forward, begged pardon for interrupting them, and cleared it up to their utter amazement.

Not that by any means all stalkers were so articulate—or so easy to understand, particularly in the tense final moments before a shot. General Crealock recorded that Chisholm, the head stalker at Achnacarry, 'religiously adhered to his golden rule of silence after handing the rifle to his gentleman':

It has happened to me once or twice, years ago, when in this position, to seek his opinion; but no, not one word or sound could I get out of him; he would lie just behind me, motionless as a statue, with his dark eyes fixed on the deer, and his face and lips quite white from suppressed excitement.

Another of the Victorian pundits, Grimble, tried to pin down the special attractions of the rifle-stalker relationship:

He will occasionally make remarks which if uttered by Mr Velveteens in a Norfolk turnip field would be downright rude and treated at once as such—not that the Mr Velveteens of Norfolk or anywhere else are in the habit of forgetting their places, or at all likely to do so ...

The whole thing is so different across the Border: for days together you and your stalker are alone, and a good one will, in a variety of small ways and good-natured little attentions to your comfort, make you feel quite friendly towards him: you cannot help seeing that all his thoughts and energies are directed to your sport and comfort. There is something about it all that you instinctively feel is rendered as a pleasure, and into which enters no thought of the tips which, whether ranging from a tenner to a sovereign, according to the depth of your pocket, will be put into his hand when with sorrow you turn from the lodge to drive to the distant station, there to meet the train which will once more take you to your usual and perhaps more sedentary occupations.

And yet, Grimble warned, no matter how good your relationship may appear, you should always be careful not to give the stalker too wide an opening:

> If you 'fancy' yourself at walking, it will be wiser not to state at the dinner table that, if your stalker carries the rifle, you never yet met the man who could walk you down, for you will be very apt to meet one the next day who will at any rate have a try, even if he does not succeed. The butler and the footman are usually good friends with the stalker, and next day you will find yourself in for a tramp which will considerably astonish you, for these sort of remarks are apt to be taken literally, and the first chance will be seized of having a 'feel' at you, just to see what you are made of; there will likely enough be more walking than stalking that day.

Because the gentlemen have always financed the whole operation, they have almost always had the final say in disputes; but on one celebrated occasion, described by several authors, the rifle hoisted himself with his own pomposity. Having killed one stag in the morning, he announced that for the rest of the day he would conduct matters himself; the stalker was to carry the rifle, and was not to speak unless spoken to, being specifically forbidden to volunteer remarks. Later that day the expert spied the antlers of a stag and he proceeded to stalk it, with his follower studiously obeying the orders he had been given. About three o'clock, to his own delight, the former found himself lying comfortably behind a rock within shot of his quarry, which was lying down. He proceeded to eat his lunch, keeping a wary eye on the beast.

About four-thirty he remarked to the stalker, 'This stag's a long time getting up.' Stalker: 'Aye, he will be verra long arising.' 5 p.m.: above remarks repeated. 5.30 p.m.: ditto. 6 p.m.: ditto. Exasperated sportsman: 'What the devil do you mean?' Stalker: 'He will be long arising, because he is deid!' The expert had carefully stalked the corpse of the stag he had killed in the morning.

Chapter Fifteen

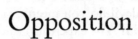

Opposition

In retrospect it is surprising that no serious opposition to deer-stalking was ever organised. By the end of the nineteenth century the deer-forests occupied 3½ million acres, or nearly a quarter of the entire area of Scotland; and yet they employed (it was calculated at the time) no more than 800 men full-time, and perhaps another 1,000 part-time. Moreover, the entire system of deer-stalking was held by many to be 'a most deplorable economical vice and public loss', since in critics' eyes it depopulated huge areas of the country, prevented those areas from being put to more productive uses, and (worst of all) demoralised the few people employed there by turning them to drink and indolence.

Several heavy-handed official attempts were made to establish the truth of such claims, among them the Crofters' Commission of 1883 and the Royal Commission on the Highlands and Islands of 1892; but the general effect of such inquiries was always to strengthen the stalkers' hands. In a paper which he wrote for the Commission of 1883, George Malcolm, factor of the Invergarry estate (and clearly a man with wide experience of the Highlands), pointed out that most of the criticism came from people who had no idea what they were talking about:

> It has been in recent years not uncommon to meet with the most sweeping condemnation of deer-forests, but rarely has any attempt been made by the authors of such attacks to approach the subject dispassionately ... There has been nothing but unreasoning denunciation by men whose position and pursuits have precluded them from acquiring that knowledge requisite to a fair consideration of the subject.

Malcolm went on to outline the economic factors which had produced such a strange situation. The most powerful was the collapse of the markets for mutton and wool and the consequent decline of the Highland sheep farm. 'The idea of importing mutton, dead or alive, from America or any of our colonies,' he wrote, 'would have been considered the height of improbability' a few years go. Yet in 1882, 488 million pounds of wool had been imported, and as a result no one wanted the Highland farms any longer:

> Excellent and most desirable holdings, which eight or ten years ago would have produced an embarrassment of offers, have been utterly without tenders ... although it was well known that the landlords were prepared to make large reductions in rent.

Far from being a 'public wrong' (as it was often called) the substitution of deer for sheep had become an economic necessity. Nor did Malcolm accept the fact that the formation of the deer-forests had caused the eviction of any humans: in the past fifty years, he wrote, the human population of the Highlands had scarcely changed. As for the claim that the morals of the gillies were undermined by employment in deer-forests – this, he said, was total invention:

> The men who are employed as gillies are generally taken from the ordinary crofter population of the neighbourhood, and are engaged as a rule for not longer than two months. In many cases the crofters' horses also are engaged ...
>
> It is certainly untrue of these men that their moral character is in any way lowered by their relations with deer-forests ... No distinct and reliable proof of these assertions of insobriety etc. has ever been given.
>
> The usual daily wage of a gillie may be stated as 3s. for himself and 3s. besides for his pony, if he has one. His pony is grazed in the forest while employed there, and he himself has a free bed and fuel for cooking etc., and generally, though not in every case, a lunch or dinner consisting of bread and meat, and one glass of whisky.
>
> Gillies seldom or never get more to eat or drink than this from their employers ... some employers give 1s. in lieu of the meal, and this gives a substantial increase to the gillie's wages, for *he* is able to provide dinner for himself for far less than a shilling.

Here Malcolm was no doubt being a little naive: the mere fact that the gillies were earning money, however little, gave them greater opportunity for buying and drinking whisky than they would have had if they had been out of work altogether. (In this context he might also have mentioned the Gillies' Ball – an annual orgy which, in many forests, traditionally brought the stalking season to a close.)

In general, Malcolm concluded, the local benefits to the Highlands 'are out of sight in favour of the forests'. Whereas the sheep farmers were never seen in the hills from one year to the next, and spent not a penny on their estates, a sporting proprietor was present for at least three months of the year, and spent immense sums in putting, or keeping, his forest in order:

> He has the lodge and other buildings, which are often extensive, to keep up for the whole year; and in repairs, alterations and additions to the buildings, in fencing, roads and path-making, in the purchase and conveyance of supplies and stores, and in various other ways, he necessarily expends every year a large sum of money, three fourths of which at least... goes into the pockets of local tradesmen, mechanics and labourers.

In one case with which Malcolm was personally familiar, the proprietor had spent £57,000 during seventeen years; and in another case, quoted during the same inquiry, a sporting owner himself gave some telling evidence:

> I have planted 8000 acres with twenty-four million trees, and that I am going on with as quickly as the seasons permit. I have put up more than seventy-six miles of my own internal fences, & I have joined with my neighbours in putting up more than thirty-four miles of march fence. I have made 473 miles of open drains. I have made over twenty miles of carriage road, & more than eighteen miles of pony tracks and walks. The whole outlay I have made during twelve years has been £180,000.

Apart from the money which they brought into the Highlands in the form of wages for staff and craftsmen, and turnover for local businesses, the deer-forests also made substantial contributions towards local rates. 'Shootings in the personal occupation of the owner are not subject to taxation,' wrote Malcolm, 'but the large rents obtained in almost every Highland parish for those shootings which are let, very materially lighten the public burden to every rate-payer.'

In one parish, he reported, the rates paid by sportsmen amounted to twenty-four per cent of the entire sum levied, and in Inverness-shire as a whole sporting rates produced twelve and a half per cent of the total. The stalkers were thus contributing a handsome amount to local government.

In most deer-forests the community to which the sporting activities gave a living was extremely small, consisting only of the stalkers, gillies and their families. Yet in some places, such as Ardtornish and Knoydart, entire villages were subsidised by the landowner. In his book about Morvern, Philip Gaskell reckoned that

the real cost of Ardtornish Estate to Valentine Smith [the proprietor] at the end of the nineteenth century may be put at anything from £6,000 to 8,000 a year, depending on how the various charges are allocated; but it was in any case a huge sum – well over £50,000 a year in modern terms – and of inestimable value as a subsidy to the district. As the *Oban Times* – no friend of the landlords – very handsomely put it in 1899: 'It is to the credit of the proprietor of Ardtornish that the officials and labourers on his estate are probably the best housed and the best paid in all Argyllshire.'

These were obviously convincing arguments in the forests' favour. Malcolm was less persuasive when he sought to prove that the system of stalking caused only a minimal loss in food production. He estimated the annual cull of deer at some 4,650 stags and 4,555 hinds, which produced about 1,226,000 pounds of venison; and this, he calculated (having worked out the number of the sheep carcases which the land could theoretically have produced), meant that 'the amount of meat lost to the nation by the use of the ground as deer-forests is 0·186 per cent. – an utterly inappreciable ratio.' It was true, he added, that most of the venison was given away, and that very little found its way on to the open market:

But it is nevertheless indisputably true that, in one form or another, it is all utilised as human food, and a full half of it is bestowed on people – the crofters, shepherds, keepers and cottars of the districts – who are not in circumstances to purchase, except at rare intervals, mutton or beef for their families.

All these points were thoroughly debated at the time; but although the Commissions of 1883 and 1892 both recommended that a check should be put on the spread of deer-forests, no positive action was taken. Despite vague talk of an artificial resettling of the Highlands, it was obvious that any such enterprise would cost an immense amount of public money. The truth—no matter how unattractive it might seem to liberal reformers—was clear: just as the deer alone had the physical stamina to withstand the rigours of the climate and the mountains, so they alone had the power of attracting money into the Highlands. The fact that the people who came to stalk were rich and aristocratic gave no small offence to politicians with egalitarian principles; yet that was the way the system worked—and no other system was feasible.

This fact, however, by no means put an end to complaints, which continued to rumble out in the press and from political platforms: in particular, the idea was advanced (in the words of S. P. J. Merlin, a barrister, who wrote a special report on the forest of Atholl) that 'the owners of the deer-forests of Scotland are keeping for the purposes of their own selfish sport a large area of the country which might be better employed for the benefit of the people, and that, in short, the pleasures of the few are standing in the way of, and over-riding, the grave needs of the many.'

To scotch this kind of fallacy, the Marquis of Tullibardine (later the eighth Duke of Atholl) conceived a novel and excellently practical plan: in August 1909 he invited a tribunal of nine working men from various urban environments to come and inspect the forest of Atholl for themselves, so that they would know once and for all what sort of land it was. The delegates were deliberately chosen 'from the very class whence the demand for small holdings [of land] arises': they were a shuttle-maker and a cycle agent from Dundee, a steel-works foreman and a joiner from Glasgow, a tanner and a compositor from Crieff, an engineer and an iron moulder from Edinburgh, and a farm labourer from Aberdeen. Three of them were keen amateur gardeners; four were conservatives, and five liberals—among them several men who had in the past attacked the deer-forests vociferously.

Their tour took place on Friday August 20th, and it must have been quite a physical challenge to the city-dwellers, for on foot and on horseback they covered thirty miles in the day. Starting from Blair Castle, and ascending several of the main hills, they directly surveyed more than 40,000 acres, or nearly a third of the entire forest.

According to S. P. J. Merlin, who himself went out with the party,

at the commencement of the enquiry a certain number of the representatives in their demeanour were obviously—and quite properly—suspicious of the whole proceedings. This attitude was however gradually displaced by the frank replies of Lord Tullibardine to the lengthy cross-examinations to which he was subjected, and by the readiness with which all suggestions, made by the representatives, as to the procedure to be adopted, were accepted.

Before the tour began a list of questions was read out by Herbert L. Tebbs, another barrister who also accompanied the party. Each delegate was asked to bear in mind such problems as '1. What is the nature of the land comprised in the Atholl Deer Forest?' and '2. In your opinion is any of the land comprised in the said Forest suitable for agricultural purposes or for small holdings, or for some other and what purposes?'

Thus primed, they set off—and it is a thousand pities that no photograph of the party survived. What did Edmund Philips, the compositor, wear? Shirt-sleeves, perhaps, for it was August. But braces over his shirt? And had he borrowed some boots, or did he mince up and down Ben Dearg in his city shoes? None of the party can have been keener than Alexander Gow, the shuttle-maker with liberal leanings, for the Marquis had promised him the free gift of any land he could discover which proved suitable for a smallholding. But he—like all the others—was time and again frustrated:

From the mountain tops we repeatedly saw spots below us which, while bathed and glistening in fleeting sunshine, looked verdant and promising sites for possible small holdings. When, however, a little while later we examined the selfsame spots, it was found that the verdure was wet moss—sometimes many inches deep—without a vestige of loam beneath it. Mr Gow ... was frequently disappointed by these views whose enchantment disappeared with the intervening distance. It is just possible that some of those who have alleged that this forest contained good agricultural possibilities were deluded by similar optical illusions to those which hereabouts deceived us.

Throughout the day the members of the party were encouraged to pick their own route, and in general they were treated with the utmost openness. Their last area for inspection was Glen Tilt—allegedly the scene of the most brutal evictions—and after viewing it they made their way wearily back to the castle, where they filled in the questionnaire.

One set of answers is enough to illustrate the striking unanimity with which they reacted to their day on the hill. To question Number 2 about the nature of the land (quoted on p. 213), they replied as follows:

A. Macpherson. 'It is of no use for small holdings or allotments. The climate and distance from markets make it still more unsuitable.'

D. Scrymgeour. 'On the edge of Glen Tilt side of the forest some part might be planted with trees. It is not suitable for small holdings. The existence of small holders would be miserable up there, owing to poor soil and distant markets.'

Alexander Gow. 'This question is met by answer to Question 1' (to which he had replied by describing the land as totally unsuitable for any farming enterprise).

George Minty. 'In my opinion none of the land is suitable for small holdings or for any other agricultural purpose.'

James Douglas. 'By no means could it, in my opinion, be utilised for any other purpose than deer forest.'

Robert Johnstone. 'In my opinion none of the land is suitable for small holdings or for any agricultural purpose.'

R. Chisholm. 'No, not in the deer forest.'

James Thomson. 'Emphatically no.'

E. Phillips. 'No, I don't think it is of any use for any such purpose, except on the very lowest parts which might be useful for sheep.'

The laird's victory was total, right through to Question 11, which asked what effect the use of the land for deer-forest had on employment in the immediate neighbourhood. Again the replies were unanimous—that the deer-forest positively increased employment, or even doubled the amount of work that sheep farms could provide, and was 'good for the working classes of the districts generally'. When asked if they would like to make any extra points about their day, several of the delegates remarked on the good relationship which obviously existed between the Atholl family and its employees; and Scrymgeour, the tanner from Crieff, was charitable enough not only to record 'the fine kindly feeling that existed between the owners and employees on the estate', but also to admit that his opinion of the Atholl deer-forest, 'formed on newspaper reports', had been 'quite changed' by his personal inspection of the ground.

Thus the Atholl family damped down–for the time being, at any rate–what the report of the inspection called 'a burning political issue' in the neighbourhood. Fuzzy Liberal ideals were no match for the harsh realities of the red deer's life–as Lloyd George found, when in 1913, as Chancellor of the Exchequer, he launched a vigorous attack on Scottish landlords, accusing them of wasting vast areas of land and selfishly evicting people from their homes. In his auto-biography, *Looking Back*, the Duke of Sutherland recalled how he had taken up the politician's wild exaggerations:

'Tens of thousands of people are turned out of their homes in order to get sport,' thundered the Chancellor ... in a vicious speech at Swindon, adding that it was his aim to repopulate the glens, reafforest the hillsides, and bring the wasted acres under cultivation ...

I decided to expose the futility of Lloyd George's allegations by writing a letter to the *Daily Mail* offering to sell the Government 200,000 acres at £2 an acre. Lloyd George's reaction was to hold an enquiry and reject my proposal on the grounds that the land was not worth the price I was asking, as I well knew. Whereupon I offered him double the acreage for just about half the price per acre–but again he declined.

The correspondence, the Duke recorded, became 'lengthy and at times extremely acrimonious', but he had easily the better of it. In one broad-side he wrote, 'Even audiences which, like yourself, have never visited a deer-forest are unlikely to be impressed by your tears for the per-version of land in the Highlands while you denounce 22s. 6d. per acre for such land as a wholly excessive price ... ' Again, the victory was to the laird, for the politician (who was guyed by a cartoon in the *Bystander*) had ventured into territory far beyond his ken.

Not until the gigantic upheaval of the First World War was there a real change in the pattern of Highland stalking–and the innovations made then were the result of practical necessity rather than of political pressure. For obvious reasons, during the war years many forests went unlet and others were let for very small sums; from 1915 there was a severe shortage both of ammunition and of able-bodied men. Even so, the annual cull of some 12,000 animals was maintained in 1916 and greatly stepped up in 1917 to about 16,000, under the direction of the

P

Venison Supply Committee set up by the Board of Agriculture. 'Only those who have had experience of bringing in deer shorthanded from difficult ground in wild weather,' said a later report, 'can realise the labour and strain which these figures represent.'

Two exceptionally severe winters, in 1917–18 and 1918–19, took further toll of deer numbers, and so helped make room for the extra stocks of cattle and sheep which were put to graze on the Scottish hills, sometimes at the suggestion of the owner, and sometimes under pressure from the authorities. Another change was that, in the absence of fit young keepers, the fox population increased substantially. The war thus considerably altered the animal balance in the Highlands.

Even so, the government thought fit, in November 1919, to set up yet another inquiry, this time appointing a departmental committee to report on the 'Lands in Scotland used as Deer Forests' and to advise 'which, if any, of these lands might profitably be put to other uses'. Under the chairmanship of Sir John Stirling Maxwell (the owner of Corrour Forest, in Inverness-shire), the committee held twelve sittings, heard evidence from 287 witnesses, inspected fifty-six deer-forests, and circulated a questionnaire to still more owners and tenants. But on January 22nd, 1921, when the inquiry had already cost some £3,000, the chairman was instructed that 'owing to the financial stringency' his inspections were to be discontinued. The inquiry thus came to a premature end, and the committee's report – though containing some sensible recommendations for such policies as better heather-burning and heavier stocking with domestic grazers – concluded with the usual rather futile remarks: that there were too many deer and too many forests, and that any further extension of the deer ground should be forbidden by statute.

Needless to say, no statute was passed; but in fact a slackening of demand during the inter-war years put a natural stop to any further expansion. For the first time stalking was blighted by a form of social stigma. 'The first and major difficulty is that the average woman quite definitely and rather naturally dislikes deer forests,' wrote Sir Iain Colquhoun in an essay called *The Future of Deer-Stalking* published in 1925; and he added:

In these days, when they are no longer content to sit indoors most of the day, but on the contrary expect to be entertained and spend as much time in the open air as the men, their point of view must be studied.

Colquhoun, who had a forest of his own and habitually went to the hill barefoot, acting as his guests' stalker, was all too familiar with the problem:

> The rifles are off to the hill long before the ladies appear for breakfast, returning as a rule about half-way through dinner, dead tired. Afterwards, having refused to play bridge, they make a spasmodic series of unintelligent remarks, and having obtained early permission from their hostess, yawn themselves gratefully to bed.

Colquhoun had also 'noticed with sorrow' that among the young there appeared to be 'no tradition of hardihood' and – perhaps in an attempt to galvanise them – he poured scorn on the new generation:

> They are fundamentally soft, and not the least ashamed of it ... If they are wet and cold, and unwilling to suffer further discomfort, they do not hesitate to let the stalker know. 'Very sensible,' say the ladies; 'after all, they are out for their own amusement.' Possibly so; but when our young men cease to find pleasure in overcoming hardship, when they find no joy in scornfully refusing to admit the weariness of the flesh or in taking the last ounce out of themselves, then personally I have but little use for that 'sensible' type of sportsman. He had better confine his activities to the low ground and the drawing-room.

The 1920s and 1930s, then, were a period of retrenchment for stalking. Probably the biggest innovation was the gradual introduction of motor transport, which enabled the remotest glens to be reached and stalked more easily. In 1924 the presence of cars in the Highlands was novel enough for Lady Evelyn Cobbold, proprietor of Glencarron, to cut quite a dash when she took a photograph of her head stalker, Grant, bringing home five hinds lashed on the back of a two-seater Calcott. Thereafter the use of cars for stalking must have steadily increased.

Occasionally there was a brief return to the style of the old days – as in 1928, when the Duke of Sutherland entertained King Alfonso of Spain to a grand deer-drive at Loch Choire, the most remote and beautiful of all his forests. The King – dapper and roguishly moustachioed – arrived at Dunrobin Castle by battleship and proceeded to the hinterland wearing a pair of immense striped bloomers. The party, which included the Marquess and Marchioness of Londonderry, drove to the lodge at the north end of Loch Choire and went on by boat to take up their positions in the *bheallach*, or pass, at the far end of the water. The whole of the Klibreck range was then driven towards them, and even though the wind changed, sending many of the deer back through the line of beaters, Alfonso killed seven stags. So excited was he by the day's sport that he sent a telegram announcing his bag to King George V at Balmoral.

Extravagant entertainments of this kind became increasingly rare; but the 1920s did at least produce the best known of all novels about stalking — *John Macnab*, which was first published in 1925. The author, John Buchan, was an experienced and enthusiastic stalker; most years he went north for an autumn holiday, staying one week at Ardtornish, on the west coast, and another at Glenetive, in Argyllshire — both excellent forests. He was a good rifle shot, a better fisherman, and an exceptional walker, able to cover twenty miles over the hill one day after another.

He thus knew exactly what he was writing about when he came to tell the story of how three professional men in London — a lawyer (Sir Edward Leithen), a cabinet minister (Lord Lamancha) and a banker (John Palliser-Yeates) — seek to throw off the lethargy which besets them all by issuing a challenge to three Highland lairds under the composite pseudonym of John Macnab. Between midnight on a certain date and midnight on the next (their provocative letters state) John Macnab will poach a salmon or a stag from each of the three lairds and return the fish or carcase to its rightful owner.

Clearly the author had enormous fun in putting his heroes through their Highland paces: the book contains a great deal of hard hill walking and running, some first-class stalking and fishing scenes, and much rather elephantine manoeuvring as the threatened estates deploy their defences (in one case, a small army of navvies). Apart from its romantic elements, which now strike an embarrassing note, the novel still reads extremely well. The hill country described — and indeed the map showing the layout of the forests under attack — bears striking similarities to Ardtornish; and the book was dedicated to Rosalind Maitland, sister of Gerard Craig Sellar, who had so often been Buchan's host on the west coast.

Yet perhaps more interesting than the book itself is the man who is said to have inspired it. In the novel the three leading characters attribute their idea to 'poor old Jim Tarras', who 'had a little place somewhere in Moray', had spent time big-game hunting in Africa, and used to

write to the owner of a deer forest and present his compliments, and beg to inform him that between certain dates he proposed to kill one of his stags. When he killed it, he undertook to deliver it to the owner, for he wasn't a thief.

It is well known that the original of 'Jim Tarras' was Captain Jimmy Brander Dunbar, a Lowland laird who had an estate called Pitgavenie near Elgin, on the coast of Morayshire, and became a notorious poacher. (His home territory, oddly enough, was much the same as that of Charles St John.)

Yet probably very few readers realise the degree to which the author romanticised both the character and the exploits of his original, who was not very attractive. People who met Dunbar in his old age, when he had mellowed, thought him a splendid character—eccentric, certainly, but benevolent, and basking in his reputation as a great sportsman. In fact he was quite different. His whole life seems to have been soured by his experience as a boy at Rugby, where, a Scot speaking only rough English, he could at first scarcely make himself understood, and in consequence was persistently bullied. The experience left him with an ineradicable hatred of anyone in authority, and in particular of anyone connected with public schools.

Even before he went to Rugby his character had been shown up as less than admirable. When he was ten, and his brother Archie eight, their father gave them both ·410 shotguns and a box of cartridges apiece. The first of these cartridges the boys fired at each other's kilted backsides, from progressively decreasing ranges, until they were knocked over by the impact of the pellets. Having thus ascertained the effective range of their guns, Jimmy set about poaching his father's pheasants, which he sold in the town to finance the purchase of more ammunition.

Though he shot freely without permission on other people's land, be became exceedingly annoyed if he discovered anyone at large on his own. Once, finding a strange youth loading turnips into a cart, he knocked him unconscious, only to learn later that the boy was the son of the new farm tenant. On another occasion he was walking round Loch Spynie, armed (as always) with a ·22, when he saw a man he did not recognise fishing in a boat some fifty yards from the shore. Without

warning he put up his rifle and shot the pipe from the man's mouth –
only to discover afterwards that he was the local solicitor to whom he
had just let the fishing.

Once at breakfast in a neighbouring lodge, where the party was
staying for a few days' grouse shooting, he startled the company by
describing with relish one of his favourite weekend recreations. His
habit (he told the horrified ladies) was to row out into the loch with
the dinghy full of terriers and a cat in a sack. When he was a good
distance from land he would throw the cat over the side, give it a
minute's start, and then hunt the terriers at the animal as though it
were an otter.

On his 3,000-acre estate he took care to employ illiterates only, so
that his keepers, foresters and farm workmen, being unable to read or
write, could not know how badly he was cheating them. On and off
the estate he squabbled constantly with local people. Although he
married a charming woman, who bore him two daughters, she left
him, taking the children, never to return.

Thereafter his house was in a disgusting state. Visitors were welcomed
by the skull of a German sniper whom Dunbar had decapitated during
the First World War. Normally he never cleaned or polished anything
except his firearms; but this human skull was the object of regular
maintenance, and it hung like a trophy of the chase over the front door.
Inside, the house stank bestially of the dogs which lived indoors, and
the ceilings were pitted with craters and stained with livid blotches,
for whenever the laird was annoyed by flies, he would sit in his chair
and shoot them with an air-rifle. He habitually wore shoes which he
had made himself from cow-hide, and a kilt that was older than
himself.

This strange character's connection with John Buchan was both
fortuitous and slender; and it is hard to say exactly how the idea of
John Macnab originated, for Dunbar, on different occasions, told
several different versions of the story. One claimed that during his time
in the army he had made a bet one evening in the mess for £20, boasting that he would kill a stag in any forest in Scotland – and that he
succeeded in Inverlochy. But the most frequently heard version related
simply that, for three consecutive summers, he rented small crofts of
about fifty acres in deer country. As usual he shot and caught everything – deer, grouse and salmon – which passed over, through or near
his territory.

All that happened, it seems, was that Buchan met him one evening in the pub, primed him with whisky (to which he was extremely partial) and, by leading him on to boast about his exploits, invented the story of John Macnab there and then. But there is no evidence that Dunbar himself ever issued a challenge to the lairds on whose land he proposed to poach, as John Macnab does in the novel. 'Poor old Jim Tarras' was handsomely served by the novelist: the whole concept of the book was far more romantic and amusing than the person who inspired it.

No connection with poachers could be ascribed to Frank Fraser Darling, the distinguished naturalist who in 1937 produced one of the most delightful books ever written about the Highlands, *A Herd of Red Deer*. Based on two years of intensive observation in the forests of Dundonnell, Gruinard and Letterewe in Wester Ross, this book is a classic example of how detailed scientific and ecological information can be presented in human fashion. Modest, perceptive, accurate, realistic yet romantic as well, the author makes an ideal companion for a stay in deer country.

His descriptions of the deer are of absorbing interest, for he watched them and reported their behaviour in every season and every kind of weather. Yet almost more fascinating is his account of the west coast hills, their effect on him, and his own reactions:

Nowhere have I felt more the ephemeral nature of individual man than after spending some days alone in this grey, broken country. I have lain sometimes on the western slopes of Beinn a' Chaisgein Beag, 'the hill of cheese', which are rich and pleasant, and where, doubtless, man's animals have grazed in past times. The burns fall to the waters of the Fionn Loch, gleaming as white as its name in the June sun, and there are traces of the dwellings of men. I have heard the singing of women's voices and the laughter of little children in this place. Perhaps the play of wind and falling water made these sounds – I neither know nor care – I was content to listen in the beauty of the moment.

These strange qualities of the country, inviting or repelling, are real to men ... There are many ... places in the Scottish Highlands where seasoned men – myself too – have had to move out at nightfall. The sensation is not fear, for intimate knowledge of the place disposes of that; but there is discomfort sufficient to make a man move. These problems of the character of individual places must remain.

In spite of these unnerving incidents, Fraser Darling found that the country as a whole had 'a joyful quality' which delighted him; and to feel its pulse more clearly he spent the summer of 1935 barefoot. After a fortnight of discomfort, he recalled, he had his reward:

> The whole threshold of awareness was raised, I was never fatigued, and stalking became very much easier. This ease in approaching animals was something more than what was gained by leaving off heavy and possibly noisy shoes. The whole organism worked in better co-ordination.

For anyone with an interest in the Highlands, it is well worth going back forty years to accompany Fraser Darling on his barefoot patrols, to share the deer's environment, day and night, to marvel at the way a man's eyesight improves if he lives in the open, and to ponder the question of how the brain of an experienced observer can elicit so much information from the almost imperceptible data that the eye receives – how it is possible to tell at once that the animal sighted nearly half a mile away is a stag, even though its antlers are invisible, or that the beast which before was facing down the hill is now looking in your direction.

During both world wars a number of Highland stalkers had a chance of turning their peacetime skills to military advantage, by becoming snipers. In both the great conflicts, history repeated itself with uncanny precision. At the start of the First World War the Germans soon showed themselves to be highly effective snipers, but the British, believing that sniping was an old-fashioned method of warfare, had entirely neglected the art. Then a man called Hesketh Pritchard – a well known stalker and game-shot – visited the lines and saw what could be achieved by accurate sniper fire in terms of casualties inflicted and morale undermined; so on his own initiative he collected some sporting rifles and himself trained a cadre of men, including a large proportion of Highlanders, who soon became every bit as proficient as the enemy.

In the Second Word War the same thing happened. The British had once more decided that snipers had no place in the modern battle line, and the sniper wing of the Small Arms School at Hythe had been closed down. Finding that the Germans were again extremely proficient, the War Office approached the Lovat Scouts (many of whose

officers and men came from the Highlands) and asked them to form a
new sniper wing that could train men in 21 Army Group, in preparation
for the Normandy Landings of 1944. The task was carried out initially
by Lord Dulverton (an officer in the Lovat Scouts), who collected a
group of non-commissioned officers and set about harnessing their
lifelong knowledge of rifle-shooting, fieldcraft, camouflage and
spying with telescopes for use against human targets. These pioneers,
reinforced by instructors from the Small Arms School, trained officers
and N.C.O.s from every battalion in 21 Army Group, and after the
crossing of the Seine in 1944 took the sniper school to Holland – with
great success.

In general it was found that the professional stalker's natural skills
formed an excellent basis for a sniper's education: and apart from the
obvious need for a man to be a good shot, the most rewarding skill –
and one of the most difficult to acquire – was that of using a telescope.

Even the experience of the two world wars did not convince the
pundits that the sniper's profession was one worth keeping up, and the
knowledge gained was once more allowed to die away. But the
efficacy of highly trained marksmen has again been demonstrated in
Northern Ireland, and the sniper wing at the School of Infantry is once
more very active. Some of its members go to Scotland every winter for
practice on live targets, in the form of hind shooting, always finding
their excursion to the Highlands immensely valuable.

Chapter Sixteen

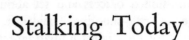

Stalking Today

Since the Second World War there has gradually evolved – both at state level and on the part of individual landowners – a far more responsible and thoughtful attitude towards the deer. Instead of being regarded simply as sporting targets, they are seen as a substantial national asset, of scientific as well as sporting interest, and as a result they are being managed in an increasingly professional way.

The first steps towards a methodical policy were taken in 1952, when the government set up a committee of inquiry to examine the possibility of introducing close seasons for deer in Scotland. Two factors provoked this move – one, the increase in the numbers of deer marauding on farm land, and the other the public outcry against organised poaching; yet after two years' work the committee found itself unable to agree on when the close seasons should be, and not until 1959 did the Deer (Scotland) Act become law. This set close seasons for red deer (for the first time since the Middle Ages) and also brought into being the body that has ever since been most closely connected with the deer's welfare – the Red Deer Commission.

The Commission has always been a small body, with headquarters in Inverness and a field force of six or eight professional stalkers who move about the Highlands as their work dictates. Its task is twofold and – at first glance – contradictory: both to conserve the deer, and at the same time to control (i.e. reduce) their numbers. At first the Commission was held in low regard, for its early work consisted largely in eliminating pockets of deer that had established themselves in unsuitable places. Because their job was to go about exterminating whole groups of deer, rather than merely culling some, as would have been done on the hill, the Commission's stalkers inevitably gained the reputation of being butchers.

This, however, they gradually lived down, and it is now universally acknowledged that they have contributed enormously to the general fund of knowledge about deer in Scotland. The Commission's Field Officer, or senior stalker, Louis Stewart, probably has greater experience than anyone else alive of the Scottish deer and their habitat, and his reputation is much enhanced by the quiet authority with which he deploys his knowledge. His greatest single contribution has been the introduction of the system of deer-counting, which the Commission has progressively refined in the light of each season's experience, and which is now applied with a degree of precision that would have been thought impossible a few years ago.

As soon as the hind-shooting has finished, in the middle of February, the Commission's team takes to the hill, eight or ten strong, often reinforced by men from the Nature Conservancy and by stalkers from the estates on which the count is being held. By this time of year the deer are at their weakest, and will not move much unless they are pushed hard; even so, the weather must be right for the operation to succeed – that is, the days must be reasonably clear, and the snow must be lying at least down to the 2,000-foot contour. With the ridges thus turned into Arctic barriers, the deer will not leave the glen in which they are sheltering, and because they are hefted to the same ground day after day, there is little chance of any being counted twice.

When conditions are favourable, the counters set out, armed with maps for precise navigation, binoculars for scanning, telescopes for positive identification, and two-way radios for communication with each other. By moving the deer gently, one herd at a time, they can gain an accurate idea of the population of every glen. The ground to be covered in each day's count is marked off in advance on large-scale maps, and each major self-contained area – such as, for instance, the 250,000 acres of the Monadhliath mountains – is selected to take advantage of lochs, main roads and strips of farm land which the deer are not likely to cross.

By this process, and by collecting statistics from the various forests, the Commission has gradually built up the first comprehensive picture of the Highland deer population. During the 1960s numbers remained steady at about 180,000, but during the past five years the total has climbed steadily to its present level in the late 1970s of some 270,000. The increase has been due largely to a succession of mild winters, for although the human cull is 16,000 stags and 20,000 hinds a year, nature, in a winter of normal severity, also kills a great many.

Very few of the sportsmen who enjoy the Highlands from August to October have any conception of how vicious the environment and the weather become during the winter. Often the mellow autumn days are spiked with hints of the bitterness to come—with gales and rain, and storms that leave the high tops romantically dusted with snow. Yet winter does not show its claws until December, and even then the deer can survive heavy falls of snow by drawing on the physical reserves which they have built up earlier in the year. By March, however, they are at their lowest ebb, and if the snow lies on into April, thousands of them simply lie down and die from starvation and cold. The oldest and youngest are the first to go: the aged stags and hinds whose constitution has been weakened by the years, and the calves that were born too late in the summer to gain enough strength for the ordeal ahead. The Commission estimates that a bad winter may kill half the annual crop of 45,000 calves.

By no means all the forests have seen their stocks build up in keeping with the national average of fifty per cent. But that is the size of the overall increase, and most people concerned agree that the deer population is now far too high. Yet to reduce it drastically is far from easy: many estates are doing everything they can to increase their cull, but without much success. One problem is the wariness of the deer, which are exceedingly alert in any case, and become ever wilder and more difficult to approach the more they are harassed. Another difficulty is that of getting the carcases of shot deer home. In many forests ponies or boats are still the only means of transporting them; but even when these traditional methods are reinforced by the use of Land Rovers and various kinds of cross-country vehicle such as Snotracs, Argocats and Garrons, the number of deer that can be shot in a day is usually limited by the physical impossibility of bringing more into the larder by nightfall.

Ironically enough, the financial incentive to shoot more deer has never been stronger. In 1977 the price of venison reached an all-time record of more than 80p a pound, making a good stag worth at least £150 and a hind about £80; at last the estates began getting a substantial return for their produce—and even at that price the dealers were searching feverishly for more carcases, as the demand (almost entirely from the Continent) seemed insatiable.

The history of the venison trade is in itself a curious story. In Victorian and Edwardian times, as we have seen, almost all the meat from the deer forests was given away, and none was sold. The two world wars galvanised proprietors into making some form of wider distribution, but even after the Second World War venison was still held in astonishingly low regard, and entire stag carcases were sold for as little as 15s. Frank Gillon, head stalker to the fifth Duke of Sutherland, recalled the appalling (but typical) waste that occurred one autumn in the late 1940s. As usual, the Duke had taken a stalking party to Loch Choire, and the stags shot during the ten days of the party's residence were skinned and butchered in the larder, so that the meat could be distributed among the tenants of the estate when the Duke returned to his main home, Dunrobin Castle, at Golspie.

The weather, however, turned unseasonably warm, and by the time the meat was dispatched — three whole trailer-loads of haunches, saddles and shoulders — much of it was starting to turn green. At the end of the sixty-mile journey to Dunrobin it was in no condition to be given to anybody, and, because it arrived on Friday evening, Gillon could not find a butcher or dealer to take any of it. As a result, several tons of venison had to be dumped in a wood.

According to Band of Perth — now one of the most active dealers — the event that first gave impetus to the venison trade was the onset of myxomatosis in the early 1950s. With almost the entire rabbit population suddenly wiped out, game dealers found themselves abruptly deprived of their staple asset, and in looking about for something to replace it, turned to venison. Then in 1956 a dealer in Hamburg called Herbert Dietrich began making tentative approaches through the German consulate in Glasgow about buying venison, and so laid the foundations of a flourishing trade. Such is the Germans' appetite for venison that by the early 1970s they were taking eighty-five per cent of Scotland's output, and clamouring for more.

In recent years their proportion has fallen, partly because other countries such as France and Belgium have become keener to share the Highland harvest, but mainly because the Germans themselves announced regulations for the handling of venison that were so stringent that Scottish dealers feared they would be unable to comply with them. Every carcase, for instance, must reach a larder chilled to forty-five degrees Fahrenheit within ten hours of the beast being shot, and the plant in which it is to be processed within twenty-four hours. Many Scottish forests are so remote as to make compliance with such requirements extremely difficult, if not impossible.

As a result, much of the trade has been redirected to countries whose requirements are less stringent. At the same time, the threat of the German proposals has brought about a much-needed improvement in the general handling of venison, which until recently tended to be old-fashioned and amateurish. The new rules have also put an end to several scurrilous tricks – among them the practice (which was standard on one estate) of launching stag carcases into the loch and towing them home four miles behind a boat, so that by the time they reached the larder they had increased handsomely in weight, both hide and meat being thoroughly saturated. (Nor are such tricks used only on deer. One Scottish dealer recently received a salmon which weighed ten pounds: since it felt exceptionally hard, it was opened up, and the post-mortem revealed that it was in fact a six-pound fish which had been posthumously stuffed with four pounds of pebbles.)

It is a curious fact that there is scarcely any demand for venison in this country. On the Continent it is among the most highly prized meat of all, and the price per pound which Scottish dealers now pay for a carcase is nearly twice that of first-class cattle. Of Scotland's annual output of 1,300 tons of venison, worth £1½ million, only about seven per cent is sold in Britain – and at present it is just as well that the demand here is no greater, for it would be extremely hard to increase production by any significant amount.

For the future, one means of doing so may prove to be deer farming, which has recently been shown to be feasible by an experimental project carried out by the Rowett Research Institute and the Hill Farming Research Organisation at Glensaugh in Kincardineshire. The experiment began in 1970, when 500 acres of hill land were fenced in and stocked with a number of calves caught in the wild soon after birth; and already the project has yielded some fascinating information, not least the fact that deer raised by man become as tame as cattle, and come readily to the herdsman's whistle or to the rattle of a bucket.

The farm has also confirmed scientifically what has been apparent to generations of Highlanders – that the deer are easily the most efficient animals in Scotland for converting rough herbage into protein. Moreover, when fed intensively on a diet of barley-based concentrates and dried grass, they still outclass the cattle and sheep that have been bred selectively for meat production for many years: whereas cattle eat about six pounds of food to gain one pound in live weight, and sheep about three and a half, deer need only three.

Naturally enough, the animals cosseted with good feeding on the farm at Glensaugh put on weight and reach maturity far more quickly than those on the open hill, and stags are ready for market in the September of their second year, when they are only fifteen months old.

There is thus no doubt that deer can be farmed; it remains to be seen whether they can produce a high enough return to offset the costs of feeding, management and, above all, fencing.

That deer will have to be farmed in some way – on the open hill as well as in enclosures – is evident from the fact that at the same time as the population has built up, the amount of land available to the wild herds has progressively declined. Competition for the use of the mountains is far stronger that it was a hundred years ago. Once the deer shared the hills only with the sheep, but now they are pushed about and hemmed in by ever-increasing pressures.

One malign influence is that of hikers, climbers and skiers, who have taken to the Highlands in such numbers that the deer have abandoned some areas altogether, among them Cairn Gorm, Glencoe, and the Cuillins in Skye. Since there is no law of trespass in Scotland, it is impossible to keep tourists under firm control: during the stalking season most estates display notices in the glens warning walkers that it is dangerous to leave the footpaths, but many people ignore these and swarm over the hills regardless. It is only a matter of time before one of these wanderers stops – or at any rate slows down – a high-velocity bullet.

Another competitor for the land is the sport of grouse-shooting, which flourishes on the relatively dry moors in the eastern half of the country. Although deer can, and do, live happily enough on grouse moors, the more the ground is disturbed by regular shooting, the less congenial they find it.

Yet by far the greatest threat to the deer, paradoxical though it sounds, is that posed by the expansion of commercial forestry. In theory the re-establishment of the woods on a large scale is an excellent prospect for the deer: they would benefit enormously if they could winter in the shelter of mature plantations rather than on the open hill – and indeed it is the ambition of the more imaginative landowners to make this possible. In practice, however, the establishment of new forestry is as inimical to the deer as they are to forestry. Because they are such voracious browsers and bark-strippers, there is no alternative but to exclude them from new plantations by means of six-foot wire fences, which now cost £2,500 a mile. Because of the expense, the temptation is to fence in a few big blocks rather than a greater number of smaller ones; thus large areas of the best grazing on the lower slopes are put out of the deer's reach, and all too often they are denied access to the glens by miles of continuous fencing along the valley-sides. The result is that they are deprived not only of food but also of vital shelter – with deadly results.

The Forestry Commission were at first notoriously insensitive in this respect. In the years after the Second World War they condemned thousands of deer to death in the winter by sealing off mile after mile of glen with unbroken fences. Now both the Commission and private owners show far greater consideration, leaving corridors down to the low ground between the plantations, even though this necessitates more fencing and therefore greater financial outlay.

The efficiency with which, on open ground, deer prevent any natural regeneration is strikingly confirmed by a number of experiments now in progress, one of them on the royal estate at Balmoral. The great Scots pines in the Ballochbuie Woods are all between 200 and 300 years old, and the ground beneath them is mown by the deer to a smooth, undulating sward. Yet in one small block, which has been fenced off to exclude all grazing animals, Scots pine and rowan seedlings have sprouted by the hundred, a dozen or more to every square yard. If the deer were kept out altogether, the Ballochbuie Woods would renew themselves naturally; but as long as the deer are present, not a single new tree will grow.

Whether it will ever be possible to reopen plantations to the deer on a large scale is a matter of some dispute. Much depends on the types of tree that are planted: rough-barked species such as larch and the native Scots pine are relatively immune to bark-stripping; but the kinds that grow best in Scottish conditions, among them sitka spruce and lodgepole pine, are highly vulnerable, and even in a mature plantation the presence of deer would lead to an intolerable amount of damage. The idea of deer living comfortably in some sort of replica of the ancient Caledonian forest is thus – unfortunately – no more than a dream.

With all these pressures on them, it is clear that the deer need better management than ever. For at least a century some forests have fed their stags during the winter: if maize or sheep-nuts are put out behind the stalker's house, word soon goes round among the senior gentlemen in the herd, who then foregather in the glen every evening and restore the strength which they have lost during the rut. But it has never been feasible to feed the hinds, which need building up just as much, if not more than, the stags. The main reason is the prohibitive expense; but the sheer physical difficulty involved is also a major impediment. Unlike the stags, which become fairly tame during the winter, the hinds never lose their fear of man, and for as long as the weather remains open, they cling to the highest pastures. Even when the snow comes, they tend to heft to remote corries and glens into which food simply cannot be transported.

It is now recognised that the most effective way of increasing the food supply is to drain and fertilise the best grazing ground in the forest – or at any rate that which can be reached by mechanical vehicles. To open new drains and spread basic slag during the spring is a far better investment than carting out hay and sheep-cobs in the depths of winter. Thus in many forests a simple form of deer hus-bandry is already being practised – and although deer-stalking is still primarily a form of sport, it is also a fact that the deer give a yield of excellent meat from the poorest of hill grazings, and the rifle is the only practical means of gathering this harvest.

With the possible exception of fox-hunting, Highland deer-stalking is the most exciting field sport that the British Isles can offer, and it is practised now with at least as great enthusiasm as it attracted a hundred years ago. Today, however, a far more humane code of behaviour is observed than in Victorian times. Every rifleman who goes to the hill is expected to have zeroed his weapon the day before. The beasts shot are carefully chosen, and every effort is made to approach within a hundred yards, so that a clean, immediate kill is possible. If a beast *should* be wounded, any professional stalker will make the most strenuous efforts to follow it up and dispatch it quickly. Almost every-body uses telescopic sights – the idea of bringing off a pretty or unusual shot having long since gone out of fashion.

Like all other field sports, stalking has become far more democratic. No longer the privilege of the aristocracy, it is now enjoyed by anyone who can afford it. Although a few lairds still have the financial resources to do all their own stalking, the majority of forests are let. Rents on the best grounds have risen to more than £100 a stag, and, because of the expense, an increasing proportion of tenants come from abroad – from Germany, France, Belgium, Norway, Holland, Switzerland and America. For an American, who is used to getting one deer (or maybe two) in an entire season – and that in ferocious competition with a press of other hunters – it is an astonishing experience to be able to watch several hundred stags in a single herd, choose the best one to shoot, and to go on repeating this agreeable process for as long as his money holds out.

One recent innovation has been the introduction of the Continental

Q

system of charging much higher fees for the right to shoot exceptional animals. Whereas the policy on most estates is to cull the
mature and old stags with relatively poor heads, the tendency now is
for each forest to allow its tenants to shoot perhaps a couple of royals
and a few ten- or eleven-pointers each season, charging up to £500
extra for the privilege of securing one such beast.

Fortunately it is also possible to stalk at a much more modest level —
and most stalking parties are now modest affairs. No longer does the
Limited Mail bear armies of butlers, housemaids, cooks and nannies
northwards in the autumn: if anyone now accompanies the stalkers, it
will be probably be a girl engaged to do the cooking for the fortnight,
and in the lodges which they briefly inhabit the holidaymakers usually
do all the menial chores themselves, stoking the boiler, laying the fires,
and doing the washing-up with a lack of pretension that would have
appalled the Victorians.

Yet for the modern rifleman, the most fascinating aspect of Scottish
stalking is that in the past century it has scarcely changed. Many of the
peripheral details are different, it is true: the stalker probably rides out
to his starting-point in a Land Rover rather than on a pony; the rifle
he now uses is a miracle of power and precision compared with the
weapons of a century ago; if his stalk is disturbed by interlopers, it will
not be by ''Arry' in appalling checks, but by hikers clad in fluorescent
anoraks; if he shoots a beast, it may come home on an Argocat or a
Snotrac rather than on a horse; and at the lodge in the evening, the
horrors of the Victorian smoking-room have given way to relaxed
informality.

Yet all these are marginal details: the central operation — of using
field-craft and physical stamina to come within a hundred yards of a
surpassingly vigilant quarry in open country — this is precisely the
same. Once the stalker has set foot on the hill, he is just as dependent
on his legs, his wind and his wits as were his Victorian predecessors.
Like them, he is alone with the grouse, the ptarmigan, the eagles and
the deer. Like them, he finds in the Highlands an incomparable
escape from the pressures of normal life.

Besides, many forests are still invincibly romantic and remote.
Knoydart, for instance, has no access by road; to reach this wonderful
west coast peninsula one must take a boat from Mallaig; and no one
who has made the brief voyage will forget the sight of the jagged
rocks of Skye and Eigg settling slowly into the sea astern as Sgurr-na-
Ciche and the other peaks of the mainland loom steadily larger ahead.

Save for one track which runs up the central glen, and another that skirts the coast, the hundred square miles of the forest are penetrated only by pony-paths, and often the stalking parties are deployed by boat from Loch Nevis and Loch Hourn.

Letterewe, in Wester Ross, is another forest to which boats provide the only access. The lodge stands by Loch Maree on a wonderfully peaceful site and behind it stretches a hinterland of peaks and ridges, corries and glens which has not changed for centuries. Loch Choire, in the heart of Sutherland, is also magnificently remote. There is an approach road, it is true—twelve miles of private track—but this runs only through the low ground to the north, and the lodge, facing south-west, looks down seven miles of its own water lying cradled in a fastness of untouched hills.

In an age when so much of Britain has been ravaged by development, it seems something of a miracle that these places have remained unspoilt. The reason is simple: they are deer country, reduced partly by deer to their present state of desolation, but preserved in that state by the nobility of the sport which the deer provide.

Now, when a stalker climbs towards the high tops, he enters a world which has not changed since Scrope described it with such relish 150 years ago. The hills are as steep, the gales as strong, the hail as fierce, the air as clean. The smells are the same—of peat, wet heather, rain coming. The sounds are identical—the thin singing of the wind in the grass, the gurgle of the burns, the scream of the eagle, the whirr of the ptarmigan, the *go-back, go-back, go-back* of the grouse, and, above all, the roaring of the stags.

Before the rut starts in September, the herds seem to be mute; only if one manages to come really close can one hear the mewing of the calves and the occasional soft answer of a hind. But once the fires of procreation are alight, the long, melancholy roars echo from one face to the next, like the lowing of gigantic bulls, loud enough to set the rifleman's hair crawling a mile away.

In the final stages of an approach, one returns to the most basic and age-old methods of the hunter, hugging the earth, using every dip or hollow in the ground, watching, listening, testing the wind, freezing if the quarry lifts its head, moving on only when it relaxes. For anyone in whom primeval instincts still burn, it is both thrilling and utterly absorbing to approach deer in this way.

For a few minutes, modern man becomes ancient again. His links with the past are re-forged. His natural instincts once more take over.

An attack of stag-fever may shake him—but no doubt something similar often shook his ancestors too. The ghosts of a thousand Highland hunters are at his shoulder, yet in the final moments he is on his own: only he can hold the rifle steady when, with the chosen stag standing clear, the stalker whispers in his ear the terse and fateful order: 'Take him now!'

Acknowledgments

I am indebted to Her Majesty the Queen for her gracious permission to include unpublished material from the Royal Archive at Windsor, and for her permission to work in the library at Balmoral.

I am grateful to Colonel William McHardy, the Resident Factor at Balmoral, for showing me round the forest with such friendly enthusiasm; to Lord Charteris of Amisfield, formerly the Queen's Private Secretary, for arranging these royal connections on my behalf; and to Sir Robert Mackworth-Young, the Librarian at Windsor Castle, for making research there such a pleasure.

I should also like to thank the following people, who contributed ideas or original material: Professor R. J. Adam, His Grace the Duke of Atholl, Geoffrey N. Baggott, Hugh Blakeney, Jock Cairney, J. C. M. Campbell, G. A. D. Chalmer, Major N. Chamberlayne-Macdonald, Frank Debenham, Isabella Doble, Lord Dulverton, Lord Elphinstone, Cuthbert Fitzherbert, the late Richard Fleming, Valentine Fleming, Roger Fulford, Frank Gillon, Niall Graham-Campbell, Ian D. Grant, Major-General F. C. Horton, James Hughes-Onslow, Andrew Hugh Smith, Edward A. Hyde, Diana Keith Neal, W. Keith Neal, Campbell Lennie, P. N. Locke, Malcolm Lyell, David Lyon, Donald Maxwell-Macdonald, Norman MacLeod, Lea MacNally, Innes Miller, Viscount Mountgarret, Michael J. O'Brien, John Ormiston, Alexander Scrymgeour, Christopher Shaw, Louis Stewart, The Countess of Sutherland, James Teacher, R. S. Thackeray, Major George Thorne, Captain F. H. P. H. Wills, Dennis Winton.

I should like to report what a delight it is to work in the National Library of Scotland and the Scottish Record Office – both havens of peace and efficiency. In the south, the facilities offered by the London Library are unrivalled and indispensable.

I am grateful to the Alistair Horne Foundation at St Antony's

College, Oxford, whose generous research grant enabled me to extend my Highland investigations; and to Lord Dulverton, Kenneth Rose and Sir Alan Lascelles, all of whom read my typescript with eagle eyes, removing many inaccuracies.

I am grateful to the following for permission to reproduce copyright illustrations:

Her Majesty the Queen, by gracious permission, for plates nos. 8, 9, 10 and 11.

The Honourable Michael O'Brien, nos. 24, 27, 30; the Courtauld Institute of Art, no. 13; John Dewar and Sons Ltd, no. 14; Lt.-Col. A. S. Gemell, no. 26; Major W. G. Gordon, no. 32; Lea MacNally, nos. 38–48; the Mansell Collection, no. 29; Lt.-Col. P. Mitford, nos. 19 and 20; the National Library of Scotland, no. 12; the Countess of Sutherland, no. 36; the *Tatler and Bystander*, no. 34.

The sources for the other illustrations are: the author, nos. 17 and 37; Breadalbane: *The High Tops of Black Mount*, no. 28; Crealock: *Deer-Stalking in the Highlands*, no. 22; Grimble: *The Deer Forests of Scotland*, nos. 5 and 23; Millais: *British Deer and their Horns*, nos. 2 and 21; *Punch*, nos. 15 and 16; Ritchie: *The Influence of Man on Animal Life in Scotland*, no. 1 and text figure page 9; Ross: *The Book of Red Deer*, no. 35; St John: *Wild Sports and Natural History of the Highlands*, no. 7; Scrope: *The Art of Deer-Stalking*, no. 6; W. McC. Smith: *The Romance of Poaching*, nos. 3 and 33; Thornton: *A Sporting Tour*, no. 4; the Wills Collection, no. 18; Winans: *The Sporting Rifle*, nos. 25 and 31.

Finally, I should like to thank the skilled and patient typists who helped bring the book into being: Cordelia Salter, Jill da Silva and Betty Stacey

Sources

Unpublished

Various manuscripts in the Royal Archive at Windsor Castle, including passages from Queen Victoria's diary not included in *Leaves from the Journal of Our Life in the Highlands.*

The Atholl Family Muniments in the Charter Room at Blair Castle.

Muniments of the Dukes of Richmond and Gordon in the Scottish Record Office, Edinburgh.

The Breadalbane Muniments (S.R.O.)

The Seaforth Muniments (S.R.O.)

The Ellice Family Papers in the National Library of Scotland, Edinburgh.

Papers relating to the creation of Coulin Forest, 1866–71 in the possession of Captain F. H. P. H. Wills.

The Journal of George Ross, Stalker at Corriemulzie, 1870–1905, a typed copy of which is now in the possession of Niall Graham-Campbell, Factor of the Benmore Estates, Sutherland.

The memoirs of Robert Campbell, stalker at Guisachan, Altnaharra and elsewhere, c. 1860–90.

Published

ADAM SMITH, JANET, *John Buchan* (Hart-Davis, 1965). Excellent modern biography.

AKEHURST, RICHARD, *Game Guns and Rifles* (Bell, 1969). Useful short history.

ANDERSON, MARK L., *A History of Scottish Forestry* (2 vols, Nelson, 1967). A monumental work, packed with an astonishing accumulation of detail.

ATHOLL, JOHN, SEVENTH DUKE OF (Editor), *Chronicles of the Atholl and*

Tullibardine Families (6 vols, privately printed, 1908). A selection of material from the Atholl muniments.

BAKER, SIR SAMUEL, *Wild Beasts and their Ways* (2 vols, 1890). Big-game hunting in many climes.

BLAKEY, R., *Shooting* (Routledge, 1854). An early paperback containing an excellent chapter on stalking, which includes an extract from Mr Cooper's novel, *The Smugglers*.

BREADALBANE, ALMA G., *The High Tops of Black Mount* (Blackwood, 1907). Classic account of stalking in Argyllshire.

BROMLEY-DAVENPORT, W., *Sport* (Chapman & Hall, 1885). Somewhat choleric description of field sports.

BROWN, IVOR, *Balmoral: the History of a Home* (Collins, 1955). Agreeable, if otiose, account of the castle and estate.

BUCHAN, JOHN, *John Macnab* (Hodder & Stoughton, 1925). Classic adventure novel set in the Highlands.

CAMERON, ALLAN GORDON, *The Wild Red Deer of Scotland* (Blackwood, 1923).

CHALMERS, PATRICK R., *Mine Eyes to the Hills: An Anthology of the Highland Forest* (A. & C. Black, 1931). A comprehensive and well chosen anthology.

CHRISTIE, JAMES, *Instructions for Hunting, Breaking Pointers and Finding Out Game* (privately published, Banff, 1817). The instructions are perfunctory; but the book contains the excellent poem 'Journal of a Hunting Party from Auchry to Reenacula'.

COLQUHOUN, IAIN, *The Future of Deer-Stalking* (1925).

CREALOCK, LT-GEN. HENRY HOPE, *Deer-Stalking in the Highlands of Scotland* (Longmans, 1892). Magnificent edition of reminiscences and lore, illustrated by the author and published posthumously, edited by the author's brother, Maj.-Gen. John North Crealock.

CUPPLES, GEORGE, *Scotch Deer-Hounds and their Masters* (Blackwood, 1894). Specialist history containing much of interest.

DARLING, FRANK FRASER, *A Herd of Red Deer* (Oxford, 1937). Classic naturalist's study.

——*Natural History in the Highlands and Islands* (Collins, 1937). An able exposition.

EDWARDS, LIONEL, and WALLACE, HAROLD FRANK, *Hunting and Stalking the Deer* (Longmans, 1927). A pleasant anthology.

ELLANGOWAN (J. G. Bertram), *Outdoor Sports in Scotland* (W. H. Allen, 1889). Useful, if sometimes foolish, contemporary account.

FRASER, HUGH, *Amid the High Hills* (A. & C. Black, 1923). Pleasant essays on stalking, shooting and nature study.

GASKELL, PHILIP, *Morvern Transformed* (Cambridge, 1968). Detailed and fascinating account of one Highland parish in the nineteenth century.

GATHORNE-HARDY, A. E., *Autumns in Argyllshire with Rod and Gun* (Longmans, 1900). Pleasant recollections of stalking and fishing.

GOWER, LORD RONALD. *My Reminiscences* (Kegan Paul, Trench, 1883). Autobiography, with occasional references to stalking in Sutherland.

GREENER, W. W., *The Gun* (Cassell, 1881). History of the development of weapons, cantankerous when the author approaches his own time.

GRIMBLE, AUGUSTUS, *Deer-Stalking* (Chapman & Hall, 1886). An excellent manual of practical advice and reminiscences.

——*The Deer Forests of Scotland* (Kegan Paul, 1896). Valuable and handsome historical account, later reissued combined with the author's first book in a single volume.

HALL, ROBERT, *The Highland Sportsman* (Simpkin Marshall, 1882). Sporting guide to the Highlands.

HART-DAVIS, CAPTAIN H., *Stalking Sketches* (Horace Cox, 1904). Slight but pleasant stalking reminiscences, illustrated by the author.

HARTING, J. E., *British Animals Extinct Within Historic Times* (1880). Valuable historical study.

HARTLEY, GILFRID W., *Wild Sport and Some Stories* (Blackwood, 1912). Excellent anecdotes of stalking in Scotland and Ireland. Good account of a stalker seeing a ghostly party of four men in black carrying a coffin over the hill.

LENNIE, CAMPBELL, *Landseer: the Victorian Paragon* (Hamish Hamilton, 1976). Life of the artist.

LONDONDERRY, THE MARCHIONESS OF, *Henry Chaplin: a Memoir* (Macmillan, 1926). Her father's life, including some stalking reminiscences.

——*Retrospect* (Muller, 1938). Her autobiography: some stalking references.

MCCONNOCHIE, A. I., *The Deer and Deer Forests of Scotland* (1923). An excellent historical, descriptive and sporting survey.

——*Deerstalking in Scotland* (1924). Reminiscences of various forests.

——*Deer Forest Life* (1932). Pleasantly discursive memories.

MACDONALD, DUNCAN GEORGE FORBES, *Cattle, Sheep and Deer* (1872). Boastful, inaccurate account of natural history by an agricultural engineer who specialised in plagiarism.

MACKENZIE, EVAN G., *Grouse Shooting and Deer-Stalking* (Love & Malcolmson, 1907). Highland reminiscences.

Q*

MACKENZIE, OSGOOD, *A Hundred Years in the Highlands* (Edward
    Arnold, 1921). Charming and discursive account of life on the west
    coast in the nineteenth century.
MacNALLY, LEA, *Highland Year* (Dent, 1968).
——*Highland Deer Forest* (Dent, 1970).
——*The Year of the Red Deer* (Dent, 1975).
    Three admirable accounts of the Highlands by a stalker-naturalist,
    illustrated with his own outstanding photographs.
MACRAE, ALEXANDER, *A Handbook of Deer-Stalking*, Foreword by
    Horatio Ross (Blackwood, 1880). Short, practical manual, full of
    sensible advice.
MALCOLM, GEORGE, *The Population, Crofts, Sheep-Walks and Deer-
    Forests of the Highlands and Islands* (paper privately printed by
    Blackwood, Edinburgh, 1883). Contains also *A Defence of Deer-
    Forests* by Donald Cameron of Lochiel.
MARTIN, THEODORE, *The Life of His Royal Highness the Prince Consort*
    (2 vols, 1876). A few references to stalking in Scotland.
MILLAIS, J. G., *British Deer and their Horns* (Henry Southeran, 1897). With
    illustrations by the author. A specialist work on deer heads, finely
    illustrated, and containing much information on the history of deer-
    stalking.
MITCHELL, JOSEPH, *Reminiscences of My Life in the Highlands* (2 vols,
    privately published, 1883). Entertaining memoirs of a distinguished
    engineer.
OLD STALKER, AN, *Days on the Hill* (Nisbet, 1926). Reminiscences of
    David Taylor, second stalker at Glenisla.
PARKER, ERIC, *English Wild Life* (Longmans, 1929). A pleasant survey.
PEEL, E. LENNOX, *A Highland Gathering* (London, 1885). Pleasantly
    written sporting tales, mainly about stalking. Some fishing also.
PORTLAND, THE DUKE OF, *Fifty Years and More of Sport in Scotland*
    (Blackie, 1933). Many stalking reminiscences.
——*The Red Deer of Langwell and Braemore, 1880–1934* (Blackie, 1934).
    Very little text; mainly photographs of outstanding heads.
PREBBLE, JOHN, *The Highland Clearances* (Secker and Warburg, 1963).
    Vivid, if overwrought, account of the Clearances.
RITCHIE, JAMES, *The Influence of Man on Animal Life in Scotland* (Cam-
    bridge University Press, 1920). A labour of love, full of historical
    information.
ROSS, JOHN (Editor), *The Book of the Red Deer* (Simpkin Marshall, 1925).
    Collection of essays on stalking in Scotland and elsewhere.

ST JOHN, CHARLES, *Natural History and Sport in Moray* (Edmonton and Douglas, 1846). A collection of marvellously well observed pieces. Contains the account of the Muckle Hart of Benmore.

——*A Tour in Sutherlandshire* (2 vols, Edmonton and Douglas, 1849). An eccentric expedition.

Note: Natural History and Sport in Moray was later reissued in several new editions, under the title *Wild Sports and Natural History of the Highlands.*

A memoir, *Charles St John's Note Books,* edited by Admiral H. C. St John, appeared in 1901.

SCOTT, WALTER, *Waverley* (first published in 1814). First of the Waverley novels.

SCROPE, WILLIAM, *The Art of Deer-Stalking* (Edward Arnold, 1838). The first work devoted to the subject: a classic, often reprinted. In some editions called *Days of Deer-Stalking.*

SINCLAIR, SIR JOHN, *The Statistical Account of Scotland* (21 vols, 1791–9). An immense collection of historical fact, contributed by the ministers in various parishes. Generally known as *The Old Statistical Account,* to distinguish it from *The New Statistical Account,* published in 1843.

SMITH, MRS E., *Memoirs of a Highland Lady* (John Murray, 1898). Amusing recollections of life at Rothiemurchus, 1797–1830.

SMITH, W. MCCROMBIE, *The Romance of Poaching in the Highlands* (1904).

SPEEDY, THOMAS, *Sport in the Highlands and Lowlands of Scotland* (1884). General survey.

STEVEN, H. M. and CARLISLE, A., *The Native Pinewoods of Scotland* (Oliver and Boyd, 1959). Scholarly study.

STEWART, JOHN SOBIESKI and C. E., *Lays of the Deer Forest* (2 vols, Blackwood, 1848). Vol. 1 contains poems in Gaelic and English. Vol. 2 is an entertaining and opinionated history of deer-stalking in Scotland to that date. The authors, claiming descent from Prince Charles, lived on Eilan Aigas, an island in the river Beauly.

SURTEES, VIRGINIA, *Charlotte Canning* (John Murray, 1976). Agreeable biography, with many lively extracts from the subject's diary.

SUTHERLAND, THE DUKE OF, *Looking Back* (Odhams, 1957). Autobiography: some references to stalking in Sutherland.

TAYLOR, JOHN (The Water Poet), *The Penniless Pilgrimage and Other Pieces.* Contains the account of his Highland journey, 1618.

THORMANBY (J. W. Dixon), *Kings of the Rod, Rifle and Gun* (2 vols, 1901). Some good material on Horatio Ross and others.

THORNTON, COLONEL T., *A Sporting Tour through the Northern Parts of*

England and Great Part of the Highlands of Scotland (Vernon and Hood, 1805). Diverting reminiscences of sport in the north.

VICTORIA, QUEEN (Edited by Arthur Phelps), *Leaves from the Journal of Our Life in the Highlands* (Smith Elder, 1868). Extensive descriptions of early visits to Scotland and life at Balmoral.

WALLACE, HAROLD FRANK, *British Deer Heads* (1913). Illustrated record of an exhibition organised by *Country Life*.

——*Happier Years* (Eyre & Spottiswoode, 1944). Autobiography, with many references to stalking.

WHITEHEAD, G. KENNETH, *The Deer Stalking Grounds of Great Britain and Ireland* (Hollis & Carter, 1960). A mine of statistical information, with some historical commentary.

——*The Deer of Great Britain and Ireland* (Routledge, 1964). Another indispensable work of reference.

WINANS, WALTER, *The Sporting Rifle* (Putnam, 1908). Pugnacious combination of memoirs and advice.

YOUNGSON, A. J., *Beyond the Highland Line* (Collins, 1974). Entertaining accounts of three eighteenth-century travellers – Burt, Pennant and Thornton.

Reports

Information has also been taken from the annual reports of the Red Deer Commission, the Forestry Commission, and the Nature Conservancy, the reports of the Crofters' Commission (1883), the Royal Commission on the Highlands and Islands (1892) and the Committee on the Scottish Deer Forests (1923). Individual reports used include the *Report on the Deer Forest of Atholl* by S. P. J. Merlin (privately printed in 1909), the Nature Conservancy Council's *Reserve Handbook* about the reserve on the Isle of Rhum (1974); and *Farming the Red Deer*, the first report on the Glensaugh experiment by the Rowett Research Institute and the Hill Farming Research Organisation (1974).

Deer, the journal of the British Deer Society, has also provided much useful background information.

Index